The Business of Rural Tourism

International Perspectives

Edited by

Stephen J. Page

Massey University – Albany,

and

Don Getz

University of Calgary

INTERNATIONAL THOMSON BUSINESS PRESS
I Ⓣ P® An International Thomson Publishing Company

London • Bonn • Boston • Johannesburg • Madrid • Melbourne • Mexico City • New York • Paris
Singapore • Tokyo • Toronto • Albany, NY • Belmont, CA • Cincinnati, OH • Detroit, MI

The Business of Rural Tourism: International Perspectives

First published by International Thomson Business Press

I⟨T⟩P® A division of International Thomson Publishing Inc.
The ITP logo is a trademark under licence

British Library Cataloguing-in-Publication Data
A catalogue record for this book is available from the British Library

First edition 1997

Typeset by J&L Composition Ltd, Filey, North Yorkshire
Printed in the UK by The Alden Press, Oxford

ISBN 0–415–13511–7

International Thomson Business Press
Berkshire House
168–173 High Holborn
London WCIV 7AA
UK

International Thomson Business Press
20 Park Plaza
13th Floor
Boston MA 02116
USA

http://www.itbp.com

The
Inte

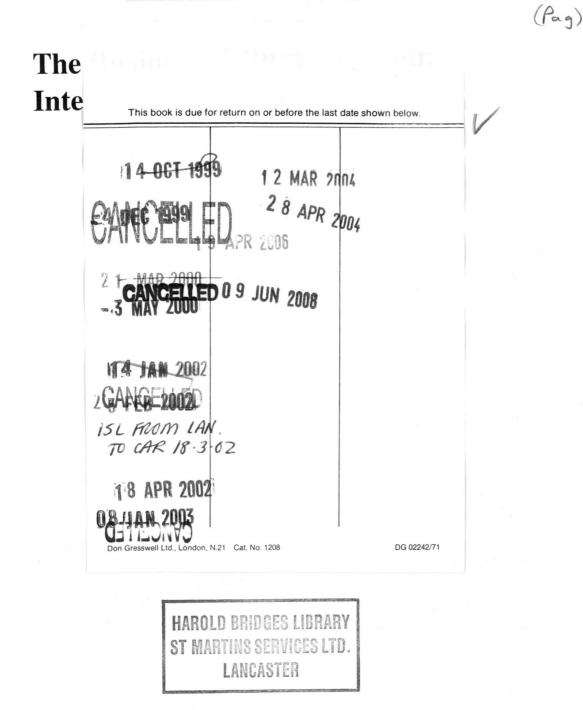

This book is due for return on or before the last date shown below.

14 OCT 1999   1 2 MAR 2004

CANCELLED   2 8 APR 2004

18 APR 2006

2 1 MAR 2000

CANCELLED 0 9 JUN 2008

-.3 MAY 2000

14 JAN 2002

CANCELLED

ISL FROM LAN.
TO CAR 18·3·02

1 8 APR 2002

08 JAN 2003

CANCELLED

Don Gresswell Ltd., London, N.21   Cat. No. 1208   DG 02242/71

041 513 5117

Tourism and Hospitality Management Series

Series Editors:

Stephen J. Page
Massey University – Albany, New Zealand

Professor Roy C. Wood
The Scottish Hotel School, University of Strathclyde, UK

Series Consultant:

Professor C. L. Jenkins
The Scottish Hotel School, University of Strathclyde, UK

Textbooks in this series:

Books in this series are available on free inspection for lecturers considering the texts for course adoption. Details of these and any other International Thomson Business Press titles are available by writing to the publishers (Berkshire House, 168–173 High Holborn, London WCIV 7AA) or by telephoning the Promotions Department on 0171 497 1422

Contents

List of figures

List of tables

Acknowledgements

Stephen Page wishes to acknowledge the assistance provided by Massey University through its research funds (MURF), overseas leave provision and the University Research Award in 1996, which all assisted with the editing and completion of the chapters. In addition, the secretarial assistance provided by Barbara Rom and Rachel Fitchett, Department of Management Systems, Massey University – Albany, was greatly appreciated in the final stages of editing the manuscript. Research assistance for Chapter 1 was undertaken by Brenda Rudkin, Massey University – Albany, and the help is duly acknowledged.

Support and assistance from the Faculty of Management, University of Calgary, is also acknowledged by Don Getz.

The help and advice provided by Steven Reed at International Thomson Business Press are also acknowledged, together with the support and encouragement provided by Francesca Weaver at the commissioning stage of the book.

The permission from the Helicopter Line to use the photo reproduced in Figure 1.2 is gratefully acknowledged. Lastly, thanks to Lisa Williams for the copy-editing and efficient turnaround of the manuscript.

List of contributors

Nitha Dolli is a Lecturer in Marketing, Massey University – Albany, Private Bag 102 904, North Shore Mail Centre, Auckland, New Zealand.

David Edgell is Commissioner of Tourism, the United States Virgin Islands.

David Fennell is Associate Professor, Faculty of Physical Activity Studies, University of Regina, Regina, Saskatchewan, Canada.

Don Getz is a Professor of Tourism Management, Faculty of Management, University of Calgary, 2500 University Drive NW, Calgary, Alberta, Canada.

Walter Jamieson is Professor of Planning, Faculty of Environmental Design, University of Calgary, Canada.

S. Fung mei Sarah Li is in the Department of Tourism, James Cook University of Northern Queensland, Townsville, Queensland 4811, Australia.

Patrick Long is Associate Professor of Tourism Management, College of Business and Administration, University of Colorado, Boulder, Colorado, USA.

Martin Operman is a Senior Lecturer in Tourism Management, Waiariki Polytechnic, Private Bag RO1, Rotoura, New Zealand.

Stephen J. Page is a Senior Lecturer in Tourism Management, Massey University – Albany, Private Bag 102 904, North Shore Mail Centre, Auckland, New Zealand.

John Pinfold is a Senior Lecturer in Finance, Massey University – Albany, Private Bag 102 904, North Shore Mail Centre, Auckland, New Zealand.

Chris Ryan is Professor of Tourism Management, School of Tourism and Hospitality, Faculty of Business, Northern Territory University, Casuarina Campus, Darwin, NT0909, Australia.

Trevor Sofield is a Senior Lecturer in the Department of Tourism, James Cook University of Northern Queensland, Townsville, Queensland 4811, Australia.

David Weaver is a Senior Lecturer in Business and Hotel Management, Griffith University, Gold Coast Campus, Queensland 4217, Australia.

Series editors' foreword

The International Thomson Business Press Series in Tourism and Hospitality Management is dedicated to the publication of high quality textbooks and other volumes that will be of benefit to those engaged in tourism, hotel and hospitality education, especially at degree and postgraduate level. The *Tourism and Hospitality Management Series* is based on core textbooks on key areas of the curriculum and is complimented by highly focused and shorter texts on particular themes and issues. All the authors in the series are experts in their own fields, actively engaged in teaching, research and consultancy in tourism and hospitality. Each book comprises an authoritative blend of subject-relevant theoretical considerations and practical applications. Furthermore, a unique quality of the series is that it is student oriented, offering accessible texts that take account of the realities of administration, management and operations in tourism and hospitality contexts, being constructively critical without losing sight of the overall goal of providing clear accounts of essential concepts, issues and techniques.

The series is committed to quality, accessibility, relevance and originality in its approach. Quality is ensured as a result of a vigorous refereeing process, unusual in the publication of textbooks. Accessibility is achieved through the use of innovative textual design techniques, and the use of discussion points, case studies and exercises within books, all geared to encouraging a comprehensive understanding of the material contained therein. Relevance and originality together result from the experience of authors as key authorities in their fields.

The tourism and hospitality industries are diverse and dynamic industries and it is the intention of the editors to reflect this diversity and dynamism by publishing quality texts that enhance topical subjects without losing sight of enduring themes. The Series Editors and Consultant are grateful to Steven Reed of International Thomson Business Press for his commitment, expertise and support of this philosophy.

Series Editors

Dr Stephen J. Page
Massey University – Albany
Auckland
New Zealand

Professor Roy C. Wood
The Scottish Hotel School
University of Strathclyde
UK

Series Consultant

Professor C. L. Jenkins
The Scottish Hotel School
University of Strathclyde
UK

Preface

S. J. Page and D. Getz

The worldwide growth of tourism has generated a considerable interest in research which focuses on the impact of tourism in different environments, at different scales and with varying emphases, often dependent upon the disciplinary bias of the researcher. It is increasingly being acknowledged that the multidisciplinary research skills needed to understand the operation, organization, impact and management of tourism in different destinations and areas requires a greater degree of interdisciplinary cooperation and research which is able to broaden our understanding of tourism phenomena. The processes shaping the development and organization of tourism activities in destination areas often remain poorly understood when researchers begin to address the issue of tourism supply (Sinclair and Stabler 1991). The absence of research which considers the supply chain in relation to the organisation and business activities associated with the tourism industry (Witt et al. 1991) means that the role of entrepreneurs and their activities in terms of new firm formation, business practices and tourism development remain poorly understood with a number of exceptions (Shaw and Williams 1990).

One consequence is that the business activities and management problems faced by tourism enterprises at different spatial scales – ranging from the international, transnational and multinational hotel chains (Go and Pine 1995) at a worldwide level through to the activities of business within countries – and different regions within countries are based on aggregated data which provides very little detailed information on how 'typical' tourism businesses operate in different destination areas. Furthermore, the prevailing paradigms within tourism epitomized by state of the art reviews of tourism research (e.g. Pearce and Butler 1993; Seaton 1994; Butler and Pearce 1995) highlight the need for a greater methodological sophistication in research studies, often overlooking the paucity of data and knowledge which results from aggregated information contained in surveys and reports. Such calls for greater methodological sophistication may be appropriate for research focusing on studies of tourism demand, but the continued neglect of tourism supply issues cannot sustain such calls. Therefore the continued growth of supply-side research inevitably requires some degree of data-gathering which utilizes existing methodologies and methods of analysis that continue to build the knowledge base in tourism. While critics of supply-side research may continue to complain about the descriptive nature of studies which use a case study approach, popularized in business research (especially in marketing – see Lovelock 1991: 513-16 for a review of the case study method), the criticisms are premature in many cases given the absence of definitive studies of tourism businesses. The continued problems associated with supply-side research in tourism are well documented (see Sinclair and Stabler 1991) and need not be reiterated here. However, one recurrent theme of significance is the difficulty of obtaining specific business information related to individual enterprises due to the highly competitive nature of the tourism business.

It is within this context that this book was conceived by the editors as an attempt to address a number of fundamental questions in tourism:

- What is the nature of existing research on rural tourism?
- How do specific enterprises establish a rural tourism business?
- What are the operational, management and business problems associated with such enterprises?
- How are these issues reflected in the case of individual enterprises?

The book aims to develop a greater understanding of how rural tourism enterprises operate, and of the similarities and differences associated with such businesses in various countries, while providing detailed information generated from case studies of individual enterprises. In this respect, the book seeks to address the prevailing dearth of knowledge on rural tourism, while drawing on hitherto unpublished studies associated with individual operators who have allowed tourism researchers access to their enterprise and business activities. While it is not possible for such research to provide data on business turnover or financial results, many other aspects of the business development process, operation and managerial issues (including human resource and marketing requirements) are discussed in many of the studies, together with the problems, prospects and potential for such businesses. *The Business of Rural Tourism* also explores the nature, development and management of rural tourism, with emphasis on individual enterprises and operators, and on what destinations and governments can do to develop and improve this sector. No previous study has combined international case studies of rural tourism businesses with an in-depth review of the rural tourism literature. Accordingly, this book provides a new and unique source of ideas, facts, case studies and strategies which will be of value to students of tourism, researchers and policy-makers, destination planners and marketers, and – in particular – the owners and operators of rural tourism businesses.

An opening question is: what is rural tourism? Indeed, what is rurality? A detailed discussion in Chapter 1 presents the diversity of theory and opinion on these subjects, while the concluding chapter employs lessons from the case studies to provide practical answers.

Chapter 1 also explores many of the issues pertaining to rural tourism, such as potential costs and benefits, and relevant planning, development and management challenges. Attention is then given to the rural tourism business and especially to entrepreneurs, owners and operators. There has been little research on this dimension of rural tourism, so the concluding chapter makes business operation its primary focus.

THE CASE STUDIES

Every case study was especially commissioned and written for this book. Each of the authors has substantial experience in researching and/or planning rural tourism, and their combined publications are too numerous to mention. While it would have been wonderful to get owners and managers to write the cases, it is seldom possible for these business people to make the time for such activities. The editors and authors are greatly indebted to all the owners/operators who took the time to be interviewed and provide details and documents about their businesses.

Global coverage was attempted, but it is a big world! Rural tourism is truly global in nature, but complete coverage is not possible owing to the researchers' limitations and the lack of information about many regions. Indeed, we are very fortunate in having new material from China, which has only recently become a player in international tourism but has a lengthy history of domestic rural tourism. In some regions and countries, notably Europe, North America, Australia and New Zealand, rural tourism is well established and big business. Hence our cases are drawn mostly from these regions (see the Map section). While absolute consistency among the cases was not attempted, most of them provide the following:

● an overview of the country or region's rural tourism environment;
● a profile of a single business and its owners or operators;
● details of management practices and issues and some discussion of the implications.

At the editors' request, authors paid particular attention to the issue of sustainable tourism, which is of critical importance in rural areas. This theme runs through the book and is an important part of the strategies recommended in the concluding chapter. The case studies provide interesting and useful information about particular regions and enterprises, but one cannot generalize from them and conclude that rural tourism is now completely understood. In the Conclusions sections we use the cases to the fullest in drawing a number of conclusions and suggesting strategies, but there is much more to study and learn than is covered in this book.

USING THIS BOOK

As a reference for entrepreneurs and managers, the case studies provide detailed examination of how a range of rural tourism businesses operate and cope with various challenges. In itself, each case offers insights into the business venture and the personal strengths and weaknesses of the owners/operators. New ideas can easily be generated by reading cases, even if the circumstances are quite different from the reader's. After reading the cases, the conclusions will be important in summarizing major issues and developing strategies.

In formal education and training settings it will be important to read the introductory chapter before tackling the cases. A great deal has been written about rural tourism, so familiarity with the basic concepts and issues is essential. The case studies can be used as readings to familiarize students with a range of business environments and issues or to investigate more closely the nature of entrepreneurship and management practices. Used to its fullest, each case can be the subject of separate analyses to address questions such as:

- Can this operation ever be profitable?
- What would the student recommend to improve this enterprise's marketing?
- Were mistakes made?

Another use is to have students develop a business concept and plan for a rural tourism enterprise, using the cases as starting points.

REFERENCES

Butler, R. and Pearce, D. (eds) (1995) *Change in Tourism: People, Places, Processes*, London: Routledge.

Go, F. and Pine, R. (1995) *Globalization Strategy in the Hotel Industry*, London: Routledge.

Lovelock, C. (1991) *Services Marketing: Text, Cases and Readings*, Hemel Hempstead: Prentice Hall.

Pearce, D. and Butler, R. (eds) (1993) *Tourism Research: Critiques and Challenges*, London: Routledge.

Seaton, A. (ed.) (1994) *Tourism: State of the Art*, Chichester: Wiley.

Shaw, G. and Williams, A. (1990) 'Tourism, economic development and the role of entrepreneurial activity', in C. Cooper and A. Lockwood (eds) *Progress in Tourism, Recreation and Hospitality Management*, Vol. 3, London: Belhaven.

Sinclair, M. T. and Stabler, M. (eds) (1991) *The Tourism Industry: An International Analysis*, Wallingford, Oxon: CAB International.

Witt, S., Brooke, M. and Buckley, P. (1991) *The Management of International Tourism*, London: Routledge.

Issues in rural tourism: the literature and business issues

The business of rural tourism: international perspectives

1

S. J. Page and D. Getz

RURAL TOURISM: AN INTRODUCTION

Rural tourism has continued to suffer from a neglect among tourism researchers, often being subsumed under or confused with recreation and leisure activities, since many studies assume that rural tourism equates with simple concepts such as 'the countryside': therefore the assumptions are that users of 'the countryside' are predominantly recreationalists and that tourists are not the main user groups. While these assumptions are invalidated by research, such beliefs still affect the image of what constitutes rural tourism. The neglect of tourism as a rural business activity has also been compounded by the absence of any theoretical research published in mainstream tourism journals. As a result, much of the research on rural tourism has, with a number of exceptions, failed to contribute to a growing awareness of its role, value and significance in the wider development of tourism studies and its importance as a mainstay of many rural economies. In this context, Butler and Clark's comments are relevant that:

> The literature on rural tourism is sparse and . . . conceptual models and theories are lacking. . . . Many of the references in tourism are case studies with little theoretical foundation. . . or they focus on specific problems . . . Some take a broader perspective focusing on issues and process. . . . There is, therefore, a lack of theory and models placing rural tourism in a conceptual framework.
>
> (Butler and Clark 1992: 167)

Much of the research on rural tourism has been published in a diverse range of social science journals (e.g. *Sociologia Ruralis, Tourism Recreation Research*), reports and edited collections of essays which have been poorly disseminated, as well as in specific texts (e.g. Sharpley 1993; Sharpley 1997; Butler et al. 1997). Consequently, rural tourism has remained peripheral to the focus of tourism research, while also remaining poorly defined: it continues to be a general term which encapsulates a wide range of interest groups not only from tourism studies, but also from economics, planning, anthropology, geography, sociology and business studies. There has also been a lack of integration between these interest groups, each cultivating its own view and approach to rural tourism. As a result few researchers have attempted to define the concept of rural tourism.

A CONCEPT OF RURAL TOURISM

Keane et al.'s (1992) innovative, but little-known study on rural tourism offers a number of insights into the definition of rural tourism, acknowledging that there are a variety of terms used to describe tourism activity in rural areas: agritourism, farm tourism, rural tourism, soft tourism, alternative tourism and many others which have different meanings from one country to another. Keane also points out that it is difficult to avoid some of this confusion in relation to labels and definitions because the term 'rural tourism' has been adapted by the European Community to refer to the entire tourism activity in a rural area (Keane et al. 1992).

But such definitions do little to convey the true meaning of tourism in rural areas because of the difficulty of establishing what is 'rural'. Robinson's (1990) invaluable synthesis of rural change illustrates that the term 'rural' has remained an elusive one and difficult to define in academic research, even though popular conceptions of rural areas are based on images of rusticity and the idyllic village life. However, Robinson argues that:

> defining rural . . . in the past has tended to ignore common economic, social and political structures in both urban and rural areas. . . In simple terms, . . . 'rural' areas define themselves with respect to the presence of particular types of problems. A selective list of examples could include depopulation and deprivation in areas remote from major metropolitan centres; a reliance upon primary activity; conflicts between presentation of certain landscapes and development of a variety of economic activities; and conflicts between local needs and legislation emanating from urban-based legislators. Key characteristics of 'rural' are taken to be extensive land uses, including large open spaces of underdeveloped land, and small settlements at the base of the settlement hierarchy, but including settlements thought of to be rural.
>
> (Robinson 1990: xxi)

Therefore any definition of rural tourism needs to recognize the essential qualities of what is 'rural'. While national governments use specific criteria to define 'rural', often based on the population density of settlements, there is no universal agreement on the critical population threshold which distinguishes between urban and rural populations. Robinson (1990) summarizes the principal approaches used by sociologists, economists and other groups in establishing the basis of what is rural in the developed world, and these need not be reiterated here. What is important is the diversity of approaches used by many researchers, who emphasize the concept of an urban–rural continuum as a means of establishing differing degrees of rurality and the essential characteristics of ruralness. In contrast, Hoggart's (1990) provocative article 'Let's do away with rural' argues that 'there is too much laxity in the treatment of areas in empirical analysis . . . [and] . . . that the undifferentiated use of "rural" in a research context is detrimental to the advancement of social theory' (Hoggart 1990: 245), since the term rural is obfuscatory due to intra-rural differences and urban–rural similarities. Hoggart (1990) argues that general classification of urban and rural areas is of limited value. For this reason, recent advances in social theory may offer a number of important insights into conceptualizing the rural environment and tourism-related activities.

According to Cloke (1992), rural places have traditionally been associated with specific rural functions – agriculture, sparsely populated areas, geographically dispersed settlement patterns – and rurality has been conceptualized in terms of peripherality (see Page 1994a for a discussion of tourism and peripherality), remoteness and dependence on rural economic activity. However, new approaches in social theory have argued that rural areas are inextricably linked to the national and international political economy. As Cloke (1992) rightly argues, changes in the way society and non-urban places are organized and function have rendered traditional definitions of rurality less meaningful due to the following changes:

- increased mobility of people, goods and messages has eroded the autonomy of local communities;
- delocalization of economic activity makes it impossible to define homogeneous economic regions;
- new specialized uses of rural spaces (as tourists sites, parks and development zones) have created new specialized networks of relationships in the areas concerned, many of which are no longer localized;
- people who 'inhabit' a given rural area include a diversity of temporary visitors as well as residents;
- rural spaces increasingly perform functions for non-rural users and in these cases can be characterized by the fact that they exist independently of the action of rural populations (Mormont 1990: 31, cited in Cloke 1992).

Consequently, Mormont (1990) conceptualizes rural areas as a set of overlapping social spaces, each with their own logic, institutions and network of actors (e.g. users and administrators). This reiterates many of the early ideas of behavioural scientists – that a rural space needs to be defined in terms of how the occupants perceive it, as a social construct where the occupiers of rural spaces interact and participate in activities such as tourism. In this context, recent developments in social theory imply that the nature and use of rural areas for activities such as tourism are best explained by examining the processes by which their meaning of 'rural' is 'constructed, negotiated and experienced' (Cloke 1992: 55). One approach favoured by Cloke is the analysis of the way in which the commodification of the countryside has occurred, leading to the emergence of markets for rural products where:

the countryside . . . [is] . . . an exclusive place to be lived in; rural communities as a context to be bought and sold; rural lifestyle which can be colonized; icons of rural culture which can be crafted, packed and marketed; rural landscapes with a new range of potential from 'pay-as-you-enter' national parks, to sites for the theme park explosion; rural production ranging from newly commodified food to the output of industrial plants whose potential or actual pollutive externalities have driven them from more urban localities.

(Cloke 1992: 55)

In this respect, rural areas are places to be consumed and where production is based on establishing new places for tourism. Cloke (1992) cites privatization in the UK as a major process stimulating this form of rural production focused on rural recreation and tourism. The new political economy influencing agriculture in the EC has also facilitated farm diversification into new forms of tourism accommodation (e.g. farm-stays) and attractions. Yet the critical processes stimulating the demand for the mass consumption of rural products have been essential in affecting such changes. Urry (1988) points to changes in taste, following the emergence of a new service class, which have led to greater emphasis on consumption in rural environments. These tastes have also influenced other social groups, who have adopted similar values in the consumption of rural areas including:

● the pursuit of a pastoral idyll;
● acceptance of cultural symbols related to the rural idyll;
● a greater emphasis on outdoor pursuits in such environments.

While the detailed social and cultural interpretations of such trends are dealt with in detail by Urry (1988), Poon (1989) illustrates the practical implications of such changes for the tourism industry. Poon interprets these changes in terms of a 'shift from an 'old tourism' (e.g. the regimented and standardized holiday package) to a 'new tourism' which is segmented, customized and flexible in both time and space. In fact, recent research on services has analysed the change in society as one from a 'Fordist' to 'post-Fordist' stage which has involved a shift in the form of demand for tourist services from a former pattern of mass consumption 'to more individual patterns, with greater differentiation and volatility of consumer preferences and a heightened need for producers to be consumer-driven and to segment markets more systematically' (Urry 1991: 52).

Hummelbrunner and Miglbauer (1994) support both Poon's (1989) and Urry's (1991) assessment, arguing that these changes to the demand for and supply of tourism services have contributed to the emergence of a 'new rural tourism'. From a supply perspective, this has manifested itself in terms of 'an increasing interest in rural tourism among a better-off clientele, and also among some holidaymakers as a growing environmental awareness and a desire to be integrated with the residents in the areas they visit' (Bramwell 1994: 3). This not only questions the need to move beyond existing concepts such as 'core' and 'periphery' with rural tourism as a simplistic consumption of the countryside, but also raises the question of how rural areas are being used to provide tourism experiences and how businesses are pursuing market-oriented approaches to the new era of commodification in rural environments. If the 1990s is a 'new era of commodifying rural space, characterised by a speed and scale of development which far outstrip farm-based tourism and recreation of previous eras' (Cloke 1992: 59), then a critical review of this process is timely on an international and national scale to assess the extent and significance of rural tourism in the 1990s. Yet this raises again the question posed by Bramwell:

> Does the physical existence of tourism in rural areas create a rural tourism that has a significance beyond the self-evident combination of particular activities in a specific place? In other words, do the special characteristics of rural areas help shape the pattern of tourism so that there is a particular rural tourism?
>
> (Bramwell 1994: 2)

One way of addressing this seemingly tautological proposition is to examine what makes rural tourism distinctive.

What makes rural tourism distinctive?

Lane (1994) discusses the historical continuity in the development of rural tourism and examines some of the key issues which combine to make rural tourism distinctive. Bramwell (1994: 3) suggests that, despite the problems of defining the concept of 'rural', 'it may be a mistake to deny our commonsense thoughts that rural areas can have distinctive characteristics or that these can have consequences for social and economic interactions in the countryside'. The views and perceptions people hold of the countryside are different from those they have of urban areas, which is an important starting-point for establishing the distinctiveness of rural tourism. Lane (1994) actually lists the subtle differences between urban and rural tourism, in which individual social representations of the countryside are a critical component of the ways in which people interact with rural areas. In fact Squires (1993) acknowledges that both social representations and personal images of the countryside condition whether people wish to visit rural areas for tourism, and what they see and do during their visit.

Lane (1994) also highlights the impact of changes in rural tourism since the 1970s, with far greater numbers of recreationalists and tourists now visiting rural areas. As Patmore's (1983) seminal study on recreation and leisure acknowledges, the impact of car ownership has led to a geographical dispersion of recreationalists and tourists beyond existing fixed modes of transport (e.g. railways). Consequently, tourism has moved away from a traditional emphasis on resorts, small towns and villages to become truly rural, with all but the most inaccessible wilderness areas awaiting the impact of the more mobile tourist. Despite this strong growth in the demand for rural tourism, Lane (1994) acknowledges the absence of any systematic sources of data on rural tourism, since neither the World

Tourism Organization nor the Organization for Economic Cooperation and Development (OECD) have appropriate measures. In addition, there is no agreement among member countries on how to measure this phenomenon. One way of establishing the distinctive characteristics of rural tourism is to derive a working definition of rural tourism. Here the work by Lane (1994) is invaluable since it dismisses simplistic notions of rural tourism as tourism which occurs in the countryside. Lane cites the following seven reasons why it is difficult to produce a complex definition of rural tourism to apply in all contexts:

1 Urban or resort-based tourism is not confined to urban areas, but spills out into rural areas.
2 Rural areas themselves are difficult to define, and the criteria used by different nations vary considerably.
3 Not all tourism which takes place in rural areas is strictly 'rural' – it can be 'urban' in form, and merely be located in a rural area. Many so-called holiday villages are of this type; in recent years, numerous large holiday complexes have been completed in the countryside. They may be 'theme parks', timeshares, or leisure hotel developments. Their degree of rurality can be both an emotive and a technical question.
4 Historically, tourism has been an urban concept; the great majority of tourists live in urban areas. Tourism can be an urbanising influence on rural areas, encouraging cultural and economic change, and new construction.
5 Different forms of rural tourism have developed in different regions. Farm-based holidays are important in many parts of rural Germany and Austria. Farm-based holidays are much rarer in rural USA and Canada. In France, the self-catering cottage, or gîte, is an important component of the rural tourism product.
6 Rural areas themselves are in a complex process of change. The impact of global markets, communications and telecommunication have changed market conditions and orientations for traditional products. The rise of environmentalism has led to increasing control by 'outsiders' over land use and resource development. Although some rural areas still experience depopulation, others are experiencing an inflow of people to retire or to develop new 'non-traditional' businesses. The once clear distinction between urban and rural is now blurred by sub-urbanisation, long distance commuting and second-home development.
7 Rural tourism is a complex multi-faceted activity: it is not just farm-based tourism. It includes farm-based holidays but also comprises special-interest nature holidays and ecotourism, walking, climbing and riding holidays, adventure, sport and health tourism, hunting and angling, educational travel, arts and heritage tourism, and, in some areas, ethnic tourism. There is also a large general-interest market for less specialised forms of rural tourism. This area is highlighted by studies of the German tourism market, where a major requirement of the main holiday is the ability to provide peace, quiet and relaxation in rural surroundings.

(Lane 1994: 9)

Consequently, rural tourism in its purest form should be:

1 Located in rural areas.
2 Functionally rural – built upon the rural world's special features of small-scale enterprise, open space, contact with nature and the natural world, heritage, 'traditional' societies and 'traditional' practices.
3 Rural in scale – both in terms of buildings and settlements – and, therefore, usually small-scale.
4 Traditional in character, growing slowly and organically, and connected with local families. It will often be very largely controlled locally and developed for the long-term good of the area.
5 Of many different kinds, representing the complex pattern of rural environment, economy, history and location.

(after Lane 1994: 14)

Lane (1994: 16) also argues that the following factors also have to be considered in defining rural tourism:

● holiday type;
● intensity of use;
● location;
● style of management;
● degree of integration with the community.

And by using the continuum concept, one can distinguish between those tourist visits which are specifically rural or urban, or which fall in an intermediate category. Thus, any workable definition of rural tourism needs to establish the parameters of the demand for, and supply of, the tourism experience and the extent to which it is undertaken in the continuum of rural to urban environments. With these issues in mind, it is pertinent to examine the most influential studies published to date on rural tourism. While such an overview cannot be completely comprehensive, it does aim to illustrate the extent of academic development in this expanding area of research.

PROGRESS IN RURAL TOURISM

Within the literature on rural tourism, a range of themes and issues emerge, most notably the impact of rural tourism (social, cultural, economic and environmental impacts), research on different forms of rural tourism (e.g. farm tourism) and the implications for rural areas. Each of these themes have a well-established academic position within the literature, many of them dating back to the interest in tourism in the 1960s and 1970s.

The impact of rural tourism: social and cultural impacts

The literature on tourism impacts has long since assumed a central position within the emergence of tourism research, as early reviews confirm (e.g. Mathieson and Wall 1982). However, in a rural context, impact research has not been at the forefront of methodological and theoretical developments, with a few notable exceptions. One particular problem, as already noted, is the tendency for researchers to adopt well-established theoretical constructs and concepts from their own disciplinary perspective, which have subsequently been applied to the analysis of rural tourism issues. Within the social and cultural dimensions of rural tourism, the influence of rural sociology in the 1960s and 1970s (e.g. Bracey 1970) dominated sociological research while Smith's (1989) influential collection of anthropological studies of tourism highlighted the approaches adopted by anthropologists. Probably the most influential statement on the social and cultural impacts is Bouquet and Winter's (1987a) diverse anthology of studies on the conflict and political debates associated with rural tourism. For example, Bouquet and Winter (1987b) consider the relationship between tourism, politics and the issue of policies to control and direct tourism (and recreation) in the countryside in the postwar period.

In contrast, Neate (1987) considers farm-based tourism in the Scilly Isles in relation to attempts to diversify the economic base of family-owned farms in the climate of declining profitability in agriculture. The sociological implications of the research highlight the role of farm tourism as an economic activity which keeps the small family-run structure of production largely intact. Winter's (1987) study of farming and tourism in the English and Welsh uplands argues for circumspection in advocating farm-tourism as a solution to the socio-economic development problems of 'less-favoured areas', a conclusion which is widely endorsed by subsequent studies. Mormont (1987) explains how entrepreneurs and 'outsiders' (i.e. tourists) have affected the feeling, environment and sense of place among residents in rural locations. Such issues highlight the planning implications of rural tourism development for communities (see Ireland 1987 and the discussion of second-home development) as well as the sociological implications of hosting guests in farmhouse accommodation (Bouquet 1987), which is a feature also examined more recently by P. Pearce (1990). Likewise, Vincent (1987) reviews the situation in St Maurice, Italy, arguing that rural tourism development requires that close-knit communities adapt to the incursion of capitalism in the expansion of tourism, where family independence, traditional values and cultural traditions may be adversely affected (McDonald 1987). One conclusion from this anthology of rural tourism research is the reliance upon case studies to illustrate the effect of tourism in specific localities, influenced by the approach of rural sociologists in the 1960s and 1970s.

Since this landmark study, a number of researchers have sought to diversify the focus of social and cultural impact research to include concerns about the way in which tourism development may change rural cultures (Byrne et al. 1993) and the consumption of rural environments and cultures in relation to late modernity or the postmodern society. The role of women in rural tourism has also belatedly attracted interest as a highly seasonal and unstable economic activity, since tourism is one of the few opportunities taken up by women but also contributes to the marginal status of women in the rural workforce. Similar arguments are also advanced by gender studies with a tourism component, such as Redclift and Sinclair (1991). More recent studies by Edwards (1991) and Keane et al. (1992) also indicate the importance of community participation in tourism planning so that the local population, and women in particular, are not excluded from the benefits of rural tourism development. A particularly sensitive issue is that of indigenous peoples and traditional cultures, including land/resource rights and their roles as performers and entrepreneurs (see Figure 1.1). Increasingly, native people are becoming involved in tourism to help meet their own goals of independence and cultural survival, yet tourism development carries special risks for them. There are also special business problems related to obtaining financing for projects, training with cultural sensitivity, attitudes towards work and service, and making decisions communally (Smith 1977).

Considerable attention has been paid in the literature to residents' perceptions and attitudes towards tourism, including studies of small towns and rural areas (for example Allen et al. 1988; Long et al. 1990; Getz 1994a; Johnson et al. 1994). While there is no way to predict what rural residents will think, say and do about tourism, some common patterns have been detected. First and foremost is the need for residents to feel tangible benefits from tourism, and preferably some degree of control over its development and promotion. In the absence of perceived benefits, it is likely that local opposition will increase. Another key factor is that of choice: if tourism is perceived to be the only development option, support is likely to increase. Johnson et al. (1994) concluded that in communities

Figure 1.1 The temple at the Fijian Cultural Centre, Orchid Island, Fiji (S. J. Page).

with low economic activity and low tourism development there will be high hopes and expectations of tourism. It has also been noted that long-term residents of rural areas are much more likely to support growth and change than newcomers, usually because the newcomers moved there for amenities which they do not want changed (Getz 1994b). However, as Butler and Clark conclude:

> [an] area where some research is needed is in the changing relationship between tourism and its host community. Rarely is tourism the sole rural economic activity. Over the last few decades the countryside has witnessed major changes in its social composition, the main symptoms being gentrification, new forms of social polarisation, and a domination by the service class. More research is needed on the relationship between the uneven social composition of the countryside, the spatially variable development of tourism, and the problematic relationship between the two.
>
> (Butler and Clark 1992: 180)

Therefore the sociological, anthropological and cultural aspects of rural tourism appear to offer the researcher in the 1990s a large number of avenues to explore in view of the processes affecting the changing population of rural areas.

The economic impact

The economic impact of rural tourism has been a fruitful area for research among a range of social scientists, often emphasizing or challenging the role of tourism as a panacea for all the economic and social ills of the countryside. But as Butler and Clark rightly acknowledge, tourism in rural areas is not necessarily the magic solution to rural development, given its:

> income leakages, volatility, declining multiplier, low pay, imported labour and the conservatism of investors. The least favoured circumstance in which to promote tourism is when the rural economy is already weak, since tourism will create highly unbalanced income and employment distributions. It is a better supplement for a thriving and diverse economy than as a mainstay of rural development.
>
> (Butler and Clark 1992: 175)

However, a longitudinal study of the Spey Valley, Scotland (Getz 1981, 1986, 1993b, 1994a, 1994b) documents a rural area in which tourism has remained the economic mainstay. In this respect, Butler and Clark's (1992) research is useful in that it identifies the principal concerns in rural economic research and the role of tourism in development in relation to:

- income leakage
- multipliers;
- labour issues (local versus imported and low pay);
- the limited number of entrepreneurs in rural areas;
- the proposition that tourism should be a supplement to rather than the mainstay of rural economies.

The principal research in this area is by Archer (1973, 1982), whose pioneering studies of multipliers have been used to establish the economic benefits of tourist expenditure in rural areas. While these studies have remained the baseline for subsequent research on rural tourism, few studies embrace a broad economic analysis to encompass the wide range of issues raised by Butler and Clark (1992). One possible explanation for this paucity of detailed economic studies of rural tourism may be related to the persistence of a 'farm tourism' focus. For this reason it is pertinent to examine the farm tourism concept, which has attracted a great deal of interest.

Farm tourism

Kariel and Kariel's (1982) research on the socio-cultural impacts of tourism in the Austrian Alps illustrated the interrelated nature of the economy, society and landscape in the rural environment. The study also noted that in the latter stages of the diffusion of tourism to rural areas income from tourism was more easily obtained than from agriculture. In this context, farm tourism may offer one way of facilitating agricultural diversification. According to Evans (1992a), research on farm tourism can be divided into two categories:

1 An expanding literature concerned with differing types of farm diversification . . . as a major option adapted by farm families to aid business restructuring, necessitated by falling farm incomes (Evans 1992a: 140).
2 One devoted specifically to farm tourism and though these studies remain the most detailed, they are becoming increasingly dated' (Evans 1992a: 140; Evans cited those by Davies (1971), Jacobs (1973), DART (1974), Bull and Wibberley (1976), Denman (1978) and Frater (1982), which all use 1970s data).

Evans is critical of the second group of studies for their lack of definitional clarity, since they fail to distinguish between the accommodation and recreational components of farm tourism (Evans and Ilbery 1989). Evans rightly considers the analytical components of the studies to be too simplistic, focusing on the expected economic costs and benefits of such enterprises, and on the characteristics and attitudes of farm families to such development (Evans 1992a: 140). Despite these problems with the farm tourism literature and concerns with its marketing, a major problem remains the absence of accurate national studies of the growth and development of farm tourism. However, Dernoi (1983) and Frater (1983) review the situation in Europe, Wrathall (1980) examines the development of France's *gîtes ruraux* and Vogeler (1977) discusses the situation in the United States, while Oppermann (1995, 1996) considers farm tourism in Southern Germany.

Evans and Ilbery's (1992) survey of England and Wales identified almost 6,000 farm businesses with accommodation. They also undertook a geographical analysis of the distribution of such accommodation, with southwest England, Cumbria, the Welsh border counties, North Yorkshire and the southeast coast of England popular locations for this activity. The upland areas and southwest England were the dominant locations, with a diversity of modes of operation (bed and breakfast, self-catering, camping and caravanning) and niche marketing used to satisfy particular forms of tourism demand (e.g. weekend breaks, week-long breaks and traditional two-week holidays). Even so, Evans (1992b) acknowledges the absence of national studies of why farm businesses have pursued this activity and the range of factors influencing their decision to undertake it. Evans and Ilbery (1992) also point to inherent contradictions in the existing literature, since their findings illustrate that larger farm businesses have also diversified into farm tourism (Ilbery 1991). Whilst this is at odds with Frater's (1982) research, it illustrates that family labour is widely used to service farm-based accommodation. Such research also highlights the capital requirements of farm tourism ventures and the role of marketing, financial advice and the need for external agents in establishing networks to develop their business. Even so, Maude and van Rest (1985) argue that due to the limited returns for small farmers and the constraints of existing planning legislation it is not a significant means of tackling the serious problem of low farm incomes in upland areas. Thus, it is unlikely to improve the low-income problem of upland farmers in their Cumbria case study since they argue that farm tourism has been wrongly regarded as the main pillar in a diversified agricultural policy (Maude and van Rest 1985). Consequently, the continued debate and focus on farm tourism have detracted from a more critical debate on the wider significance of rural tourism within an economic context. However, in an environmental context a critical debate has continued to develop in relation to the impact of rural tourism.

The environmental effects of rural tourism

The environmental impact of tourism has been extensively reviewed in the tourism literature and rural tourism has emerged as a prominent element, with the usual caveat that tourism is destructive to different degrees of the actual qualities which attract tourists. In a rural context, the growing pressure emerging from the development-intensive nature of tourism and the expansion of mass tourism has posed many new pressures as 'new tourism' discovers the qualities of rural environments. In fact, the construction of theme parks in rural environments, second homes (Gartner 1987), timeshare, conference centres, holiday villages, and designation of environments as special places to visit (e.g. National Parks) have all contributed to the insatiable tourism appetite for rural environments. Bramwell (1991) highlights the concern for more responsible and environmental forms of rural tourism as the 1990s witness the changing focus of the sustainability debate firmly focused on the rural environment, and examines the extent to which rural tourism policy in Britain has been integrated with concepts of sustainability, outlining the role of the English Tourist Board and Countryside Commission policy-formulation process.

The Countryside Commission points to the need to improve the public's understanding and care of the rural environment, as outlined in their consultation paper 'Visitors to the Countryside'. A number of recent special issues of journals have also focused on sustainability and rural tourism (e.g. *Tourism Recreation Research* 16(1), 1991; *Journal of Sustainable Tourism* 1/2, 1994). However, it is apparent that tourism in a rural context displays many of the features of the symbiotic relationship which exists between tourism and the environment. For this reason it is appropriate to consider the tourism resource base, emphasizing supply and demand features in relation to the business aspects of rural tourism.

THE BUSINESS OF RURAL TOURISM: POLICY, PLANNING AND THE COUNTRYSIDE

The resource base

The rural tourism resource base can be defined in several ways, including by asking what attracts people to rural areas. The attractions or benefits sought will encourage country life experiences, contact with primary resource users, sightseeing (see Figure 1.2), shopping for unique goods in

Figure 1.2 Tourist sightseeing in rural areas by the Helicopter Line in Queenstown, New Zealand (courtesy of the Helicopter Line).

small-town settings, wildlife viewing or consumption, recreation, and peace and quiet. An ecological approach to classifying the rural tourist resource base focuses upon unique landscapes or ecosystems, such as, alpine, desert, coastal, wetlands, forest and uplands areas. This highlights the dependence of rural tourism businesses on the rural resource base. In each landscape there will be a blending of human and natural forces, giving rise to unique opportunities and challenges; many of these environments are sensitive to human development and use. The Australian Rural Tourism Strategy (Australia's Commonwealth Department of Tourism 1994) suggests a classification by referring to rural tourism segments including island, coastal, hinterland, country, bush, outback or remote areas. These categories seem to combine ecological and perceptual variables peculiar to that country's geography and settlement patterns. A further approach is to ask what combination of resources and supply is attractive for tourism investment. Lane (1994: 28) identified these factors when considering investment suitability in rural areas; these include scenic value, special wildlife assets, cultural assets, ease of access to large populations, special facilities for sport, effective promotion and management skills.

Rural tourism supply

While any tourism or hospitality business can be located in a rural area, Table 1.1 provides a starting-point for defining the typical rural tourism

Table 1.1 Typical rural tourism businesses

- outfitting, guiding and rentals for hunting, fishing, horse trekking, safaris, nature study, boating, off-road vehicles and other outdoor recreation and adventures (but not dependent on intense facility developments)
- fly-in services to remote areas; these are often called adventure and ecotourism enterprises
- wilderness and ecotourism lodges; small-scale resorts; retreats (sometimes called alternative or specialist accommodation)
- small roadside motels and related forms of accommodation
- spas and health resorts emphasizing rural amenities
- low-intensity campgrounds and self-catering operations; seasonal camps for organized groups
- bed and breakfast and guest houses; small country inns and taverns; farm stays and visits
- large estates with small-scale accommodation and outdoor activities
- safari parks; game and fish farms; agricultural, silvicultural, fishing and other primary activities that sell to or host visitors; pick your-own produce establishments; resource-based educational tours
- low-intensity downhill and cross-country skiing facilities
- village and roadside retailing and hospitality services
- festivals and special events in villages and nature parks
- services provided by indigenous people and traditional cultures on reserves or traditional resource-use areas
- interpretive and other rural heritage attractions
- guided countryside tours (sightseeing and cultural themes)
- community cooperatives
- native communities which provide tourist services
- nature parks with visitor services

business. To Bramwell (1993) it is also their small-scale and functional relationship with open space and nature, heritage or traditional societies that makes them rural. He also suggests that rural businesses should be traditional in design and character, and organic in structure based on the local resource base and population.

Demand for rural tourism

To a certain extent, undifferentiated or mass tourism exists in rural areas, but this phenomenon is usually manifested in large-scale developments and at some point ceases to be 'rural' in nature; mass and rural tourism are essentially incompatible and development of the former lessens the availability of the latter. Although it would be logical to assume that everyone is a potential rural tourist at some time, the range of rural tourism products and experiences is too great for generalizations. What matters, therefore, is gaining knowledge of the existing and potential rural tourist's motives, preferences and behaviour regarding the various niche markets that exist; specifically, who can be attracted to a given rural tourism product? This is a research task complicated by the fact that many domestic and international visitors experience urban, rural and resort attractions on the same trip.

Bramwell (1993: 21) notes that rural tourists appear to be more affluent and better educated, to seek quality and spend above-average amounts on holidays. As to motivations, there is little published material available. Oppermann (1996) found a surprising fact in a study of farm-based tourism in southern Germany: operators thought a 'calm relaxing environment' was the chief motivator of tourists, but to visitors the actual farm environment was only a backdrop. And although the conventional wisdom in Germany is that rural tourists are mostly middle-aged couples with children, Oppermann (1995) found a bimodal distribution defined by couples and groups of four. Families were much more likely to stay on farms.

Identifying and segmenting the rural tourism market is probably the least researched and understood process in the rural tourism system. There are few studies that focus on the rural tourist, although one could assemble market facts from diverse sources and aggregate them into a comprehensive rural tourism market evaluation. Lane (1994) recommended research into price sensitivity, the importance of particular types of landscape, heritage and interpretive facilities, and on demand for certain types of accommodation. Better understanding of perceptions, motivators and consumption patterns (such as repeat visits) is also important.

Organization, management and policy issues for rural businesses

Who sets rural tourism policies? What are the relative roles and the partnership potential among the diverse public agencies and private associations which in some way influence rural tourism? In many parts of the world, tourism organizations and their promotion focus on urban areas and resorts. Often, rural areas have been marginalized as sightseeing territory or have been viewed as space in which development might occur, rather than as a distinct and important tourism product or market segment. Pigram (1993) observed that rural tourism often constitutes a disjointed and reactive policy field, while Long and Nuckolls (1994) concluded that support for local and regional tourism in the United States is fragmented or non-existent, and although Luloff et al. (1994: 49) reported that thirty out of fifty states have some form of programme aimed at rural tourism, they concluded it was often 'more rhetoric than action'.

The development of specific approaches to tourism planning and their application in a rural context has attracted comparatively little attention. Phillips and Williams (1984) argue that traditional forms of rural planning were related to development control by designating landscapes as specially protected areas. However, with changes in the economic structure of rural areas, as agricultural employment has declined in the post-war period, rural planning has also adopted a more positive strategy towards rural tourism as a form of employment generation to offset out-migration and a declining population base and to sustain thresholds for service provision. In this context, tourism has been perceived as one activity to assist in rural development in declining areas. In other contexts, rural planning has needed to exercise development controls to prevent rural tourism development (e.g. second-home ownership) from dominating villages and other rural settlements to the detriment of the local community. In other words, rural planning has been used in both a facilitating and a controlling role for rural tourism to develop, protect and enhance the quality of rural environments.

Long and Nuckolls (1994: 19) argued that 'developing a sustainable industry . . . will only be possible if a rural community has the necessary leadership, is effective in its planning efforts, and can access technical assistance to supplement local expertise and eliminate the information and resource gaps'. They stressed key factors in organizing resources for rural tourism planning, including:

- the leadership of individuals or groups, leading to balanced community representation;
- education of residents and other stakeholders;
- the adoption of planning strategies that fit the local situation;
- access to technical information and expertise.

Their strategic planning process involves ten steps, which are:

- gathering information;
- identifying community values;
- developing a vision;
- identifying critical concerns and opportunities;
- formulating a mission;
- developing goals;
- developing objectives;
- outlining actions and funding strategies;
- evaluating progress;
- updating or modifying the plan.

This process is much more than an economic planning exercise, and must blend with all aspects of rural life. One of the most important aspects of rural strategic tourism planning is the 'soft' nature of evaluating community values and formulating a vision. This process must consider the meaning and substance of rural or small-town life and how tourism can and will alter it. But values might very well be diverse, especially where the tourism industry already has a hold, in commuter zones around cities and in retirement areas.

According to the Minnesota Extension Service (1991), values should encompass authenticity and a sense of place, assess the true benefits and costs of using tourism as a diversification strategy, develop and deliver quality services while sharing the benefits and encouraging local control. Likewise, the Australian National Rural Tourism Strategy (Australia's Commonwealth Department of Tourism 1994: 13) examined the stakeholder organizations and their roles, noting that they are 'many and varied'. Specifically, the strategy discussed private operators, host communities, tourism industry bodies, non-tourism industry bodies (e.g. agriculture and automobile clubs), transport operators, educational institutions and financial institutions. Although development is primarily an industry function, governments are involved in research and planning, development assistance schemes, facilitation, infrastructure supply, regulation and accreditation, demonstration projects, awareness campaigns, provision of information, attractions and services, and marketing. Various strategies arising from the Australian review of rural tourism are indicative of the kinds of roles government and industry partnerships can pursue, as illustrated in Table 1.2.

The community cooperative is a form of organization that has particular relevance to small towns and rural areas. In parts of Ireland and Scotland, for example, cooperatives – assisted by public agencies – have launched and continue to manage a number of tourism projects such as accommodation and retailing. In Canada's far north some indigenous people work through formal cooperatives to supply guides

Table 1.2 The Australian National Tourism Strategy 1994: strategic actions

- encourage the sustainable development of high-quality tourism products and product variety in rural areas
- support accreditation and introduction/recognition of standards for rural tourism ventures
- ensure that educational and training needs are known and are being met
- promote coordinated and cooperative marketing of rural tourism opportunities
- encourage the provision of reliable regional data and research on rural tourism supply/demand functions
- encourage and support industry and community leadership as a means of developing tourism in rural areas and contributing to regional growth
- encourage improvements in rural transport and infrastructure
- further enhance local-government understanding of the benefits and requirements of tourism, and the value of integrated industry and government planning

and crafts, while in other rural communities tourism is part of more comprehensive development schemes (Clarke 1981). While policy and planning issues associated with the supply of and demand for tourism are important in a strategic context, individual rural tourism businesses also need to recognize that there are specific operational issues which affect, shape and in some cases determine the nature of rural tourism business activities.

Operational issues affecting the establishment and development of rural tourism businesses

In the ensuing discussion it is useful to consider how each business transcends resources, supply, demand and organizational issues; as far as possible these connections are specified. Naturally there are many issues and sub-issues that could be added to this discussion, all with varying importance under different circumstances. For example, the Minnesota Extension Service (1991) provides a thorough discussion of both obstacles to rural tourism development and major challenges and it is a useful starting point. In this discussion the most prominent issues are outlined and their significance highlighted.

Accessibility and spatial factors

Many recreational activities are inherently or preferably rural, and those which require very large tracts of open space are rural almost by definition. As a consequence, urbanites seeking a skiing, fishing, golfing, hiking, boating or camping experience often seek the countryside. Some of these activities are subject to distance-decay functions and must be nearby to attract frequent use, while others attract travellers because of remoteness. Resorts and second-home communities can generate frequent trips, longer stays and a feeling of ownership in a rural community. To some individual rural tourism businesses, like restaurants and retailing, high-volume accessibility is essential. Highway and town locations are a must. To others, remoteness is advantageous, but getting to the area presents a cost which is usually passed on to or directly absorbed by the customer. In a shrinking world where travel reduces the problems of access and distance, remote experiences will certainly become more rationed by planning and price, presenting substantial long-term competitive advantages for certain businesses.

Access issues are also complex, with large potential costs – both for remote and near-urban rural areas. Very early research on urban-centred recreational travel was conducted in the landmark ORRRC (1962) studies in the USA, which found that same-day travel dominated outdoor recreational patterns. Research in central Scotland by Duffield and Owen (1970) discovered differences between physically active recreation, which was close to the city, and pleasure driving, which went further afield. Cracknell (1967) used the term 'living space' to describe the countryside around cities, while Mercer (1970) referred to 'hinterlands' for day and weekend recreational zones. Mercer (1970) and others realized, however, that distance was important in conjunction with other factors such as supply, quality and access routes.

Modelling the processes of spatial variations in the urban–rural travel continuum and the factors which explain them has been of considerable research interest for geographers (see D. Pearce 1987: 5–12). Lundgren (1983), for example, concluded that increasing mobility over time led to increasing penetration of rural areas for recreational and tourism development, and that a life-cycle related to these patterns plus changing recreational preferences could be observed to affect rural tourism businesses. One aspect of the life-cycle was a tendency for personal ownership to be replaced by corporate holdings, especially as resorts developed. The Recreation Opportunities Spectrum (ROS) (Clarke and Stankey 1990) and Tourism Opportunities Spectrum (TOS) (Butler and Waldbrook 1991) are related concepts with planning and management implications. ROS is more applicable to protected areas and encompasses zones from highly accessible and developed to remote and inaccessible, each catering to different recreational interests. The TOS could be applied to urban-centred regions, or rural areas adjacent to resorts, involving a continuum from intense use through dispersed traffic to inaccessible protected areas.

A number of other spatial planning concepts applicable to rural tourism have been suggested. Gunn's (1979) regional tourism development concepts have been widely adopted. Gunn distinguished between attraction/service clusters and touring corridors, and also noted the importance of gateways, clustering and linkages in developing regions. Fagence (1991) argued for a hierarchy of country towns acting as service centres, transit and interchange stops, gateways to specialized activity zones, and focal points for special events or other attractions. In contrast, Lundgren (1983) showed that the process of rural tourism development could be shaped through direct means such as traffic and transport controls or indirectly through facility location and area marketing advocating use of existing service centres, to minimize negative impacts. A uniquely rural tourism concept is the touring route, as manifested in the Cultural Routes in Europe scheme, which incorporates cross-border routes emphasizing rural heritage (see *Tourism Recreation Research*, 1991, 16(1): 43), and scenic roads in the USA (Lew 1991). In Arizona, for example, routes were classified into historic, recreation, park or native American themes. By including these designations in travel guidebooks, it is possible to influence travel patterns directly. It is difficult to counter the common attitude that rural areas are merely spaces waiting to be filled or accessed. Until rural tourism resources are highly valued for their unique qualities, and until it is widely recognized that improved access and development tends to destroy rural attributes, the dominant planning and marketing concepts are likely to be related to rural development, not conservation.

Multiple use: the integration of tourism businesses into the locality

The rural tourism resource base in most localities is mixed with the different sectors of the economy represented, especially the primary sector. This may pose problems of compatibility and in others areas competitiion for the same resource. Primary-resource users have often been dominant or favoured, with tourism being viewed as an economic supplement or development tool of last resort. Tourism is a natural ally of farming, to preserve rural landscapes and farm-related cultural elements, the interrelationships are often complex: forestry and tourism are invariably compatible, but those dependent on forestry are not usually sympathetic to the tourism industry's pleas for banning clear-felling. Farmers and tourists can also be in opposition over rights of way, litter and interference with animal husbandry.

Business operators might have to accommodate or make arrangements for multiple use, especially of public lands. This is often highly regulated, but in the absence of controls the typical problems of overuse associated with the 'law of the commons' tend to apply. In such cases industry self-regulation is preferable to open and destructive competition, and business associations might find it advantageous to appeal for enforceable regulations. Another multiple-use issue of importance to rural tourism businesses is that of incompatible uses. Rivers cannot simultaneously accommodate power boats and rafters without risk of serious accidents. Temporal and spatial zoning is increasingly necessary, either through interbusiness agreements or formal regulations. Sooner or later capacity becomes an issue. Can farmers and other rural residents physically and socially accommodate large numbers of tourists? How many small-scale eco-lodges constitute an environmental threat to sensitive areas? Will rural tourism overstrain the capacity of villages to absorb the traffic, or of rural authorities to provide infrastructure and manage growth? Between-use conflicts can grow to a point where one resource user group suffers or is displaced. Cumulative long-term impacts might be almost invisible and difficult to monitor.

Seasonality

Seasonal and other short-term cyclical demand for rural tourism is largely dependent on institutional and climatic factors. However, primary resource uses can hinder or encourage seasonal visits, such as the desire for urbanites to participate in harvesting, and through the cultural rhythms of rural communities which result in festivals at certain times of the year. The normal range of rural tourism activities results in a peak summer season, largely based on sightseeing, second-home and farm stays, water sports and hiking. A winter sports season has been created in many rural areas, although the infrastructural and investment requirements are quite different. Autumn and spring seasons usually experience much lower demand, although for many people they are the best times to visit the countryside or wild areas. Strategies for extending the rural tourism season typically include new product development (especially all-year sports), price and packaging incentives, special events and segmented marketing. Such strategies might be resisted by communities which value their own peace and quiet most of the year. A further complication occurs through second-home purchases, thereby introducing urbanites into the rural community outside normal tourism seasons. In the future it is likely that rural depopulation in many regions will be more than matched by in-migrants and seasonal-home owners seeking the rural or alternative lifestyles. This suggests a major shift in how people will perceive and experience 'rurality'.

Many businesses subject to intense seasonality simply shut down for part of the year, and some operators enjoy that option. Employment of seasonal and part-time workers is the only option for many businesses, while others market hard to attract off-peak clients so as to retain their cash flow and keep permanent staff. Investors and lenders always look very hard at seasonality when determining the attractiveness or viability of financing rural tourism ventures.

Infrastructure and technology

Rural tourism planners will usually be confronted with infrastructural problems – in terms either of quantity (e.g. insufficient electrical or water supply) or of quality (e.g. poor roads and communication systems). Often rural infrastructure is highly concentrated in a few towns or located along major highways. This is both a blessing for those seeking a true 'getaway' experience and an obstacle to growth. A further concern is that development of roads or electricity supplies will simply encourage more traffic and diminish the original attractiveness of the area. Residents, on the other hand, often welcome such improvements. Information provision and interpretation are also related issues. Rural areas often lack adequate sign-posting for visitors, and information centres will likely be concentrated in a few towns or resorts. Can technology be developed which will allow tourists to access appropriate information from their vehicles, wherever they are? Use of the Internet is rapidly increasing, and an initiative in the United States has been designed to give rural tourism greater exposure to potential customers using this new medium.

The planner must evaluate the relative costs and benefits of concentration and dispersal strategies for rural tourism (Getz 1981): is it better to concentrate infrastructure and supply in towns or resorts where impacts can be managed, or to disperse improvements widely so as to spread benefits and avoid overcrowding? Isolated resort towns or service centres are likely to suffer from congestion and overuse of critical services at peak times, yet they might not be able to afford improvements to meet peak demands. Will residents approve expenditures aimed at improving tourism infrastructure? The traditional arguments about creating jobs and a stronger tax base might not be compelling unless residents also see improvements in the services they use. Policy-makers have to evaluate their investments carefully in this context, all the while hoping to take advantage of grants from senior levels of government aimed at tourism infrastructural improvements. Additional costs are often borne by rural businesses to secure and service basic infrastructure, including roads, electricity, water, waste disposal and telecommunications. Remote establishments might have to become reliant on some or all of these services.

Finance

Costs are often much higher in rural areas, and especially in remoter areas, both for development and operations. Availability of insurance and high costs were cited as a problem for rural tourism businesses in Australia. The costs of public infrastructure, such as roads, will also be higher, and the local authorities are often unable to finance ambitious projects or ensure adequate maintenance. To a large extent the additional costs of rural tourism are passed on to tourists, ensuring that many rural tourism experiences will remain expensive. In other places, however, such as densely populated Europe, rural tourism might be looked upon as a less costly holiday option, though without the absolute sense of isolation one can find in more remote areas, where access can artificially restrict visitor numbers.

Obtaining finance for tourism and hospitality projects is often difficult, and in rural areas this is normally compounded by several factors: absence of wealthy residents; inadequate infrastructure (such as fire or police, which give security to investments); absence of lending institutions (which often have an urban bias); lack of collateral (especially in depressed areas where, for example, land prices have fallen); and resource-poor public authorities. This is one reason why rural financial assistance programmes are common. In many countries grants, subsidies and other incentives have been applied strictly to rural or marginal areas as a way of overcoming their inherent weaknesses, and tourism has frequently been a major recipient. Canadian tourism planning and development initiatives in the 1970s and 1980s favoured rural areas explicitly. The most substantial tourism-related programmes have been joint federal–provincial agreements called TIDSAs (Tourism Industry Sub-Agreements). Beginning in 1974 and lasting about ten years (individual agreements usually lasted five years), most provinces took advantage of the shared funding provisions (half provincial and half federal government-sponsored) to prepare tourism plans and establish funding programmes for development, upgrading or training. This period was marked by a flurry of rural tourism schemes because urban areas were, for the most part, specifically excluded. Each TIDSA resulted in varying programmes aimed at province-established priorities. The 1979 TIDSA for Eastern Ontario, a large rural area without a major city (Ottawa being excluded), provided funding for feasibility studies, selected capital infrastructure, historical restorations, and local events with tourism potential.

Labour

According to Hohl and Tisdell's study (1995) of the remote Cape York Peninsula in Australia, the main obstacles to developing and expanding local tourism business were seasonality and the lack of a skilled workforce. Labour supply and quality are issues both for establishments who need staff and with regard to entrepreneurial potential. Many rural tourism businesses are small in scale, and often family-operated. This exacerbates the financing problems. Families can provide additional support for business initiatives, or can offer resistance to experimentation in new sectors like tourism. Multi-job families are not uncommon, with many tourist operators also running farms or even commuting into cities. The complexity of running a tourism business is accordingly greatly increased. A related problem is that of training. There is much less flexibility in time and working conditions for small tourism operators, and they miss out on the training opportunities available to larger employers. To reach many rural tourism operators, therefore, more flexible programmes are required, including distance education, off-season opportunities and economic incentives. This issue is clearly related to improving standards of product and service quality, and to certification and accreditation of operators. In some cases, the accreditation or certification process can be made conditional on training. Increasingly, families moving to rural areas for lifestyle reasons are finding that tourism offers the potential for earning income, so there might develop an entrepreneurial split between local residents and newcomers; newcomers are likely to have more money and more business experience.

The quantity and quality of labour in rural areas is a global problem for the tourism industry. Residents might be inexperienced in the service industry, or hostile towards such jobs. Training opportunities are normally limited. If rural tourism businesses are successful in attracting local workers, commuting and housing problems prove difficult and expensive to overcome, such as the necessity to provide transport or on-site housing for workers coming from far afield. It might prove easier to attract female workers than males, both because of competition with primary industries and due to attitudes. There is also a need to employ indigenous people. Accordingly, more sensitivity to cultural issues is required and owner–worker relations can be highly situational. Whereas tourism has proved to be successful at creating many jobs in rural areas, it has sometimes been to the detriment of primary resource industries, and especially to agriculture. A guaranteed service-sector wage might be looked upon by many as being preferable to unpredictable farming income, with the lure of resort or urban living adding to the problem. In this way tourism might serve to increase rural depopulation and harm local food supplies or an existing export industry.

Sustainability

The type, scale, location and pace of tourism development in rural areas requires special planning considerations. Tourism can easily overwhelm a small town or traditional society, particularly through an inability effectively to plan and manage development, disruption of lifestyle and weakening of cultural traditions, drastic alterations to work and leisure patterns and overloaded services and community infrastructure. Moreover, in rural landscapes the problem of 'common pool resources' frequently emerges. Healey (1994) notes that landscapes are susceptible to overuse and derogation of their attractiveness because of a lack of incentive for individuals or businesses to invest in conservation or productivity enhancements.

Determining the appropriateness of tourism in rural areas means achieving a good fit between tourism demand and the supply and management system in place, or between the needs of the industry and the wants of the residents. Murphy (1985) calls this process determining the 'community tourism product', and it requires a fully informed and involved community. Closely related to the question of appropriateness is the emerging paradigm of sustainability (Anon. 1994). What forms or pace of development can be absorbed to the benefit of rural residents, but without impeding the future social and economic health of the community? It can be argued that serious disruption of viable primary resource industries is not sustainable; on the other hand, tourism often creates more jobs and can keep the rural population on the land. So sustainability is not an easy issue to resolve.

Two systems are needed in order to ensure that sustainable development is debated and applied to planning decisions: monitoring through impact research, and ongoing community involvement. Residents will be much more likely to identify threats to sustainable development than outsiders, and their perspectives on sustainability are likely to be much different. But this is not to say that external evaluation is unnecessary. Conflict between environmental activists and logging communities demonstrates precisely how difficult it is to achieve consensus on what sustainable development actually means. Klejdzinska (1991) documented a number of environmental issues for rural tourism planning, many of which are generic to any rural developments, or to any recreation and tourism activity. Of particular interest here are those impacts which are uniquely rural, such as the effects on farming (e.g. loss of grazing land) and resultant landscape modification.

Healey (1994) discussed several methods for overcoming the common pool problem, and these can also be thought of as strategies for sustainable development. The first is to privatize resources to ensure one owner has control; usually this will apply only to specific developments. Parks and reserves can be created to ensure that public agencies protect the resource base. A variety of direct development and land-use controls are available, such as zoning and permits. Private owners can cooperate through associations to overcome overuse problems. Although they are usually focused on economic development and growth, increasingly rural areas must cope with tourism-generated problems and devise defensive and ameliorative strategies. Barker (1994) examined the development of tourism in the European Alps, showing how planning evolved. At first planning was dominated by a focus on quantitative growth, followed by a shift to qualitative growth in response to market competition. Then came recognition of the need for change as a result of congestion and use pressures, and most recently a fundamental reorientation to break out of the uncontrolled growth spiral.

Businesses in rural areas, and especially those in sensitive environments, must face unique conditions not found in the city. Weather can become a more intense and expensive factor, especially if the business operations must be halted when roads are closed by snow, when river and lake levels are too high for recreational uses, or when winds or temperature make a rural visit undesirable. Environmental factors might add additional operating costs (especially heating or airconditioning), add to transport costs and generate extra construction costs. Seasonal variations might easily lead to closure of rural tourism businesses for large blocks of time, some planned and others unexpected. Managing cashflow therefore becomes a major challenge, especially if lending institutions are unsympathetic. Being 'green' – that is reducing and effectively treating or removing wastes, conserving water and energy, recycling and avoiding ecological damage – is fast becoming a necessity for many rural tourism businesses. This is because of government regulations or the response of operators to customer demands. The very nature of rural and remote tourism experiences requires extra environmental sensitivity and therefore costs. Suggested principles for achieving sustainable rural tourism would commence with these and related goals. These goals might be difficult to achieve, and some might prove to be incompatible, yet they are all worthwhile in their own right.

Design

Blending into the rural environment and preserving the rural ambience are important to rural tourism businesses. Not only should the development be architecturally appropriate, but siting related to views and wildlife is important, and so is avoidance of disturbance to primary resource uses. Tourists expect resorts and rural tourism experiences to be different from urban experiences, especially in terms of providing direct environmental experiences. Authenticity is an important issue where traditional styles of design are found. Austria and Switzerland, for example, are noted for their traditional designs and themes which run through all urban and rural development. Incorporation of traditional motifs is generally desirable and possible, even where no single style predominates. Heritage conservation is clearly a feasible goal for rural tourism, as many old buildings can be creatively adapted to modern uses. The retail sector often leads this process, finding that old buildings and traditional designs help create a desirable social and shopping environment. Regional and national themes can be expressed through physical design, but also through cultural events, arts and crafts, dress and other traditions. Rural enterprises are able to foster traditions through many aspects of their design and operations.

Planning, research, management and marketing capabilities for rural tourism businesses

Rural areas and small towns will usually lack the sophisticated management systems found in cities and in higher levels of government. This includes fewer resources and perhaps less expertise in research, planning, marketing, and operational and project management. This applies to private and public sectors alike. Tourist operators need to organize for marketing (Middleton 1982; Gilbert 1989), planning (Holland and Crotts 1992), lobbying and self-help purposes, and in rural areas this process is more difficult – due to fewer numbers, greater distances, fewer resources, and perhaps cultural factors which act against collaboration. Dependency on joint marketing initiatives and on intermediaries is likely to be heightened in rural tourism situations. A small, remote operator lacks marketing and political clout, and must make up for this problem with greater participation in organizations.

Keane et al. (1992) insisted that rural tourism must be integrated with community-based development initiatives and not planned as a single sector, a theme developed by Jones (1993). Other prerequisites to successful rural tourism are: supports being available to community-based, not individual, initiatives; working capital funds; professional development co-ordinators; and marketing supports, including coordination with wider product and marketing structures. A distinct image must also be cultivated – one that appeals to consumers looking for specific, attractive products.

IMPLICATIONS FOR RESEARCH ON THE BUSINESS OF RURAL TOURISM

In this review of the rural tourism literature and its significance for rural tourism businesses, it is acknowledged that the small-business sector is a major growth sector in many industrialized and less-developed countries, with the individual entrepreneur and family-run business being prominent features of rural environments. In the case of rural tourism, there have been few attempts to consider the literature on small businesses and their relationship to tourism enterprises. A recent survey of tourism businesses in New Zealand (Deloitte Touche Tomatsu 1994) highlighted the small-firm nature of many rural tourism businesses, and the factors which characterize this sector most notably are:

- the prevalence of small-scale operations with less than five employees;
- development from family-run businesses;
- the difficulty in accessing finance to initiate, develop and expand their business;
- expansion into tourism during the preceding five to seven years as a new growth sector in the New Zealand economy.

These features seem to be similar to the broader issues raised in the study, in the UK by Keeble et al. (1992), *Business Success in the Countryside* (cited in Curran and Storey 1993) where:

- rural business founders are much more likely to be in-migrants to their local area than founders of urban businesses;
- employment has grown faster in recent years in rural small firms than urban small firms;

- rural firms are somewhat younger than urban firms, suggesting that the birth rate of firms in rural areas is higher than that in urban areas;
- rural firms occupy specific market niches, which differ from those of urban firms and which they have successfully exploited;
- there seems to be evidence that the rural firms, particularly those in accessible rural locations, are more innovative (modified from Curran and Storey 1993: 6).

The implications for rural tourism businesses are less clear, given the absence of detailed studies in different countries. Therefore, such research raises a range of questions pertinent to rural tourism businesses:

1 To what extent are rural tourism businesses based on local entrepreneurs rather than in-migrants who innovate and develop a strong product base?
2 Are rural tourism businesses offering a wide range of rural employment opportunities for the local population as opposed to imported labour?
3 Are there high growth and failure rates for rural tourism businesses and to what extent are these a diversification from an existing business? What are the rates of business formation for rural tourism and what is the motivation of entrepreneurs seeking to expand into this sector?
4 Do the motivations of rural entrepreneurs starting rural tourism businesses accord with Townroe and Mallalieu's (1993) seven categories of business start-up in rural areas: off-farm diversification; arts and crafts; early retirement; mid-life switchers; spin-out from previous employment; rebuilding earlier business and other reasons?
5 What unique problems do rural businesses face? Are they disadvantaged due to their distance from urban centres in relation to finance, employment/recruitment, and how is this counterbalanced by advantages?
6 How are rural tourism businesses performing? Are such businesses profitable despite the highly seasoned nature of rural tourism?
7 What policies are required by government to expand this sector? Are rural entrepreneurs with tourism businesses in need of training and advice? If so, who should be providing such training and advice?

It is hoped that the ensuing chapters in this book will begin to examine some of these issues given the paucity of research on them. To date, some of these issues are dealt with in an ad-hoc manner in the range of publications on rural tourism, with a limited number of studies belatedly considering such issues in a more sytematic manner (Cox and Fox 1991). The role of marketing has attracted only limited attention (Evans 1992a; Gilbert 1989), while the implications of strategic business planning (Holland and Crotts 1992) and the role of state and national government in facilitating rural tourism business development have only recently attracted attention in the UK (PA Cambridge Economic Consultants 1992) and in Ireland in the context of heritage tourism (Page 1994b; Phillips and Tubridy 1994). However, there are a range of issues associated with the rural business environment which present many policy, planning and management challenges – both for the destination and for individual business managers – that are in whole or part unique. Major elements in this system are rural tourism resources, supply (i.e. businesses), demand, and destination-level organization, policy and marketing functions. Across each of these elements run a number of key, transcending issues, such as accessibility, financing, labour and management expertise. Rural tourism businesses face many problems and challenges that urban businesses do not, but, equally, they have many opportunities to exploit. As understanding of these challenges and opportunities increases, governments, destination organizations and individuals will be better able to collaborate for sustainable rural tourism development.

REFERENCES

Allen, L. R., Long, P. T., Perdue, R. R. and Kieselbach, S. (1988) 'The impact of tourism development on residents' perceptions of community life', *Journal of Travel Research* 27(1): 16–21.

Anon. (1994) Special issue on Sustainable Rural Tourism Development, *Trends* 31(1).

Archer, B. (1973) *The Impact of Domestic Tourism*, Cardiff: University of Wales Press.

—— (1982) 'The value of multipliers and their policy implications', *Tourism Management* 3(2): 236–41.

Australia's Commonwealth Department of Tourism (1994) *National Rural Tourism Strategy*, Canberra: Australia's Commonwealth Department of Tourism.

Barker, M. (1994) 'Strategic tourism planning and limits to growth in the Alps', *Tourism Recreation Research* 19(2): 43–49.

Backman, S. J., Backman, K. F., Potts, T. D. and Uysal, M. (1992) 'International tourism: an unrecognized potential in rural tourism', *Visions in Leisure and Business* 11(1): 24–31.

Balogh, O. and Csaky, C. (1991) 'The development of rural tourism in Hungary', *Tourism Recreation Research* 16(1): 25–8.

Belford, S. (1983) 'Rural tourism', *Architects Journal* 178(29): 59–71.

Bouquet, M. (1987) 'Bed, breakfast and an evening meal: commensality in the nineteenth and twentieth century farm household in Hartland', in M. Bouquet and M. Winter (eds) *Who From Their Labours Rest? Conflict and Practice in Rural Tourism*, Aldershot: Avebury.

Bouquet, M. and Winter, M (eds) (1987a) *Who From Their Labours Rest? Conflict and Practice in Rural Tourism*, Aldershot: Avebury.

—— (1987b) 'Introduction: tourism politics and practice', in M. Bouquet and M. Winter (eds) *Who From Their Labours Rest? Conflict and Practice in Rural Tourism*, Aldershot: Avebury.

Bracey, H. (1970) *People and the Countryside*, London: Routledge & Kegan Paul.

Bramwell, B. (1991) 'Sustainability and rural tourism policy in Britain', *Tourism Recreation Research* 16(2): 49–51.

—— (1993) *Tourism Strategies and Rural Development*. Paris: OECD.

—— (1994) 'Rural tourism and sustainable rural tourism', *Journal of Sustainable Tourism* 2: 1–6.

Bramwell, B. and Lane, B. (eds) (1994) Special Issue on Rural Tourism and Sustainable Rural Development, *Journal of Sustainable Tourism* 2: (1/2).

Bull, C. and Wibberley, G. (1976) *Farm Based Recreation in South East England: Studies in Rural Land Use Report 12*, London:Wye College, University of London.

Butler, R. (1992) 'Tourism landscapes: for the tourist or of the tourist?', *Tourism Recreation Research* 17(1): 3–9.

Butler, R. and Clark, G. (1992) 'Tourism in rural areas: Canada and the United Kingdom', in I. R. Bowler, C. R. Bryant and M. D. Nellis (eds) *Contemporary Rural Systems in Transition, vol. 2: Economy and Society*, Wallingford, Oxon: CAB International.

Butler, R. and Waldbrook, L. (1991) 'A new planning tool: the tourism opportunity spectrum', *Journal of Tourism Studies* 2(1): 2–14.

Butler, R., Hall, C. M. and Jenkins, J. (eds) (1997) *Tourism and Recreation in Rural Areas*, Chichester: Wiley.

Byrne, A., Edmondson, R. and Fahy, K. (1993) 'Rural tourism and cultural identity in the West of Ireland', in B. O'Connor and M. Cronin (eds) *Tourism in Ireland: A Critical Analysis*, Cork: Cork University Press.

Cedrins, R. (1991) 'Small scale tourism in Sweden', *Tourism Recreation Research* 16(1): 85–6.

Clarke, R. (1981) *Our Own Resources: Cooperatives and Community Economic Development in Rural Canada*. Langholm, Scotland: Arkleton Trust.

Clarke, R. and Stankey G., (1990). 'The recreation opportunity spectrum: a framework for planning, management and research', in R. Graham (ed.) *Towards Serving Visitors and Managing Our Resources*, Waterloo: University of Waterloo.

Cloke, P. (1992) 'The countryside', in P. Cloke (ed.) *Policy and Change in Thatcher's Britain*, Oxford: Pergamon Press.

Cote, D. (1987) 'Valle d'Aosta and the Lake District', in M. Bouquet, and M. Winter (eds) *Who From Their Labours Rest? Conflict and Practice in Rural Tourism*, Aldershot: Avebury.

Cox, L. J. and Fox, M. (1991) 'Agriculturally based leisure attractions', *Journal of Tourism Studies* 2(2): 18–27.

Cracknell, B. (1967) 'Accessibility to the countryside as a factor in planning for leisure', *Regional Studies* 1: 148.

Craik, J. (1987) 'A crown of thorns in paradise: tourism on Queensland's Great Barrier Reef', in M. Bouquet and M. Winter (eds) *Who From Their Labours Rest? Conflict and Practice in Rural Tourism*, Aldershot: Avebury.

Curran, J. and Storey, D. (eds) (1993) *Small Firms in Urban and Rural Locations*, London: Routledge.

DART (1974) *Farm Recreation and Tourism in England and Wales*,

Report to the Countryside Commission, English Tourist Board and Wales Tourist Board, Publication No. 14, CCP 83, Cheltenham: Countryside Commission.

Davies, E. (1971) *Farm Tourism in Cornwall and Devon – Some Economic and Physical Considerations*, Report No. 184, Exeter: Agricultural Economics Unit, University of Exeter.

Deloitte Touche Tomatsu (1994) *Small Business Survey 1994: New Zealand Tourism Industry*, Christchurch: Deloitte Touche Tomatsu.

Denman, R. (1978) *Recreation and Tourism in Farms, Crofts and Estates*, Report to the Highlands and Islands Development Board and the Scottish Tourist Board, Edinburgh.

Dernoi, L. A. (1983) 'Farm tourism in Europe', *Tourism Management* 4(3): 155–66.

DiPersio, C., Hayden, G. and Goeldner, C. R. (1993) 'National Rural Tourism Development Foundation established', *Journal of Travel Research* 32(1): 62.

Dornbusch, D. M. and Kawczynska, C. J. (1992) 'Tourist oriented directional signs: a self-supporting program to promote rural business and economic development', *Journal of Travel Research* 31(1): 3–9.

Duffield, B. and Owen, M. (1970) *Leisure + Countryside =: A Geographical Appraisal of Countryside Recreation in Lanarkshire*, Edinburgh: University of Edinburgh.

Edwards, J. (1991) 'Guest–host perceptions of rural tourism in England and Portugal', in M. T. Sinclair and M. J. Stabler (eds) *The Tourism Industry: An International Analysis*, Wallingford: CAB International.

Evans, N. (1992) 'Towards an understanding of farm-based tourism in Britain', in A. W. Gilg (ed.) *Progress in rural policy and planning*, vol. 2, London: Belhaven Press.

Evans, N. J. and Ibery, B. W. (1989) 'A conceptual framework for investigating farm-based accommodation and tourism in Britain', *Journal of Rural Studies* 5(3): 257–66.

—— (1992a) 'Advertising and farm-based accommodation: a British case study', *Tourism Management* 13(4): 415–22.

—— (1992b) 'The distribution of farm-based accommodation in England and Wales', *Journal of the Royal Agricultural Society of England* 153: 67–80.

Fagence, M. (1991) 'Rural tourism and the small country town', *Tourism Recreation Research* 16(1): 34–43.

Fowler, J. E. (1991) 'Farmhouse holidays in Ireland', *Tourism Recreation Research* 16(1): 72–5.

Frater, J. (1982) *Farm Tourism in England and Overseas*, Research Memorandum 93, Birmingham: Centre for Urban and Regional Studies, University of Birmingham.

—— (1983) 'Farm tourism in England', *Tourism Management* 4(3): 167–79.

Garcia-Olaya, D. L. C. (1991) 'Farm tourism a possible resource for the rural population (Spain)', *Tourism Recreation Research* 16(1): 83–4.

Gartner, W. C. (1987) 'Environmental impacts of recreational home developments', *Annals of Tourism Research* 14(1): 38–57.

Getz, D. (1981) 'Tourism and rural settlement policy,' *Scottish Geographical Magazine* 97 (December):158–68.

—— (1983) 'Capacity to absorb tourism, concepts and implications for strategic planning', *Annals of Tourism Research* 10(2): 239–63.

—— (1986) 'Tourism and population change: long term impacts of tourism in the Badenoch-Strathspey District of the Scottish Highlands', *Scottish Geographical Magazine* 102(2): 113–26.

—— (1993a) 'Impacts of tourism on residents' leisure: concepts, and a longitudinal case study of Spey Valley, Scotland', *Journal of Tourism Studies* 4(2): 33–44.

—— (1993b) 'Tourist shopping villages: development and planning strategies', *Tourism Management* 14(1): 15–26.

—— (1994a) 'Students' work experiences, perceptions and attitudes towards careers in hospitality and tourism: a longitudinal case study in Spey Valley, Scotland', *International Journal of Hospitality Management* 13(1): 25–37.

—— (1994b) 'Residents' attitudes towards tourism: a longitudinal study in Spey Valley, Scotland', *Tourism Management* 15(4): 247–58.

Getz, D., Joncas, and Kelly, M. (1994) 'Tourist shopping villages in the Calgary region', *Journal of Tourism Studies* 5(1): 2–15.

Gilbert, D. (1989) 'Rural tourism and marketing: synthesis and new ways of working', *Tourism Management* 10(1): 39–50.

—— (1993) 'Issues in appropriate rural tourism development for southern Ireland', *Leisure Studies* 12(2): 137–46.

Gill, G. A. (1991) 'The effects of "on farm tourism", on the rural community and on farming in the United Kingdom', *Tourism Recreation Research* 16(1): 69–71.

Gilligan, H. (1987) 'Visitors, tourists and outsiders in a Cornish town', in M. Bouquet and M. Winter (eds) *Who From Their Labours Rest? Conflict and Practice in Rural Tourism*, Aldershot: Avebury.

Government of Canada and the Province of British Columbia (undated) *Travel Industry Development Subsidiary Agreement: An Introduction* (brochure).

Government of Canada and the Province of Ontario (1979) *Canada-Ontario Subsidiary Agreement*, Eastern Ontario Tourism Program of the Eastern Ontario Subsidiary Agreement.

Groome, D. (1993) *Planning and Rural Recreation in Britain*, Aldershot: Avebury.

Gunn, C. (1979) *Tourism Planning*, 1st edn, New York: Taylor & Francis.

Healey, R. (1994) 'The common pool problem in tourism landscapes', *Annals of Tourism Research* 21(3): 596–611.

Hoggart, K. (1990) 'Let's do away with rural', *Journal of Rural Studies* 6: 245–57.

Hohl, A. and Tisdell, C. (1995) 'Peripheral tourism: development and management', *Annals of Tourism Research* 22(3): 517–34.

Holland, S. M. and Crotts, J. C. (1992) 'A strategic planning approach to tourism development in rural communities', *Visions in Leisure and Business* 11(1): 14–23.

Hummelbrunner, R. and Miglbauer, E. (1994) 'Tourism promotion and potential in peripheral areas: the Austrian case', *Journal of Sustainable Tourism* 2: 41–50.

Ilbery, B. W. (1991) 'Farm diversification as an adjustment strategy on the urban fringe of the West Midlands', *Journal of Rural Studies* 7(3): 207–18.

Ireland, M. (1987) 'Planning policy and holiday homes in Cornwall', in M. Bouquet and M. Winter (eds) *Who From Their Labours Rest? Conflict and Practice in Rural Tourism*, Aldershot: Avebury.

Jacobs, C. (1973) *Farms and Tourism in Upland Denbighshire*, Tourism and Recreation Report 4, Denbighshire County Council.

Jess, N. (1991) 'Farm tourism comes of age in Northern Ireland', *Tourism Recreation Research* 16(1): 21–4.

Johnson, D., Snepenger, J. and Akis, S. (1994) 'Residents' perceptions of tourism development', *Annals of Tourism Research* 21(3): 629–42.

Jones, A. (1993) 'Sustainability and community participation in rural tourism', *Leisure Studies* 12: 147–8.

Kariel, H. G. and Kariel, P. E. (1982) 'Socio-cultural impacts of tourism: an example from the Austrian Alps', *Geografiska Annaler*, 64B: 1–16.

Keane, M. J., Briassoulis, H. and van der Straaten, J. (1992) 'Rural tourism and rural development', in Briassoulis, H. and van der Straaten, J. (eds) *Tourism and the Environment: Regional, Economic and Policy Issues, Environment and Assessment*, vol. 2, Dordrecht: Kluwer Academic Publishers.

Keeble, D., Tyler, P., Broom, G. and Lewis, J. (1992) *Business Success in the Countryside: The Performance of Rural Enterprise*, London: HMSO.

Klejdzinska, M. (1991) 'Report on tourism and agriculture', *Tourism Recreation Research* 16(1): 10–14.

Lane, B. (1994) ''What is rural tourism?', *Journal of Sustainable Tourism* 2: 7–21.

Lew, A. (1991) 'Scenic roads and rural development in the US', *Tourism Recreation Research* 16(2): 23–30.

Lonc, T. (1991) 'The potential for the development of tourism in conjunction with agriculture in Poland', *Tourism Recreation Research* 16(1): 80–2.

Long, P. (1994) 'Rural tourism development in the United States', unpublished paper presented to the Japan Rural Tourism Symposium, Shirahama.

Long, P. and Nuckolls, J. (1994) 'Organising resources for rural tourism development: the importance of leadership, planning and technical assistance', *Tourism Recreation Research* 19(2): 19–34.

Long, P. T. and Perdue, R. R. (1990) 'The economic impact of rural festivals and special events: assessing the spatial distribution of expenditures', *Journal of Travel Research* 28(4): 10–14.

Long, P. T., Perdue, R. R. and Allen, L. (1990) 'Rural resident tourism perceptions and attitudes by community level of tourism', *Journal of Travel Research* 29 (Winter): 3–9.

Luloff, A., Bridger, J., Graefe, A., Saylov, M., Martin, K. and Gitelson, R. (1994) 'Assessing rural tourism efforts in the United States', *Annals of Tourism Research* 21(1): 46–64.

Lundgren, J. (1983) 'Development patterns and lessons in the Montreal Laurentians', in P. Murphy (ed.) *Tourism in Canada: Selected Issues and Topics*, Western Geographical Series vol. 21, University of Victoria.

McDonald, M. (1987) 'Tourism: chasing culture and tradition in Brittany', in M. Bouquet and M. Winter (eds) *Who From Their Labours Rest? Conflict and Practice in Rural Tourism*, Aldershot: Avebury.

Mathieson, A. and Wall, G. (1982) *Tourism, Economic, Physical and Social Impacts*, London: Longman.

Maude, A. J. S. and van Rest, D. J. (1985) 'The social and economic effects of farm tourism in the United Kingdom', *Agricultural Administration* 20: 85–99.

Mercer, D. (1970) 'Urban recreational hinterlands: A review and example', *Professional Geographer* 22 (2): 74–8.

Middleton, V. T. C. (1982) 'Tourism in rural areas', *Tourism Management* 3(1): 52–8.

Minnesota Extension Service (1991) *A Training Guide for Rural Tourism Development*, Minnesota: University of Minnesota.

Mormont, M. (1987) 'Tourism and rural change', in M. Bouquet and M. Winter (eds) *Who From Their Labours Rest? Conflict and Practice in Rural Tourism*, Aldershot: Avebury.

Murphy, P. (1985) *Tourism: A Community Approach*, New York: Methuen.

Neate, S. (1987) 'The role of tourism in sustaining farm structures and communities on the Isles of Scilly', in M. Bouquet and M. Winter (eds) *Who From Their Labours Rest? Conflict and Practice in Rural Tourism*, Aldershot: Avebury.

Oppermann, M. (1995) 'Holidays on the farm: a case study of German hosts and guests', *Journal of Travel Research* 33: 57–61.

—— (1996) 'Rural tourism in southern Germany', *Annals of Tourism Research* 23: 86–102.

ORRRC (Outdoor Recreation Resources Review Commission) (1962) *Outdoor Recreation for America: A Report to the President and to Congress by the ORRC*. Washington, DC: ORRRC.

PA Cambridge Economic Consultants (1992) *A Study of Rural Tourism*, London: English Tourist Board.

Pacione, M. (1983) (ed.) *Progress in Rural Geography*, London: Croom Helm.

Page, S. J. (1994a) 'Perspectives on tourism and peripherality: a review of tourism in the Republic of Ireland', in C. Cooper and A. Lockwood (eds) *Progress in Tourism, Recreation and Hospitality Management*, vol. 5, Wiley: Chichester.

—— (1994b) 'Developing heritage tourism in Ireland in the 1990s', *Tourism Recreation Research* 19(2): 79–90.

Palminkoski, U. and Johansson, R. (1991) 'Tourism as a form of subsidiary farm income: Finland', *Tourism Recreation Research* 16(1): 61–3.

Patmore, J. A. (1983) *Recreation and Resources: Leisure Patterns and Leisure Places*, Oxford: Blackwell.

Pearce, D. (1987) *Tourism Today: A Geographical Analysis*, 1st edn, London: Longman.

Pearce, P. L. (1990) 'Farm tourism in New Zealand: a social situation analysis', *Annals of Tourism Research* 17(3): 337–52.

Pevetz, W. (1991) 'Agriculture and tourism in Austria', *Tourism Recreation Research* 16(1): 57–60.

Phillips, A. and Tubridy, M. (1994) 'New supports for heritage tourism in rural Ireland', *Journal of Sustainable Tourism* 2(1/2): 112–29.

Phillips, D. R. and Williams, A. M. (1984) *Rural Britain: A Social Geography*, Oxford: Blackwell.

Pigram, J. (1993) 'Planning for tourism in rural areas: bridging the policy implementation gap', in D. Pearce and R. Butler (eds) *Tourism Research: Critiques and Challenges*, London: Routledge.

Poon, A. (1989) *Tourism, Technology and Competitive Strategies*, Wallingford, Oxon: CAB International.

Potthoff, H. (1991) 'Facilities offered in agriculture for leisure time and tourism (Germany)', *Tourism Recreation Research* 16(1): 66–8.

Redclift, N. and Sinclair, M. T. (eds) (1991) *Working Women: International Perspectives on Labour and Gender Ideology*, London: Routledge.

Reisegg, F. and Sjtveit, O. (1991) 'Farm tourism in Norway', *Tourism Recreation Research* 16(1): 76–9.

Robinson, G. M. (1990) *Conflict and Change in the Countryside*, London: Belhaven Press.

Schroeder, T. (1992) 'Host community perceptions of tourism's impacts: a cluster analysis', *Visions in Leisure and Business* 10(4): 43–8.

Sharpley, R. (1993) *Tourism and Leisure in the Countryside*, Managing Tourism Series, No. 5, Huntingdon: Elm Publications.

—— (1997) *Tourism in the Countryside*, London: International Thomson Press.

Sime, H. (1991) 'Wildlife holidays in Scotland', *Scottish Agricultural Economics Review* 6: 131–9.

Slee, B. and Souter, M. (1993) 'Agency structures and rural tourism in Scotland', *Scottish Agricultural Economics Review* 7: 125–34.

Smith, V. (ed.) (1989) *Hosts and Guests: The Anthropology Of Tourism*, 2nd edn, Philadelphia: University of Pennsylvania Press.

Smith, V. and Wilde, P. (1977) 'The multiplier impact of tourism in Tasmania', in D. Mercer (ed.) *Leisure and Recreation in Australia*, Melbourne: Sorrett Publishing.

Squire, S. J. (1993) 'Valuing countryside: reflections on Beatrix Potter tourism', *Area* 25(1): 5–10.

Stokes, R. (1991) 'Psychosocial, environmental, and economic factors relevant to farm tourism supply', *Australian Psychologist* 26(3): 183–7.

Szaboacute, L. (1991) 'Prospects of rural tourism in Transylvania (Romania)', *Tourism Recreation Research* 16(1): 29–32.

Townroe, P. and Mallalieu, K. (1993) 'Founding a new business in the countryside', in J. Curran and D. Storey (eds) *Small Firms in Urban and Rural Locations*, London: Routledge.

United States Travel and Tourism Administration (1989) *National Policy Study on Rural Tourism and Small Business Development*, Washington, DC: United States Travel and Tourism Administration.

Urry, J. (1988) 'Cultural change and contemporary holidaymaking', *Theory, Culture and Society* 5: 35–55.

—— (1991) 'The sociology of tourism', in C. Cooper (ed.) *Progress in Tourism, Recreation and Hospitality Management*, vol. 3, London: Belhaven Press.

Vincent, J. A. (1980) 'The political economy of alpine development: tourism and agriculture in St Maurice', *Sociologia Ruralis* 20 (3–4): 250–71.

—— (1987) 'Work and play in an alpine community', in M. Bouquet and M. Winter (eds) *Who From Their Labours Rest? Conflict and Practice in Rural Tourism*, Aldershot: Avebury.

Vogeler, I. (1977) 'Farm and ranch vacationing', *Journal of Leisure Research* 9: 291–300.

Wilkinson, P. and Pratiwi, W. (1995) 'Gender and tourism in an Indonesian village', *Annals of Tourism Research* 22(2): 283–99.

Winter, M. (1987) 'Farm-based tourism and conservation in the uplands', *Ecos: A Review of Conservation* 5(3): 10–15.

Wrathall, J. E. (1980) 'Farm-based holidays', *Town and Country Planning* 49(6): 194–5.

—— (1991) 'Canadian country vacations: the farm and rural tourism in Canada', *Tourism Recreation Research* 16(1): 15–20.

2 Managing rural tourism businesses: financing, development and marketing issues

N. Dolli and J. F. Pinfold

INTRODUCTION

Tourist ventures are one of the few development options available for many rural areas seeking to develop their local economy, especially in marginal areas (Robinson 1990). These areas are often geographically remote but possess great scenic beauty and are very attractive propositions for tourists:

> as people's leisure is increasingly being used in a space-extensive way: a move from passive recreation to participation. Growth has been fastest in informal pursuits taking the form of half day trips in the countryside. With the rise in ownership of private cars the urban population has discovered the recreational potential of the countryside on its doorstep and also more remote and less occupied areas.
>
> (Robinson 1990: 260)

It is in this context that many tourist enterprises have developed as the rural environment provided a containing context for many forms of tourist activity. This chapter examines the management challenges facing such businesses which have sought to develop the tourism market and questions the assumption that development requires central and local government initiatives to pump prime the activity.

Launching rural ventures involves overcoming two major hurdles: first, the venture must be financed; second, demand must be generated. In particular, the marketing of rural tourist ventures provides special challenges. The ability to reach the target market and convince them to travel to remote locations is a critical success factor.

This chapter starts with an analysis of the problems associated with financing rural tourism ventures, the potential sources of such funding and how investors evaluate such investments. It discusses how the availability of finance can determine the type of new ventures that are undertaken and deals with some of the aspects of financial control that are central to managing such companies. Attention is then focused on the marketing of rural tourism. First, the scope of marketing in rural tourism is outlined. The chapter then discusses the application of key marketing principles and offers a structured planning approach for rural businesses to follow. Finally, the role of regional tourism organizations in the marketing effort of rural tourism is considered.

THE FINANCING OF RURAL TOURISM

The problem of finance

Generating the idea for a business venture is not the most decisive factor in the creation of a new business. Finding the funding is the crucial hurdle only the minority of prospective new ventures overcome. Funding requirements vary greatly, ranging from the part-time venture easily funded by family, to the multi-million-dollar development requiring a syndicate of investors. Expansion brings the need for more capital, and often the growth prospects of the business are such that additional outside funding is required if it is ever to reach its potential. For a venture to be a viable business it must be able to provide its working proprietors, if any, with an income at market rates for the hours they work, as well as providing an adequate return on invested funds commensurate with the risk involved. To attract funding not only must a business have the ability to provide an adequate return, but its management must also be able to instil confidence in potential investors.

Rural tourism businesses tend to have characteristics which make them risky propositions when viewed from the financiers' perspective. They are often remotely located, which means they are distant from business services, such as accountants and consultants, which can assist the business if it gets into difficulty. A receivership or mortgagee sale to recover a defaulting loan will then be difficult and expensive. The assets[1] of a tourism business may be specialized in nature and have little resale value if the venture is not successful, and hence may be of limited value as security for a loan. Many tourist businesses are seasonal in nature, which makes them difficult to sustain through the off-peak periods. Financiers are often sceptical that entrepreneurs based in rural locations have the management and financial skills necessary to manage a business, especially when they have no track record in successfully operating such ventures.

The small size of the business proposition and its remote location will provide an additional incentive not to invest. Generally the financier will want to be able to visit and monitor the business's progress on a regular basis. Where the size of investment is small, the estimated costs of administering and monitoring the business will often be greater than the financiers' margin on the loan. Nevertheless, finance is certainly readily available to small businesses in rural locations, but will be concentrated on activities where the risks are known and business assets have recognized market values. Rural banks will lend to farmers and businesses which service the farming industry because they have a long history of financing these sectors and know the risks and rewards available. If a farmer fails to operate profitably the bank knows it will normally be possible to hold a mortgagee sale of the property and other assets to recover the money owed. On the other hand, the rural tourism enterprise will generally involve an innovative but unproven idea. The financier may decline to invest simply because the risks are not quantifiable (i.e. the financier cannot determine the likelihood of success or the value of the business assets in the event of the business failing).

Sources of funding

The difficulty experienced by small business in raising debt finance is well known. When the reasons for small businesses' lack of access to financial markets was investigated in Australia, Campbell (1981) found that it could not be attributed to any lack of efficiency in the allocation of financial resources but was directly related to the higher cost and risk of lending to small enterprises. Keasey (Keasey and Watson 1994) arrived at the same conclusions when studying the situation in the UK. A Deloitte Touche Tohmatsu (1994) study of 400 small tourism businesses in New Zealand demonstrated the consequences of banks' reluctance to lend to small business. Some 44 per cent of the businesses in the study relied totally on their own funding, and only 22 per cent sourced 50 per cent or more of their funds from banks. This means the majority of rural tourism ventures typically need to find the major source of their funding outside the banking industry. Nevertheless, seeking bank funding will be the logical first step for the rural tourist venture needing to fund its operations.

In situations where entrepreneurs cannot fund the operation from their own resources or obtain bank finances it will normally be necessary to invite other shareholders to participate in the business. While the venture capital[2] industry may be regarded as a logical source of finance in these situations, the reality is that the vast majority of ventures will not meet typical venture capitalists' requirements, and in fact the venture capital industry is not the major source of private capital. Florida (1994) reported that while US venture capitalists financed 10 per cent of new high-technology business start-ups, they invested in less than 1 per cent of business start-ups as a whole. Fried and Hirsrich (1988) asserted that fewer than 2 per cent of venture capital proposals are ever funded. Clearly, venture capital, given the limited role it plays in financing other sectors of business, cannot be considered a likely source of capital for the tourist industry as a whole, let alone for rural ventures.

The majority of capital in all new ventures comes from the entrepreneurs, their friends and relatives, with the major outside source being what are known as 'angels'. Angels are difficult to identify accurately in spite of the known importance of their role. They are wealthy individuals and companies with capital to invest in new ventures. In the tourist industry they are likely to be individuals with experience in the industry or companies which already operate in the sector; they can add expertise and create synergistic benefits such as the ability to tap into an existing customer base.

The existence of these angels does not make it easy to locate them or to convince them of the merits of an investment; however, they are the most likely outside source of capital, particularly for the expansion of proven concepts constrained by under-capitalization. Mason and Harrison (1994) found that the majority of *angels* in the UK located the companies in which they invested through sources other than the generally recognized ones such as accountants, lawyers, banks and consultants. He found that 16.3 per cent were located through friends, 24.7 per cent through business associates and 15.1 per cent through personal searches for investment opportunities. Few *angels* made investments as a result of referrals from accountants and other professional sources. The Deloitte Touche Tohmatsu (1994) study, which found that only 6 per cent of the sample of small New Zealand tourist businesses had outside investors providing half or more of their funding requirements, reflects the relatively small role outside investors currently play in financing the sector, and this is probably true in other countries.

Investment evaluation

Financial risk can be regarded in two ways: either the risk of the business failing and the investment being lost or as a measure of the variability of the possible return on the investment. Providers of debt have a fixed rate of return and hence the probability of losing all or part of their investment is the focus of their analysis. They will generally look only at propositions where the probability of such a loss is small, and this inevitably means that assets must be pledged as security for the loan. It must be remembered, however, that financiers will not lend money simply because they can recover the loan by realizing securities. They look upon this as a last resort and must be satisfied of the viability of the venture as well as of the worth of the security offered.

Risk capital investors, that is, anyone who puts up money which is unsecured, are in a different position. Here the loss of the investment is a real possibility even in well-established businesses. Taking this risk can be justified only if the investor can share in the profits. In addition to the risk of losing the investment, it is necessary for them to look at the variability of the returns which might be achieved. The more uncertain or variable the future income stream is likely to be, the greater is the risk; the greater the risk, the higher the return the rational investor will require.

Estimating investment risk is an extremely difficult task, particularly where new ventures are concerned. The risk will always be high due to the high failure rates of start-up businesses. Birch (1987) and Altman (1993) put the number of US firms failing within five years at 50 per cent. A more pertinent study by Williams (1987) in Australia showed 65.4 per cent of a sample of 13,780 businesses had failed in their first five years. Similarly, in New Zealand analysis of Statistics New Zealand's *Business Demography Database* showed only 42.5 per cent of businesses started in 1988 and 1989 survived their first five years. Failure rates varied across sectors of the economy and were high in all industries, ranging from a high of

64.5 per cent for mining and quarrying to a low of 55.2 per cent for manufacturing businesses.

Based on the reports cited above, a figure of 60 per cent can be used as a rule of thumb for estimating the probability that a start-up business will fail. The likely failure rate of individual businesses varies from this figure, and the previously mentioned characteristics of many rural tourist ventures put them at the higher end of the risk spectrum. Thus, in determining the returns required it is realistic to assume a 60 per cent or higher chance that the total amount of risk capital invested will be lost. The returns that can be achieved from the business if it is a success must be high enough to compensate for this risk.

Given the high risks faced by entrepreneurs, the rewards must be also high. One method of calculating the required return, which is probably the most useful, is to use a risk-adjusted rate of return when calculating the discounted cash flow of the investment. Exactly what rate of return is required for a particular level of risk is a vexing question and comes down largely to a matter of opinion. As a guide, a UK study by Mason and Harrison (1994) found that informal investors or *angels* required a minimum annual rate of return of 45 per cent for businesses in their pre-start-up phase, 32 per cent for start-ups and 21 per cent for established firms. Schilit (1993) put the minimum rate of return required by US venture capital firms at 38 per cent per annum, and Fried and Hirsrich (1994) gave a range of 30–70 per cent.

The evaluation of an investment to see if it meets the required rate of return is made using a discounted cashflow technique. The method most accepted as being correct is the net present value method (or NPV), although the use of internal rates of return, a very similar method, is probably more widespread in practice. The principal behind the NPV method is that investors will only invest $1 today if they expect to get $1 plus their required rate back in one year's time. The cash flow from the investment each year is therefore discounted back on an annual basis by the required rate of return to find out its value at the present time. When all the present values of the future cash flows are added together the total must be equal to or greater than the cash to be invested, otherwise less that the required rate of return will have been achieved. When calculating this return, only cash flows to the investor (i.e. dividends) are used, not accounting profits. In addition, any salary paid to owners of the business for their work in the business is excluded.

To illustrate the returns required, assume one invests $10,000 in a start-up business today and requires a return of 32 per cent. As we are dealing with a start-up business, assume that all the profits will need to be ploughed back into the business and in five years' time the business will be sold to realize this return. At what price will the investment need to be sold to get this required rate of return? The calculation is:

$$\$10,000 \times (1.32)^5 = \$40,000$$

It must be remembered that this is a start-up business and there is a 60 per cent chance that it will fail and the entire investment be lost. Assume there are only two possible outcomes: a 60 per cent chance of failure, and a 40 per cent chance the business will be profitable enough to sell at a price high enough to achieve the required rate of return. As we expect to get nothing back 60 per cent of the time we must get a higher return when the business succeeds if on average we are to receive $40,000. Therefore:

expected return = (return if business fails × 0.60) + (return if business
succeeds × 0.4)
$40,000 = ($0 × 0.6) + (return if business succeeds × 0.4)
$40,000 = ($0 × 0.6) + ($100,000 × 0.4)

This means that the investment, if successful, must sell for at least $100,000 in five years' time to achieve the required rate of return. What level of profit will the business need to be generating in five years' time to achieve this price? A reasonable estimate[3] of the price a small business will fetch is four times its after-tax earnings. For the $10,000 investment the after-tax earnings would need to be:

$$\$100,000 \div 4 = \$25,000.$$

In other words, the business will need to be generating around $2.50 per annum of after-tax profit in five years' time for each $1 of risk capital invested today.

This is a very daunting task but illustrates the type of investment performance required by so-called 'rational investors' before they will risk their money. Entrepreneurs are by nature optimistic and will base decisions on their estimates of the risks and returns available, which may be very different from the more jaundiced eye of the professional financier.

The effect of financial availability on the shape of the industry

The difficulties of meeting the debt financiers' lending criteria, coupled with the difficulties of generating sufficient return to attract outside equity investors, inevitably shapes the type of investments which are made in rural tourism. The idyllic country lodge may be very aesthetically appealing, but once it consistently fails to operate at a profit its market price may well be a small fraction of its construction cost, if it can be sold at all. A bank way well decide that if a mortgage over the property is the only security available, then the maximum size of loan that can be offered is only a small per centage of the construction cost. For the equity investor the potential profit will probably be insufficient to cover the risk, given the high capital cost coupled with the fixed revenue that can be generated. Both the bank and the equity investor will find that investing in a similar venture in an urban location provides a similar return for substantially less risk, given the concentration of tourist visitors compared to the tendency for a dispersed geographical pattern in rural areas (Page 1995).

The type of ventures able to overcome the financing hurdle will be those which have the best risk to reward ratio. These are ones where the capital investment required is small in relation to the size of the potential market, and probably small in absolute terms. Investing in outdoor recreational activities such as river rafting and wilderness trekking, for example, can be contrasted with capital-intensive and fixed facilities like accommodation. Where accommodation is built it will normally be in places where customer demand is already established, because the risks are lower. Development will therefore tend to form clusters, with each enterprise building on the success of those which have gone before. The use of home-stays will be an attractive method of accommodating tourists because it does not need significant additional capital, though it needs to be remembered that this type of accommodation does not follow the established pattern of geographical clustering, especially where the prevailing patterns of rural activity are space-extensive.

Assets purchased will tend to be ones that can be readily sold or moved to another area if a venture is not successful, such as vehicles, boats and equipment. The investments will tend to be ones which can be started on a small scale and grown once they are successful, for example an adventure tour operator starting with one or two vehicles and building to a large fleet as business grows. Additional capital for expansion will prove difficult to obtain; hence, the involvement of larger chains will often be necessary to develop more successful concepts. Those looking to start rural tourism ventures should be mindful of these characteristics. Large-scale outside funding is unlikely to be available in most cases, and business activities which can start on a small scale using personal funding have a better chance of progressing beyond the planning stage.

After the business is financed, the next major hurdle is making a success of the venture. This is dependent upon the management of the business and the marketing of its products and services. Before looking at the various aspects of marketing, it is useful to examine the principles of financial management that are crucial to the success of the business.

Financial management

The financial skills required to manage a rural tourism operation are essentially the same as those required to manage any other business, and it is well beyond the scope of this book to cover the subject comprehensively. It is worthwhile, however, to draw attention to some of the key issues. While it may seem obvious that managers must monitor the ongoing financial position of the business, in practice many businesses find out how profitable they have been only some time after year end when their accountant prepares the annual tax accounts. Haswell and Holmes (1989) pointed out the significance of a lack of accounting records and showed half of all failed businesses have deficient accounting records or none at all. Williams (1987) investigated 5,646 failed Australian firms and found that inadequate, inaccurate or non-existent books and records were one of the reasons for failure in 55.3 per cent of the businesses. The need for adequate financial records is clearly not in dispute, but many small-business owners have little perception of what is required.

Wilcox (1976) studied various financial models which were being developed to predict company failures and found that in all cases the key determinant of failure was the ratio of cash flow to total assets. While the value of these models in predicting failure is arguable, they clearly demonstrate the importance of cash flow in business survival. The old cliché that businesses do not fail because they run at a loss but, rather, because they run out of money is very true, and the event which spells the end for many companies is the day they do not have enough money to pay the wages. Cash-flow management is a key activity in financial management. It can be divided into short- and long-term cash management. The short-term cash management involves listing out, on a day-to-day basis, the cash which the business expects to receive from all sources and the cash it will pay out (e.g. to its suppliers, staff, for rent rates and taxes). From this information the company can calculate its projected bank balance and hence ensure that adequate funds are available. Typically the daily cash flow is projected out for a two-month period and is revised once a month, or more often where there are changes in projected cash flows.

The longer-term cash flows form part of a company's budgeting process, whereby at least once a year the business should project its balance sheet, profit and loss, and cash flow for the next year, and preferably for two years or longer. Longer-term projections are advisable where the business is young or expanding rapidly. The business's actual financial position should be compared on a monthly basis with these budget projections.

While budgets are notoriously unreliable indicators of actual performance, the process of generating budgets and monitoring performance against them is in itself very important, as through it management is able to understand the business and monitor its progress. In this way problems are detected early and can be dealt with before they become crises. Ask a bank manager for a temporary increase in a loan facility because you cannot pay this week's wages and the answer is likely to be a receiver walking through the door. Tell the same bank manager that you expect to need an additional short-term loan in three month's time and the chances of success are greatly enhanced.

The type of financial skill required to carry out this process may be beyond the expertise of many managers, and the accounting profession obviously provides this input for many businesses. However, the business's own managers should do as much as possible of the financial management, for only they can follow developments on a day-by-day basis. Also, the cost of a heavy input of professional services may reduce the profitability of the business and be self-defeating. Rural tourist businesses in remote locations will often find it difficult to access accounting services, and this can pose a real problem where managers lack appropriate financial skills.

THE MARKETING OF RURAL TOURISM

Definition and scope

Rural tourism is characterized by a large number of small, relatively unorganized businesses operating in a dispersed geographical region (Gilbert

1989). Faced with these constraints, the linking of supplier (the tourism organization) with buyer (the customer) becomes a difficult task. It has been suggested (Gilbert 1989) that the application of marketing techniques in rural tourism can benefit organizations by providing an effective, planned approach to development that satisfies the objectives of the organization, the customer and the interests of the region as a whole (Ministry of Agriculture, Farming and Fisheries 1994; Clarke 1996).

Although there is an increased acceptance of marketing within tourism (Middleton 1988; Laws 1991; Holloway and Plant 1992), there still appears to be a certain amount of confusion in relation to its application to rural tourism business. Negative connotations associated with marketing in tourism are often the result of misunderstanding and the association of marketing with the 'hard sell' (Hall and McArthur 1993). For the purpose of clarification, definitions of marketing can be found in the literature. According to the American Marketing Association:

> Marketing is the process of planning and executing the conception, pricing, promotion, and distribution of ideas, goods, and services to create exchanges that satisfy individual and organisational objectives.
> (American Marketing Association 1985)

The definition of marketing outlined above centres around the importance of the consumer as part of an exchange process. Customers are recognized as the starting-point for marketing activity. The process then involves analysing these needs and developing products to satisfy them. This essentially means that marketing, through the interpretation of consumer needs, provides direction for the other business functions in an organization.

On a macro level, marketing is a process that directs the flow of goods and services from the producers of the service to the consumers in a way that matches supply and demand and accomplishes the objectives of society as well (McCarthy and Perrault 1987). The macro-level dimension of marketing is of particular relevance to rural tourism, where the marketer is faced with the added issue of taking into account the fragile nature of the product that is being marketed. The public nature of many rural attractions leads to problems of access and control. Marketing, in this situation, provides a managerial framework that can help to develop a rural area while still protecting the product. It is a logical process that includes research, need assessment, analysis, planning and marketing-mix considerations.

The philosophy of marketing is applicable to both private and public sector, and both profit and non-profit organizations. Private-sector organizations are primarily profit-driven. However, within the public sector, where financial objectives are often qualified by non-financial objectives, the desire to meet customer needs must be further constrained by the requirement to consider wider social issues. The idea of applying the principles of marketing to organizations in the service and nonprofit areas (together constituting the majority of tourism organizations) is by no means new. Marketing has been adopted as a philosophy by many tourism organizations because of the tangible benefits that can be gained.

The paucity of literature in the area, however, suggests that the extent to which the principles of marketing have been applied to rural tourism can be questioned. Slee and Yells (1984/85) suggest that distance from the consumer, undifferentiated products and the nature of competition are all contributing factors to the lack of concern regarding the application of marketing in rural tourism. In addition, the multi-faceted nature of rural tourism lends itself to a complex product for which it is hard to identify a unique selling proposition.

Despite these factors, the economic climate in many countries and competition for limited resources by many small rural operators has led to the increased interest in marketing as a necessary business function in the procurement and efficient management of scarce resources. Essentially, the interest in marketing may be regarded as reactionary as opposed to demonstrating a proactive change in the way of thinking and doing business in rural tourism organizations. However, the adoption of key marketing principles provides rural tourism organizations with the opportunity to think proactively in the development of their businesses.

Rural tourism and the application of marketing

Marketing can help in rural tourism development by addressing such issues as who participates, how tourism activity is organized and the type of structures that are put in place to promote the product (Keane et al. 1992). It serves to attract funds, generate business and satisfy customer needs. However, it must be remembered that in the case of rural tourism the satisfaction of customer needs must be matched by satisfaction of the needs of the region and other interested parties.

According to Bramwell (1993), there are several key issues that need to be resolved in rural tourism. These include:

1 The need to understand and relate to the market.
2 The development, improvement and monitoring of accommodation.
3 The need to provide and manage infrastructure.
4 Research into the development and management of rural tourism.

All of these issues are effectively marketing management issues, which further illustrates the importance of marketing in rural tourism (see Clarke 1995).

The underlying concern in rural tourism marketing, however, is the issue of sustainability: how to achieve customer satisfaction while still protecting the product that is being marketed. According to Crotts (1994), unmanaged development of rural tourism attractions can have significant effects on both the natural environment and the quality of life in the locality. This social responsibility function in the marketing of rural tourism presents a great challenge. There needs to be a balance between contemporary marketing objectives and the objectives that are important in the rural tourism context.

In this situation customer satisfaction may not always be the key – successful marketing needs to give adequate consideration to the long-term implications of tourism development on the environment as well

(Wells 1993). To this end, marketing and the process of marketing planning provide justifiable tools for the management of regional or national resources.

The marketing planning approach

Marketing planning provides a structured approach to the procurement and utilization of resources. It involves research, understanding the needs of the target market, development of products and promotions, and the outlining of goals and objectives.

As mentioned earlier in the chapter, many rural tourism organizations tend to be small in size and remote in location. The problems of raising funds in small organizations are also problems that can be seen in their marketing efforts. Size, lack of funds and locational factors make marketing a hard task even to start thinking about in rural tourism firms. A vicious cycle is in effect created by lack of funds, leading to less concentration on marketing, thereby decreasing chances of increasing the viability of the business and attracting more funds.

The marketing activity and planning process in rural tourism organizations are further constrained by two major factors, those associated with the marketing of services and non-profit organizations.

The marketing of rural tourism is complicated by the involvement of non-profit organizations, as well as small, private for-profit businesses and/or public-run agencies. Kotler and Andreasen (1991) outlined various factors that complicate marketing in non-profit organizations:

1 The degree to which donations are relied upon.
2 The extent to which the performance of the organization is open to public scrutiny.
3 The extent to which marketing is seen as undesirable by some or all members of the organization and its sponsors.
4 The level of reliance on volunteers.
5 The degree to which performance is judged on non-marketing measures.

Challenges such as these are further compounded by the fact that many non-profit organizations lack staff skilled in the areas of business such as accounting, marketing and management. In addition to these factors, the marketing of services produces complicating characteristics in rural tourism, which include:

1 *Intangibility.* A service is abstract and does not lend itself to trial before purchase. Service marketers seek to add tangible evidence to their product. This can be achieved through the use of clear and relevant promotional activities. For example, in tourism this may include low price trial flights or the development of videos that produce an image of the product.
2 *Inseparability.* The consumption of a service is said to be inseparable from its means of production – the producer and consumer must interact. People are an inseparable part of the rural tourism product. The travel agent who sells our holiday, the waiter who serves us and the

hotel receptionist are all an integral part of the product we are purchasing. The process that is used to produce the service then becomes crucial to the achievement of customer satisfaction. Training of employees, therefore, becomes a very important facet of successful marketing in this area.

3 *Variability.* Each interaction in the provision of a service may produce a different outcome. Controlling variability is dependent on the selection, training and motivation of staff that are involved in the provision of the service. Standardisation and the maintenance of service quality are major concerns. Though every effort may be made to standardise the service, the consumers' experience may still be different every time. For example, no amount of standardisation is going to give the tour operator control over factors such as the weather. In such situations it is imperative that the organisation maintain a consistent standard of service quality in order to minimise customer dissatisfaction.

4 *Perishability.* An important aspect of services is that they cannot be stored. For example, unused raft spaces, or bed-nights in hotels are lost opportunities which cannot be recovered. This is crucial in rural tourism marketing where such factors as the weather and economic conditions produce continual variations in demand.

5 *Ownership.* The inability to actually own a service is related to its perishability and intangibility. The buyer is merely purchasing the right to use a leisure park or heritage site. Rural tourism marketing brings with it the additional considerations of the 'rights' or limits to use of public and community resources.

(Palmer 1994)

The negative impact of these factors on business operations can be controlled by the use of appropriate marketing strategies.

Given these constraints, the preparation of a marketing plan is important for rural tourism organizations that face a reasonable level of competition (for both customers and funding) and are functioning in a volatile business environment. The development of long-term, proactive strategies which are designed to develop the local area positively has to be the goal of marketing. A planned effort can help to achieve the principal functions of marketing. In addition, planning can help to sustain the destination, support the local community and at the same time contribute to the achievement of customer satisfaction (Wells 1993).

Despite its importance, the Deloitte Touche Tohmatsu (1994) study illustrated the lack of emphasis given to planning by small tourism operators. Only 11 per cent of the businesses surveyed had a formal plan. Of the rest, 64 per cent had an informal plan and 25 per cent had no marketing plan at all. This research, conducted in New Zealand, is comparable to UK research, indicating that tourism organizations in many countries may be at the same stage in marketing awareness (Deloitte Touche Tomatsu 1994).

The format, length and focus of marketing plans can vary greatly from organization to organization. However, most successful plans will involve examination of four basic areas:

1 Situation analysis: where are we now?
2 Marketing objectives: where do we want to go?
3 Strategy: how can we get there?
4 Monitoring and performance (Reed 1992).

A marketing plan outline is shown diagrammatically in Figure 2.1.

Situation analysis: where are we now?

It is essential that the situation analysis begins with a thorough internal analysis, including examination of the nature of the firm and historical data relating to sales and profit. For rural tourism firms sales may correspond to the number of visitors to a particular site. This first step allows the organization to develop a mission or reason for being in business and assess its current situation.

In addition, the nature of rural tourism dictates that consideration needs to be given to socio-cultural, economic, technological and political/legal factors as well. These macro-environmental forces can have a vast effect on the viability of tourism products and need to be considered through all stages in the planning process.

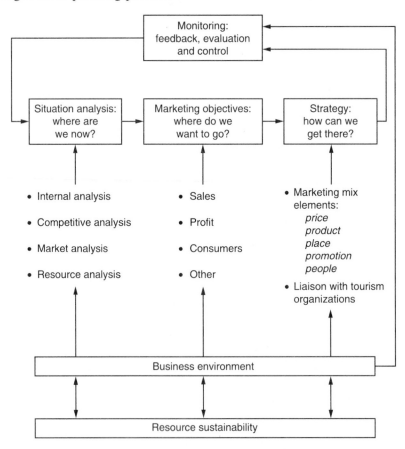

Figure 2.1 The rural tourism marketing planning process.

Any detailed situation analysis also has to include an examination of consumers (the market) and a competitive analysis. Consumers in the rural tourism context may be trying to satisfy a variety of different needs, ranging from the need for relaxation time or a stress-free environment to that for cheap accommodation and leisure activities. It is therefore necessary to have an understanding of several factors:

1 Who the firm is trying to serve.
2 How many consumers there are.
3 What motivates them.
4 How often they consume the service.

In short, the rural tourism marketer needs to have an understanding of consumer behaviour in order to ensure that their product offerings and other marketing efforts are targeting the right market (Fawcett 1996).

A situation analysis is not complete without an examination of the competitive environment. The size of key direct and indirect competitors, their characteristics and their strategies need to be examined. This will allow the firm to assess current marketing opportunities. Many small organizations fall into the trap of assuming that they have no competition if they are offering a reasonably unique service – this is not the case. In the broad sense, all tourism activities are competing for tourist expenditure and are substitutable products.

In rural tourism an additional consideration is that of the resources being used. Resource analysis, in this context, will aim to highlight the resources that are available to the company and hence ensure that the protection of key rural areas is given consideration in the planning process. It requires an understanding of the rural area, including the surrounding culture and social environment.

Conducting a situation analysis will identify strengths, weaknesses, opportunities and threats, and thereby guide the firm in isolating key issues for consideration in the marketing strategy formulation.

Marketing objectives: where do we want to go?

Marketing objectives can basically be divided into three areas: those relating to sales, profit and the consumer. Rural tourism provides a variety of different product options that will satisfy the needs of different groups of consumers – not all individuals want the same rural tourism experience. An understanding of the consumer helps to focus on how the target market is going to be satisfied. At the same time it is not always possible to design a totally unique experience for each consumer. The concept of identifying groups of consumers who have similar needs helps to overcome this problem. If groups of individuals with similar needs and motivations can be identified, the marketer can then formulate marketing activities designed to satisfy each of these segments. This process, termed 'market segmentation', should result in groups of customers of a reasonable size in order to ensure economies, to allow for future growth and satisfy the interests of consumers that are not currently being met by other operators.

In rural tourism it is vital that objectives include due consideration of the effect that marketing may have on the environment. In the case of rural tourism, non-financial objectives are likely to be as important as financial objectives. Public goals may range from raising the awareness level of a particular attraction or increasing occupancy rates for farm accommodation, to generating income into the community by marketing local accommodation. Environmental goals, such as the conservation of sensitive areas are also of vital importance in rural tourism. Clearly defined, measurable objectives provide guidance, reduce uncertainty and motivate employees (Hall and McArthur 1993). Attaching percentages, numbers and timeframes allows the objectives to be evaluated. To illustrate, compare the following goals:

- to raise the level of awareness of rural areas in the North Island as tourist destinations;
- to raise the level of awareness of rural areas in the North Island as tourist destinations by 10 per cent in the next twelve months.

The second statement both is more precise and allows results to be measured and evaluated over a specific timeframe. The results of the situation analysis will provide a guide as to realistic and achievable objectives. In particular, opportunities need to be detailed with reference to the constraints that the situation analysis highlights.

Strategy: how can we get there?

Once the rural business organization has outlined its objectives, consideration needs to be given to how these objectives are going to be achieved with the application of marketing activities.

Strategy formulation has to be preceded by situation analysis and identification of the target markets of consumers that the firm wishes to pursue. The firm could decide to concentrate on one segment or try to satisfy the needs of two or more segments based on available resources and attractions. For example, a farm accommodation operator could offer packages that concentrate on the rural home-stay aspect or alternatively try to capture a different market based on the activities that can be pursued. Rural operations such as small hotels or camp sites may have no choice but to adopt a concentrated strategy. Large tourist destinations or parks, on the other hand, will be able to identify various activities that can be used to target different segments of the population. The task of marketing is then to formulate a marketing mix that suits the needs of each of the different markets selected. This process has to give due consideration to the most appropriate generic competitive strategy for the business-cost leadership, differentation or focus/niche marketing (see Kotler and Armstrong 1996).

Step three of the marketing planning process involves designing an appropriate marketing mix through the manipulation of what are known as the four Ps in marketing: *product/service*, *price*, *place/distribution* and *promotion*. In many service organizations a fifth P – people – is added to the marketing mix. In addition to these five Ps, tourism authors such as

A. Morrison suggest a further three Ps that may be considered relevant to rural tourism marketing: *programming*, *partnership* and *packaging* (Morrison 1989: 37–8).

Product strategy highlights the nature of goods and services that need to be developed in order to satisfy the needs and wants of the target markets. According to Gilbert (1989), the rural product has two dimensions: features and benefits. Marketers need to isolate 'benefits' because it is benefits that actually bring satisfaction. The benefits that can be seen in the rural product (for example, feeling at peace with nature or the benefit of escaping the humdrum of city life) need to be stressed in the firm's marketing communications. 'Features', on the other hand, are aspects that are designed into the final product that is delivered to the customer. Normal features of a rural product would include easy access to the site or leisure activities and areas for rest and relaxation.

The core benefit of the rural product is, however, intangible. An experience or a place of relaxation is not a tangible benefit. For this reason marketing activities for rural tourism need to try to provide more tangible benefits that the consumer can recognize and remember as part of the experience. Increasing the tangibility of rural tourism services can involve consideration of such things as physical surroundings, buildings, and providing a warm and welcoming atmosphere.

Price and place are also crucial determinants of the success of the firms' marketing efforts. Among other factors, the levels of price to be charged can be based on the location of the attraction and the nature of the firm. Non-profit rural operators may have very different pricing objectives. Place, on the other hand, brings considerations of how to distribute the service, what type of facilities are needed and where it is to be located. The physical location of the tourism attraction will obviously not be easy to control – the predominant purpose of rural tourism being to attract people to a region or existing attraction. A key role of place in rural tourism, therefore, has to involve ensuring that the tourism activity is easily accessible.

Promotion decisions centre around deciding on the best mix of personal selling, advertising, sales promotion and public relations for the rural product. Strategy will be based on the communication objectives of the firm and the available budget. The small size and budget of many operators restrict the type of promotion that can be used. The Deloitte Touche Tomatsu (1994) study found that brochures, information centres and free media coverage were the most popular methods of promotion. Word of mouth was found to be the most common means through which customers had heard of the tourism activity. These results are comparable to a study of advertising and farm-based accommodation conducted in Britain, where guidebooks and group cooperation were the most popular methods of advertising (Evans and Ibery 1992). What needs to be considered, however, is the best way to reach the target market for the product that is being marketed, whether it is a farm museum, riding and hiking, or rural accommodation.

The prohibitive expense involved in many forms of advertising necessitates that rural tourism firms also examine alternative promotion tools.

Regional tourism promotion through membership of a collective organization provides a reasonably cost-effective means of communicating with the consumer. Alternatively, operators can forge links with other organizations to initiate joint marketing efforts. The Deloitte Touche Tomatsu (1994) study found that two-thirds of those interviewed had actually done this at some point.

Employees skilled in the formulation of promotional material are crucial to the success of any promotional plan. Lack of staff skilled in all aspects of marketing remains one of the problems faced by rural tourism firms. The firm needs to ensure that adequately trained staff are employed to manage the planning process in an efficient and effective manner.

The formulation of marketing strategy also needs to give consideration to financial objectives. For rural tourism organizations this is not only important in achieving objectives, but also essential in the procurement of resources.

Monitoring

No marketing plan is complete without a suitable system of evaluation and control. It is important that the organization continually review its planning process to ensure that marketing objectives that have been set are actually achieved. Results need to be measured against goals and objectives. In rural tourism, evaluation also needs to consider any negative influences on the surrounding environment. Feedback from the business environment can help to monitor resource sustainability, a crucial issue in the development of rural attractions. Any shortfalls in the planning activities of the organization need to be examined. Based on these factors, the process of evaluation will also help in determining future budgets and financial considerations.

The role of regional tourism organizations

It has been noted that rural tourism is characterized by many small operators (posing resource constraints), large distances between the supplier and the consumer, and long lead times in developing a successful presence in the marketplace. Given these factors, and the added burden of marketing in a non-profit services arena, a major requirement for success in the development of a rural business is access to marketing support. A central marketing structure can help to promote a clear image for the tourist attraction in the market. Collective resources allow for more efficient planning and control for the region as a whole (Keane et al. 1992).

Regional tourism organizations (RTOs) can play a vital role in the promotion of a region's attractions, both in the home country and overseas. Major benefits to participating rural businesses include:

- collective representation, both nationally and internationally;
- information provision, training and education;
- coordination of joint marketing opportunities;
- networks of service providers to discuss issues affecting the industry at a local level.

In New Zealand, regional tourism promotion was highlighted as a critical success factor for tourism organizations in the Deloitte Touche Tomatsu study (1994). Despite this, the study also showed that 31 per cent of those surveyed did not belong to an RTO. Reasons cited for this high figure were the lack of understanding of the requirements of small operators by the RTOs, a perceived lack of tangible benefits and expensive subscriptions. Unfortunately, low levels of membership influence the ability of the RTO to perform for the local businesses. Strong membership in turn provides collective strength, which results in a greater impact in the community.

A key feature in the development of rural tourism, however, has to be local organizations that are in turn linked to wider product and marketing structures. Links need to be established between regional and national tourism bodies. In New Zealand this would involve the RTOs forging links with organizations such as the New Zealand Tourism Industry Association Inc., whose role is to foster unity among regional organizations and encourage the development of the industry by providing a range of services. In fact there is a growing research literature now emerging on place-marketing (e.g. Ashworth and Voogd 1990) that recognizes that rural areas 'need to promote themselves in an integrated fashion in order to make themselves more attractive to tourists, investors and employees' (Butler and Hall 1997: 159).

In short, RTOs provide a crucial link between rural businesses. These organizations, if functioning effectively, can help to overcome many of the problems faced by small operators in rural areas. As research in New Zealand has shown, however, perceived returns and the costs of participating are major factors that need to be overcome.

CONCLUSION

The successful birth of new firms is an important avenue for development and change within an economy and their impact is far greater than their contribution to economic output or employment. The volume of new ventures will be a function of the ability to find funding. The success of the ventures will be a function of the ability to attract and satisfy a market and this will depend on the application of marketing principles.

Marketing principles appear to be under-utilized in rural tourism. This is due to a lack of appreciation of the benefits that can be gained and to resource constraints (finance and trained marketing personnel). In the context of rural tourism, marketing can help to achieve a balance between the product and the market: satisfying the needs of the customer while working to sustain the destination. The essential aspect of marketing planning is that it provides formal commitment to consideration of resources and the consumer. In the absence of a large resource base and marketing knowledge, the RTOs can provide a crucial service in co-ordinating and supervising the marketing initiatives of small rural operations.

NOTES

1 The assets are any property of value owned by the business, including physical assets such as vehicles and buildings, financial assets such as money owed to the business and intangible assets such as brand names, patents and other rights.
2 The venture capital industry is that sector of the finance industry that is willing to invest funds that are not adequately secured against assets. In the event that the business in which they invest fails, they expect to be unable to recover some or all of their investment. To compensate for the risk taken they expect to participate in the profits of the business.
3 The use of price–earnings multiples to value businesses, while widely used, in practice is not generally considered to be a valid method; discounted cashflow methods of valuation are preferred. It is, however, adequate for the demonstration used here.

REFERENCES

Altman, E. E. (1993) *Corporate Financial Distress and Bankruptcy*, 2nd edn, New York: Wiley.
Anon. (1995) 'AMA board approves new marketing definition', *Marketing News* March 1: 1.
Ashworth, G. and Voogd, H. (1990) *Selling the City*, London: Belhaven.
Birch, D. L. (1987) *Job Creation in America*, New York: Free Press.
Bramwell, B. (1993) *Tourism Strategies and Rural Development*, Paris: OECD.
Butler, R. and Hall, C. M. (1997) 'Image and reimaging of rural areas', in R. Butler, C. M. Hall and J. Jenkins (eds) *Tourism and Recreation in Rural Areas*, Chichester: Wiley.
Campbell, J. K. (1981) *Report of the Committee of Inquiry into the Australian Financial System*, Canberra: AGPS.
Clarke, J. (1995) 'The effective marketing of small-scale tourism enterprises through national structures: lessons from a two-way comparative study of farm tourist accommodation in the United Kingdom', *Journal of Vacation Marketing* 1(2): 79–86.
—— (1996) 'Farm accommodation and the communication mix', *Tourism Management* 17(8): 611–20.
Crotts, J. C. (1994) 'Trends and issues in sustainable rural tourism development: an introduction', *Trends* 31(1): 2–4.
Deloitte Touche Tomatsu (1994) *Small Business Survey 1994: New Zealand Tourism Industry*, Christchurch: Deloitte Touche Tomatsu.
Evans, N. J. and Ibery, B. W. (1992) 'Advertising and farm-based accommodation: a British case study', *Tourism Management* 13(4): 415–22.
Fawcett, S. (1996) 'Quality in the agritourism product', *Progress in Tourism and Hospitality Research* 2(1): 79–86.
Florida, R. (1994) 'What start-ups don't need is money', *INC* (April): 27.
Fried, V. H. and Hirsrich, R. D. (1988) 'Venture capital research: past, present and future', *Entrepreneurship: Theory and Practice* 13: 15–28.

—— (1994) 'Towards a model of venture capital investment decision making' *Financial Management* 23(3): 28–37.

Gilbert, D. (1989) 'Rural tourism and marketing: synthesis and new ways of working', *Tourism Management* 10(1): 39–50.

Hall, C. M. and McArthur, S. (1993) 'The marketing of heritage', in C. M. Hall and S. McArthur (eds) *Heritage Management in New Zealand and Australia: Visitor Management, Interpretation, and Marketing*, Auckland: Oxford University Press.

Haswell, S. and Holmes, S. (1989) 'Estimating the small business failure rate: a reappraisal', *Journal of Small Business Management* 27(3): 68–74.

Holloway, C. J. and Plant, R. V. (1992) *Marketing for Tourism*, London: Pitman Publishing.

Keane, M. J., Briassoulis, H. and van der Straaten, J. (1992) 'Rural tourism and rural development', in H. Briassoulis and J. van der Stratten (eds) *Tourism and the Environment: Regional, Economic and Policy Issues, Environment and Assessment*, vol. 2, Dordrecht: Kluwer Academic Press Publishers.

Keasey, K. and Watson, R. (1994) 'The bank financing of small firms in the UK: issues and evidence', *Small Business Economics* 6(5): 349–62.

Kotler, P. and Andreasen, A. (1991) *Strategic Marketing for Nonprofit Organisations*, Englewood Cliffs: Prentice-Hall.

Kotler, P. and Armstrong, G. (1996) *Principles of Marketing*, Englewood Cliffs: Prentice-Hall.

Laws, E. (1991) *Tourism Marketing: Service and Quality Management Perspectives*, Cheltenham: Stanley Thornes Ltd.

Mason, C. and Harrison, R. (1994) 'Informal venture capital in the UK', in A. Hughes and D. J. Storey (eds), *Finance and the Small Firm*, London: Routledge.

McCarthy, E. J. and Perrault, W. D. Jr. (1987) *Basic Marketing*, 9th edn, Illinois: Irwin.

Middleton, V. T. C. (1988) *Marketing in Travel and Tourism*, 1st edn, Oxford: Heinemann.

Ministry of Agriculture, Farming and Fisheries (1994) *Success with Farm-based Tourist Accommodation: A Guide to Meeting Customer Requirements*, London: Ministry of Agriculture, Farming and Fisheries.

Morrison, A. M. (1989) *Hospitality and Travel Marketing*, Albany, NY: Demar Publishers.

Page, S. J. (1995) *Urban Tourism*, London: Routledge.

Palmer, A. (1994) *Principles of Services Marketing*, London: McGraw-Hill.

Reed, P. (1992) *Marketing Planning and Strategy*, Marrickville, NSW: Harcourt Brace Jobanovich.

Robinson, G. M. (1990) *Conflict and Change in the Countryside*, London: Belhaven Press.

Schilit, W. K. (1993) 'The performance of venture capital funds, stocks and bonds', *International Review of Strategic Management* 4: 304.

Slee, R. W. and Yells, R. (1984/85) Some aspects of marketing farm holiday accommodation, *Farm Management* 5(8): 315–23.

Wells, J. (1993) 'Marketing indigenous heritage: a case study of Uluru National Park', in C. M. Hall, and S. McArthur (eds) *Heritage Management in New Zealand and Australia: Visitor Management, Interpretation, and Marketing*, Auckland: Oxford University Press.

Wilcox, J. W. (1976) 'The gamblers ruin approach to business risk', *Sloan Management Review* 18(1): 33–46.

Williams, A. J. (1987) 'A longitudinal analysis of the characteristics and performance of small business in Australia', *Australian Small Business and Entrepreneurship Research: Proceedings of the Third National Conference*, Newcastle, NSW: University of Newcastle: Institute of Industrial Economics.

International case studies in the northern hemisphere

Rural tourism in the United States: the Peak to Peak Scenic Byway and KOA

3

P. Long and D. Edgell

> The well-being of America's rural people and places depends upon many things: the availability of good-paying jobs; access to critical services such as education, health care, and communication; strong communities; and a healthy natural environment to name a few. And while urban America is equally dependent upon these things, the challenges to well-being look very different in rural areas than in urban [areas].
>
> (USDA 1995: preface)

INTRODUCTION

The success of tourism in the rural areas of the USA depends substantially on the ability of a region to recognize its capacity for tourism, to plan and manage its tourism economy effectively and to maximize its ability to capture tourist expenditures. Unfortunately, many rural communities have been hampered in their efforts to meet these objectives due to a lack of the human, financial and technical resources necessary to establish a sustainable tourism industry acceptable to residents and businesspeople, as well as their travelling guests. This chapter provides information on two recent federal initiatives supporting rural tourism business development in the USA and looks at the success of a rural business through two case studies. It begins with a brief overview of rural America in the 1990s followed by an historic review of rural tourism policy development. The two initiatives – first, the National Rural Tourism Foundation, a non-profit, private-sector support system for rural tourism business development and, second, the National Scenic and Historic Byway Program, a 'vehicle' for coordinated rural tourism planning and management – are then highlighted. This is followed by a case study of a Kampgrounds of America (KOA) franchise campground located along the Peak to Peak Scenic Highway in Colorado.

However, to provide a context in which to understand issues associated with rural tourism in the USA in the 1990s it is pertinent to consider the issues and characteriztics of America's rural environment and the implications for tourism.

RURAL AMERICA IN THE 1990s

Although most Americans today live in metropolitan areas with a population of over 1 million, the rural sectors of the USA have advanced over the years in many significant ways. According to Robinson (1990: 12), the USA Bureau of Census defines rural people as 'those individuals living in open country or in towns with a population of less than 2500 but this means that rurality can vary from the "extreme rural" of much of the Great Plains to the "nearly urban" of rural enclaves within the megalopolis of the north east'. In contrast to the example of New Zealand (Chapter 9), where the limit of a settlement of up to 1,000 people is the critical threshold for a rural area, in the USA the difficulty of using the term rural is compounded by problems of definition. Thus, understanding the processes of population change in rural America is fraught with problems, although a number of distinct processes have helped to shape the nature of rural America in the 1990s. For example, the fact that unemployment rates are below those in metropolitan areas has meant that losses of rural population to urban areas are lower than in the past. This is in part explained by the process of counter-urbanization, explained in simple terms as a reversal of established trends associated with the population migration from rural towns to urban areas (Champion et al. 1987). The movement has often been characterized by the movement of population from large cities to smaller towns and rural communities, often with a further movement to the rural periphery. Other terms have been used to describe this process, such as the 'population turnaround' (Dean et al. 1984). Although use of the term 'counter-urbanization' has been fraught with problems of ambiguity (Robinson 1990), the preconditions of decentralization and deconcentration of the population led to a strong growth in the rural population in the USA in the 1980s (Keinath 1982; Bohland 1988). One outcome is that rural areas are becoming an important context for retirement and recreation services, which showed substantial growth during the 1980s and early 1990s. Vast improvements in and expansion of utilities, telecommunications and the interstate highway system have placed rural America in a better position to serve its population as well as visitors. Unfortunately, real earnings per job and the ability to provide good jobs for educated youth are areas yet in need of improvement (USDA 1995: 1).

In the USA today there are 2,288 rural counties (political subdivisions of a state), which contain 21 per cent (51 million) of the nation's people and 83 per cent of its land, and 'In 1992, nonmetropolitan counties supplied 18 percent of the Nation's jobs and generated 14 percent of its earnings' (USDA 1995: 2). The economy of rural America has shifted over the years from a dependence on agriculture, forestry and mining to the provision of services (tourism and recreation, retirement, financial, insurance, real estate, retail and restaurants) and manufacturing. Today the service sector employs over half of all rural workers and manufacturing provides jobs for about 17 per cent of the rural workforce. Due to the vastness of land and the number of people in the USA, it is neither simple nor always accurate to summarize its characteristics generally. The United States Department of Agriculture (USDA) segments rural counties into a number of categories, two of which offer a particularly insightful assessment of tourism in rural America today. One category is comprised of counties which are heavily service-oriented, and the second includes those influenced by the presence of federally managed lands. A 'service' county (323 counties) is classified as one that has shown recent growth in transportation, public utilities, wholesale and retail trade, finance, insurance and real estate. Counties located close to natural and man-made amenities frequently provide recreation, tourism and retirement opportunities. The success of the service sector in federal lands counties (270 counties) is also frequently associated with the growth of tourism and recreation.

Counties which are considered service-dependent derived 50 per cent or more of their earned income from service jobs during 1987–89. This included an increase of over 3 million such jobs from 1979–89, accounting for 83 per cent of new rural jobs. The *USDA Bulletin* reported that 'The economies of services counties did well during the 1980s. Total real earnings grew by nearly nine percent (more than twice the rate for nonmetro counties as a whole), and earnings from services grew by twenty-four percent (nearly twice as fast as the nonmetro average). The number of jobs in services counties grew slightly faster (both in total jobs and services jobs) than in nonmetro counties as a whole' (USDA 1995: 16). Although, on the whole, earnings per job in the service sector were the lowest of all industrial sectors studied, service jobs in services counties tended to pay better than service jobs in other counties. It is projected that rural areas near natural amenities 'will probably see increasing demand for services associated with recreational activities and retirement populations' (USDA 1995: 17). Federal lands counties have been impacted recently by the growth of tourism and recreation. The *USDA Bulletin* notes that the 'average growth rate in services jobs in Federal lands counties has outpaced even the average total job growth rate in metropolitan areas, and the overall job growth rate in these counties was faster than the nonmetropolitan rate' (USDA 1995: 20). But again, the earnings per job have declined. The population of these counties has also grown significantly (9 per cent) due to an increase in the numbers of both retirees and working-age people. New jobs range from seasonal to full time, filling the needs of an ever-growing mobile and recreation-minded American public. The future of these lands, in terms of a concern for the environment, will be heavily influenced by a changing federal policy. Such policy will most certainly reflect a lesser role on the part of the federal government, with greater responsibility being given to local units of government.

The plight and the opportunity of an emerging, changing rural America is conveyed by Hobbs, a rural sociologist, who argued that 'There are two rural Americas–one real and the other imagined. The imagined one is a product of images, some based on experience, some created, and some based on selective perception and nostalgia. Both are important because both are exerting an influence on today's farm policy and rural development agenda' (Hobbs 1987: 43). An important component of the future success of rural tourism business development could well be the ability to capture the nostalgic – the imagined – and integrate it effectively with the real rural America.

RURAL TOURISM POLICY IN THE USA

Although the USA revisited its federal tourism policy in 1970 with the modification of the International Travel Act, creating the National Tourism Resources Review Commission, and again in 1974, through the National Tourism Policy study, it was not until 1981 that the United States Travel and Tourism Administration (USTTA) was established within the Department of Commerce. This office is headed by its own Under Secretary, and its establishment elevated the stature of tourism at the federal level (see Pearce 1992 for more detail on this issue). Despite longstanding policies in the USA affecting rural areas, the primary focus has been on agriculture and an agricultural lifestyle. It was not until 1992 that a formal policy was articulated regarding tourism development in rural America. Although one might argue that rural tourism policy initially emerged with the authorization of the National Park Service in 1916, or, even earlier, with the establishment of Yellowstone National Park in 1872, it was not until the late 1980s that a comprehensive study was conducted on the implications of tourism business development for rural economies (Economic Research Associates 1989). Entitled the *National Policy Study on Rural Tourism and Small Business Development*, this study further acknowledged that rural areas in the USA were badly in need of economic revitalization, yet that these same areas had an abundance of cultural, historical and natural resource amenities around which to expand or build a tourism economy. The study concluded that travel and tourism could be an important tool for rural economic revitalization and that it should be an essential component of broader rural economic development strategies. In addition, a need for federal policy and strategic responses on the part of the federal government regarding rural tourism was identified.

The federal policy and strategic response resulted in the creation of the National Rural Tourism Foundation (NRTF) as part of the Tourism Policy and Export Promotion Act of 1992 Act (Public Law 102–372). Established as a charitable and non-profit corporation, the NRTF is charged with 'the planning, development, and implementation of projects and programmes which have the potential to increase travel and tourism export revenues by attracting foreign visitors to rural America' (NRTF 1996). The programme's efforts are to include:

- the development and distribution of educational and promotional materials about both private and public attractions located in rural America;

- the development of educational resources to assist rural tourism development;
- participation in Federal land-management agency outreach efforts (NRTF 1996).

The authorization of the NRTF represented the first major formal effort at the federal level to support tourism business development in rural areas of the USA. In establishing the NRTF as the primary vehicle for rural tourism product development and promotion, Congress recognized the value of the 'rural' experience to both domestic and international tourism; the importance of tourism to the economy of rural areas; and the lack of a coordinated effort to establish and achieve rural tourism development goals. NRTF receives no public funding, and its activities are governed by a board of directors comprised primarily of travel industry leaders representing the private sector and public interests. Board members establish policy and set programme and funding priorities. Additionally, representatives of federal land-management agencies, including the National Park Service, US Forest Service, Department of Agriculture, Bureau of Indian Affairs, Corps of Engineers and the Bureau of Land Management, all with current and/or emerging interest in rural tourism development, hold ex-officio, non-voting status on the NRTF board. Funding for the foundation's activities is currently derived through gifts, grants and contracts tied to specific projects.

The foundation's mission is 'to contribute, in a manner that is socially and environmentally sound, to the economic development and general quality of life in rural America, by encouraging responsible development and promotion of tourism in rural areas, with a special focus on increasing international visitation and expenditures' (National Rural Tourism Foundation 1996: 1). In partnership with federal land-management agencies, one goal is to promote lesser-known federal tourism and recreational destinations and, in some cases, to divert traffic from overcrowded park, forest and recreation areas.

National Rural Tourism Foundation tourism initiatives

Four major initiatives intended to improve the competitive nature of rural tourism businesses in the USA are currently supported by the NRTF. These initiatives are centred around actions critical to the establishment, development and marketing of tourism businesses in rural areas. A brief overview of each initiative is given below.

Internet connectivity

For the tourism industry, exchanging information, whether it be to promote a particular area's attractions or to learn about how other communities have managed tourism development, is an essential ingredient for success. The NRTF, in partnership with the College of Business and Administration at the University of Colorado at Boulder, developed one of the first World Wide Web sites aimed at unifying the presence of the US travel industry on the Internet. Benefits to rural tourism businesses include global marketing of tourism by rural regions, preparation of existing tourism development and management information and its delivery to rural communities. Entitled the United States Travel and Tourism Information Network (USTTIN), this Internet initiative (www.uttin.org) is intended to serve as both a tourism marketing and management tool. It is designed to be a graphics-based, user-friendly, nationwide directory through which consumers can easily access travel, tourism and recreation-related services and resources. By serving as the 'point of presence' for US travel information, USTTIN enables users to locate accurate and reliable travel information quickly. For example, by knowing just one Internet address, a user can quickly locate any of the fifty states' travel offices. Once a user is in Colorado, all twenty-one scenic byways are just a few clicks away. Commencing February 1996, USTTIN has been licensed as a commercial enterprise and is being transformed and integrated with other Internet services targeted at rural America. Efforts are being made to coordinate activities with other organizations providing comprehensive travel-related information.

State Tourism Partners' Program

Every state in the USA has a substantial rural land base and thus the opportunity to enhance its rural tourism offerings. Since states and their respective rural communities will be the ultimate benefactors of any NRTF efforts, relationships are being developed with a variety of public and private tourism interests in each state, the initial point of contact being the state travel office. This partnership programme includes the establishment of a rural tourism specialists' advisory council, identification of the resource needs of rural areas pursuing tourism, and provision of information and contacts to rural communities seeking technical assistance in developing and managing their rural tourism products and services. One current project, in partnership with the state travel offices, is a nationwide assessment of the specific needs of rural tourism businesses. The objectives of this assessment are to identify the training and resource requirements of existing and emerging tourism businesses and to determine what public policies are needed to create an environment for their success. Study findings will provide important insights that will impact upon long-term strategies to support rural tourism businesses nationwide.

International Tourism Initiative

The NRTF is interested in pursuing relationships with a number of countries whose residents have expressed interest in a rural tourism experience in the USA. These travellers are particularly intrigued by the beauty, history and culture that rural America can provide. Foreign visitors typically spend more than their domestic counterparts; thus the former are a particularly appealing target market. A model programme is currently being developed and tested in cooperation with the Japanese Travel Bureau International, Inc. (JTB), and complements initiatives in both Japan and the USA that aim to increase tourism visits between residents of both countries (e.g. Tourism Exchange Promotion Programme[1]).

The International Tourism Initiative is intended to encourage the development of rural tourism programmes and tour packages targeted at the Japanese market. Representatives of the NRTF first met in Tokyo with JTB and Ministry of Transport executives to determine the level of interest. This meeting resulted in representatives of the Research Division of the JTB touring the northern tier of western states (from Minnesota to Washington State) and preparing a marketing report for distribution by the NRTF.[2] The 'Development of Japanese Tourism in Rural America' report has been distributed widely both to state travel offices and to private businesses interested in pursuing the Japanese market, and is also being used by the JTB to determine which appropriate tour packages it is to market internally. Private-sector support for the familiarization tour came from KOA. Earlier research suggested that the Japanese visitor to the USA is more inclined to travel independently, seek natural amenity and outdoor recreation experiences, and shop for reasonably priced, quality merchandise, at factory outlet stores and conventional shopping malls. The Japanese are also very intrigued by the history and culture of the western USA, including the cowboy and Native American Indian. The conclusion reached by the JTB research team was that rural America, particularly the West, was well positioned to attract and fulfil the expectations of the new Japanese market segment that today is comprised of individuals seeking a non-urban tourism product. The effect of this model of international cooperation between the NRTF and Japan on rural tourism businesses is being assessed and it will ultimately be applied to other foreign markets.

US forest service case study project[3]

In cooperation with the US Forest Service, the NRTF has prepared twelve case studies about rural tourism development adjacent to or within Forest Service-managed lands. Many of these case studies highlight successful tourism and recreation partnerships along scenic corridors between Forest Service Districts and local communities. They include examples from Alaska, Arkansas, California, Colorado, Idaho, New Mexico, Oregon, Pennsylvania, Utah and Virginia. Each case study highlights the cooperative efforts of public entities, as well as recreational and visitor services frequently provided by tourism businesses. Examples of the services represented include hunting and fishing guides, cabin and campground rentals, swimming beach access, horseback riding, llama trekking, snowmobile or all-terrain vehicle riding, boating, water-skiing, winter sledding, cross-country and downhill skiing, and re-enactments of historic events. This information is now available both in hard copy and on the Internet.

The Scenic and Historic Byways Program

According to the *Colorado Byways Resource Manual*, 'Scenic byways are special routes offering travellers access to the beautiful scenery and the cultural and natural riches of our country. They provide an antidote to the monotony of linear, high-speed travel; open up vistas; and introduce us to places we might otherwise pass by. They may be spectacular destinations sought after by travelers, and they may be local routes long admired by a local community for a Sunday drive. They may be rural, suburban, and urban. They come with different names; rustic roads, scenic highways, historic roadways, or backways. As long as a community regards a roadway as a special resource to be promoted and protected, it is a scenic byway' (Colorado State Scenic and Historic Byways Program 1995: n.p.). Scenic and historic byway designation programmes exist throughout the USA and, depending upon their origination, are administered by local, state or federal government units, or by the private sector. These designation programmes are generally established to help preserve unique environmental, scenic or historical qualities along roadway corridors. Many programmes emphasize economic development as a desired outcome; however, this must be balanced with preservation of the amenity.

The 1991 Intermodal Surface Transportation Efficiency Act (ISTEA)[4] included a National Scenic Byways Program to encourage the planning, design and development of state scenic byway programmes. To qualify as a National Scenic Byway or an All-American Road, a road or highway must possess at least one of six characteristics or types of attraction, those being scenic, historic, natural, cultural, recreational or archaeological. An interim grants programme was authorized to encourage early development, with grant priority given for model projects with corridor management plans, strong local support and multistate corridors. States are also required to spend 10 per cent of their Surface Transportation Program funds for enhancements including bike facilities, scenic easements, historic preservation, landscaping, preservation and enhancement of abandoned railway corridors, conversion to bike and walkways, and archeological planning and research. It should be noted that in addition to the ISTEA scenic designation programme, both the US Forest Service and Bureau of Land Management also have scenic corridor designation programmes.

Colorado Scenic and Historic Byways Program

The Colorado Scenic and Historic Byways Program was authorized by the Governor in 1989 (Executive Order B 045 89), with the creation of the Scenic and Historic Byways Commission. This fifteen-member Commission is charged with the responsibility of 'find[ing] ways in which the State could reap significant benefits from an increased effort to identify, interpret, and promote its exceptional scenic, natural, ecological, historical, and cultural resources' (Colorado State Scenic and Historic Byways Program 1995: 5). The Commission includes representatives from the State Legislature, Department of Transportation, Department of Local Affairs, Colorado Tourism Board, Department of Natural Resources, Colorado Historical Society, US Forest Service, Bureau of Land Management, State Wildlife Commission, State Transportation Commission, local government, local historical museums and Native American tribes, and has designated twenty-one scenic byways since the programme's inception.

To qualify for existing and future funding for byway enhancements and management, all Colorado scenic byways must develop official 'Corridor management plans'. Such plans detail management strategies and policies for enhancement, protection and marketing activities within the defined corridor. The formal purpose of these plans is to 'establish community-based goals and implementation strategies for the scenic byway, to utilize community resources efficiently, to conserve intrinsic qualities of the scenic byway, and enhance its value to the community' (Colorado State Scenic and Historic Byways Program 1995: S.5, 3). Thus, the corridor management plan sets the stage for rural tourism business development by setting standards that are complementary to the region's social, historical and environmental priorities.

The Peak to Peak Highway, a 55-mile corridor located in a rural area of north-central Colorado, was the state's first scenic and historic byway. Approved by the Colorado Legislature in 1989, this designation distinguishes the route as an outstanding scenic and historic resource, and formally encourages local leaders to protect the unique attributes that set it apart from other roads. In addition to the highway's potential as a tourism and recreation resource, the Peak to Peak Highway serves as a major transportation corridor for residents and property owners of numerous communities in the region.

Recently, due in part to opportunities for state and federal financial support, interest in cooperative management of the Peak to Peak Highway has increased. Community leaders, representing public and private interests of both the incorporated and un-incorporated areas of three counties, as well as the US Forest Service and National Park Service, have formed a working group known as the Peak to Peak Scenic Byway Interest Group. A memorandum of understanding has been created, outlining a framework of cooperation between these public and private interests. The group continues to work to develop a plan to guide management decisions and secure funding to implement objectives. A major thrust of the Peak to Peak plan is to ensure that proposed strategies and policies will preserve the integrity of the environmental, cultural, historical and recreational resources while maintaining a satisfactory quality of life for local residents. Over 140 tourism-related businesses exist along the Peak to Peak Highway. These businesses provide food and beverage, accommodation, recreation opportunities and retail services; they also employ over 1,700 people, of which 670 are full time. The products, services and experiences offered are primarily consumed by individuals or groups other than local residents, making these businesses heavily reliant on tourism-generated revenues for their survival. The future projections by the owners and managers of these businesses are for growth and expansion, but not at the expense of the Peak to Peak region's social and environmental integrity (Nuckolls et al. 1993: i-iv). In the case of this byway, the values of the business owners are closely aligned with the goals of the state byway designation programme.

The authorization of scenic byway programmes and the establishment of the NRTF have provided long-overdue formal recognition of the fact that tourism business development is important to rural economic revitalization and stabilization. These initiatives also provide programmes and services that will improve the success rate of both existing and new tourism businesses. Effective planning and management of tourism development in rural areas coalesced around a scenic corridor, coupled with better policies, training, and technical assistance designed to influence tourism business creation, can greatly increase the potential for economic enhancement.

KAMPGROUNDS OF AMERICA: A RURAL TOURISM BUSINESS VENTURE

Kampgrounds of America is North America's largest system of privately owned, full-service overnight and destination campgrounds, offering more than 75,000 camping sites at over 500 properties, both domestic and international. KOA was established in 1962 by a group of enterprising business leaders who saw an opportunity to provide a service to motorists travelling cross-country to the World's Fair in Seattle, Washington. In the 1990s KOA continues to offer its original services of clean toilet facilities, individual hot showers and a camp store – a successful formula for creating a uniform system of campgrounds across the USA and throughout the world (KOA Information Bulletin 1996). KOA developed the franchised campground concept. Seventy per cent of all KOAs are owner-operated, eleven are company-owned and operated, and the remaining properties are owned by investors who employ managers to operate their campgrounds. Eight out of ten KOAs are located within 100 miles of metropolitan areas with a population of 50,000 or more. Many locations are destination campgrounds, offering economical lodging near to popular tourist attractions. In addition to the basic services, most campgrounds offer recreation, playgrounds, utility hook-ups and swimming pools; and some provide hot tubs, saunas, mini golf, boat docks and other amenities. Campground bookings can be made at each KOA or through an international system-wide reservation service.

KOA has also developed Tent Villages and Kamping Kabins. Tent Villages provide a covered cooking and eating area with running water and electricity, a lockable storage cabinet and a private grassy tent site. Kamping Kabins, available at more than three-quarters of all KOAs, sleep four or more people. Guests provide their own sleeping bags or bed linen, a lantern, and camp stove and utensils for meal preparation. Many of these units are equipped with air conditioning. A *KOA Directory, Road Atlas and Camping Guide* (referred to as the camper's bible) is available free of charge at any KOA campground. Patrons can also purchase a low-cost KOA Value Kard which entitles cardholders to a 10 per cent discount on all daily registration fees.

Central City/Dory Hill KOA

The Central City/Dory Hill KOA is a 3.7-acre mountain campground located half a mile west of the Peak to Peak Scenic and Historic Highway (State Highway 119), approximately 5 miles north of Black Hawk, Colorado. Built in 1969, the campground was originally operated on a seasonal basis. It is now open year-round with thirty recreational vehicle (RV) and tent sites and eight Kamping Kabins. Services include a grocery store, gift shop, liquor store, swimming pool, video game room, gasoline, showers, water, electricity, propane, sewage dump station, air compressor and video rental. In addition to providing these services for campers, the owners are 'good neighbours', providing area residents with water and showers in the winter should they have frozen pipes, access to groceries, gasoline and propane, a shelter in bad weather for children using the neighbouring outdoor recreation facilities, and a gathering spot for distribution of community notices, purchase of newspapers and family reunions. The campground has also been the site of swimming lessons for the local high school (a 'chilling' experience) and even a baptism. A frequent statement among area residents is 'I'll meet you at KOA!'. The campground is fully booked from the second week in June to Labour Day (early September) and is a quarter- to half-full during the autumn season. Due in part to the addition of casino gambling in the neighboring communities of Central City and Black Hawk, the occupancy rate during the rest of the year has increased, especially on weekends and holidays. Besides the owner/operators, the campground provides employment for twelve full-time and four part-time staff in the summer, and two full-time and five part-time staff during the winter months.

The Central City/Dory Hill KOA is the first KOA property west of Denver, Colorado, and thus is a frequent first stop for both international and domestic visitors seeking a camping and outdoor experience. Its location on the Peak to Peak Highway and just 15 miles off Interstate 70 makes it a popular destination. In addition to being able to appreciate the area's scenic beauty, visitors gain easy access to Rocky Mountain National Park, Rollins Pass, Mount Evans, US Forest Services lands, and neighbouring rural mountain communities. Since this portion of State Highway 119 has formal scenic byway designation, the route is highlighted on Colorado's state highway map. Overall promotion of the Peak to Peak appears to be increasing visits along the route and thus potential campground visitors. Primary summer markets hail from many of the neighbouring 'hot weather' states of Texas, Oklahoma, Missouri, Kansas, Nevada and New Mexico. Residents of New York, New Jersey, Illinois and other parts of Colorado are also represented. Foreign visitors are most frequently from Europe, Canada, Australia, New Zealand and Japan. Summer registrations appear to be dominated by family campers, while the off-season draws more older couples. Common advertising outlets are the *KOA Directory* and KOA promotional efforts in Europe, publications of the Colorado Travel and Tourism Authority and local and regional promotional materials such as the *Peak to Peak Visitor Guide*, the *Front Range Visitor Guide* and the *Clear Creek Courant* (a local newspaper insert). The Central City/Dory Hill KOA also benefits from those seeking lodging to attend the Central City's world famous opera, which opens its doors each summer season. Competition for campers comes mainly from nearby state and federal government campgrounds and a private youth camp. But these same competitors provide important recreation outlets that draw campers to KOA as well. In addition, the current market trends of wilderness camping and trail-bike riding seem to influence campground visits.

As with most small tourism businesses, there is virtually no financing available for purchase or capital improvements for KOAs. In the case of the Central City/Dory Hill KOA, the current owners[5] received financing from the previous owners for a two-year time period. The installation of the eight Kamping Kabins was possible due to financing from the manufacturer, but no financing was available for the recent renovation/expansion of the shower facilities. It appears that being a multi-service operation is an additional drawback to securing bank financing. In the owners words, 'There is no place to get a loan; lending institutions don't take it seriously'. The campground has a substantial economic impact on the area's economy beyond wages and benefits paid to employees. Purchase of products such as gasoline, propane, grocery supplies, beer and alcohol, and campground maintenance materials is significant. KOA receives weekly deliveries of food and supplies, including products from the popular Schwann's Dairy, known for its nationwide rural delivery network. Being affiliated with a franchise organization such as KOA offers some distinct advantages. In addition to name recognition, group marketing benefits and a consumer understanding of available services, owners/operators have access to a variety of support services through the KOA network. First and foremost, the Central City/Dory Hill KOA campground, as is the case with many KOAs, was an affordable property that could be purchased and operated by a husband-and-wife team. Its location was near the couple's life long residence (nearby Golden, Colorado), and it was capable of generating a profit.

The KOA organization offers franchisees access to an existing pool of campers who have grown to depend upon the security and safety, as well as comforts and supervision, provided by the KOA system. Mandatory training for owner-operators every five years, state campground owners' association meetings, state and national conferences, and technical advice for almost any aspect of campground ownership and development are available through the KOA system. And the opportunity to share experiences and information with other franchisees is most helpful. But being a franchisee also means the payment of some combination of an annual franchise fee, royalties on camping fees, and fees to an advertising fund. It also means adherence to a common set of standards for liability coverage, construction, services, signage, swimming pools and cabins that are not always readily supported by each individual property.

Purchasing the Central City/Dory Hill KOA offered its owners a retirement business opportunity. The property was purchased prior to the husband's full retirement and managed in the early years of ownership by his wife. In 1996 the couple and other employees shared in the responsibilities of maintaining the property with campground supervision and hosting of campers being attended to by a host couple who live on site. Major property improvements are contracted out, while record-keeping is done by the owners, using up-to-date computer technology. In addition to the important income stream, the rewards of running this campground include the variety of things to do and the fun of meeting and interacting with the campers. The owners did note the value of being able to leave the property from time to time and the importance of having dependable employees to look after the operation when they are away. For small rural tourism businesses such as this KOA, adhering to state and federal regulations can, at times, be challenging. Sometimes conflicting interpretations of health and safety standards and practices, the frequency of completing required paperwork and reporting, and costly improvements to maintain ever-changing standards can burden a business with limited personnel and resources. An unusual positive note is that this KOA (and all county residents and businesses) has benefited substantially from the introduction of gambling in the two nearby historic mining towns, as this has meant a reduction in excess of 50 per cent in real estate taxes. It has also meant better dining and entertainment experiences for the area.

IMPLICATIONS FOR RURAL TOURISM BUSINESS DEVELOPMENT

A rural tourism business such as the Central City/Dory Hill KOA faces many challenges in remaining an economically viable entity. Until the early 1990s no formal policy existed in the USA that acknowledged the importance of tourism business development in rural areas. Without such a policy, the legitimacy of rural initiatives and political support is often limited. Also, there have been virtually no 'focal points' in rural areas such as scenic corridors around which tourism businesses could organize and actively participate in a region's tourism development, management and marketing activities. All too often, individual businesses have been left to fend for themselves. Limited access to information, training, financial capital and markets has made it difficult for many to survive and thrive.

Two recent federal initiatives, the authorization of the National Scenic Byways Program and the creation of the National Rural Tourism Foundation, offer existing and potential rural tourism businesses legitimacy as well as new resources to support their efforts. Scenic byway designation provides a catalyst and structure for effective planning and management along a rural highway corridor, offering all interested parties the opportunity to participate in its governance, development and promotion. The notation of scenic byways on state highway maps, in promotional materials and on the Internet increases byway visibility and traffic flow, and thus the potential for economic gain. The ability and willingness to balance such gain with the preservation of the region's natural and cultural amenities increases with the participation of those most likely to benefit long term.

CONCLUSIONS

The NRTF is currently developing a resource base of all printed materials available throughout the USA on rural tourism and rural tourism business development, to be made available on request and through the Internet. An annual national conference and regional seminars on such topics as 'entrepreneurship', 'business start-up' and 'accessing capital' are being established. And, local, state and federal policy is being reviewed to determine the future changes necessary to ensure rural tourism business success – success that can be brought about without sacrificing natural and cultural amenities. Each of these efforts provides new support for economic development in America's rural areas. There is new excitement and acceptance surrounding the tourism experience in the rural areas within the USA by policy-makers, business owners, residents, and the domestic and international visitor. However, unless rural regions provide products and services to attract and satisfy the marketplace and outlets for their visitors to spend money, there can be little overall improvement to the local economy. The emergence of scenic corridors and a national foundation offers rural tourism businesses a new perspective and resources to support their efforts. The Central City/Dory Hill KOA is simply one of many tourism businesses in rural areas that can benefit from these new federal initiatives. It is a business that must be sensitive to its place in the natural environment and its commitment to a sustainable regional tourism economy. Without a wealth of tourism amenities it is unlikely tourists will visit a region and spend money, thus the scenic corridor becomes a rallying point for long-term development and management. To complement this effort, the NRTF can provide training, technical assistance and access to information, all important to a rural tourism business's success.

ACKNOWLEDGMENTS

The authors wish to thank Mr Art Peterson, Executive Director/CEO of Kampgrounds of America, Inc. and Chairman of the National Rural Tourism Foundation, Norman and Kathleen Condreay, owners and operators of the Central City/Dory Hill KOA campground, and Jonelle Nuckolls, Research Associate, University of Colorado at Boulder, for their assistance with this chapter.

NOTES

1 A cooperative effort of the US Department of Commerce and the Japan Ministry of Transport to double the number of tourists between the United States and Japan to 8 million by the year 2000.
2 To obtain a copy of the report, call or write to the NRTF Japan Initiative, c/o National Rural Tourism Foundation, 3704 Collin Drive, Billings, Montana 59102, USA.
3 To obtain a copy list of the twelve case studies, call or write to the NRTF Case Study Project, c/o National Rural Tourism Foundation, 3704 Collin Drive, Billings, Montana 59102, USA, or visit the USFS website on the Internet at www.usfs.gov.
4 In December 1991 the Intermodal Surface Transportation Efficiency Act (ISTEA) (Public Law 102–240) was signed by then President George Bush. ISTEA represents a federal effort to establish a competitive network of air, port, truck and rail services to facilitate distribution of goods in the evolving global market as a US priority. The Secretary of Transportation was charged with establishing an Office of Intermodalism to start a national database and coordinate federal research, with all states required to have an intermodal transportation plan by 1995. Congress also created a Bureau of Transportation Statistics to enhance data collection and analysis.
5 The Central City/Dory Hill KOA is owned and operated by Norman and Kathleen Condreay, 422 DeFrame Court, Golden, Colorado 80401, USA; telephone (00 1) (303) 582–9979.

REFERENCES

Bohland, J. (1988) 'Rural America', in P. Knox, E. Bartless, J. Bohland, B. Holcomb and R. Johnston *The United States: A Contemporary Geography*, London: Longman.

Champion, A., Green, A., Owen, D., Ellin, D. and Coombes, M. (1987) *Changing Places: Britain's Demographic, Economic and Social Complexion*, London: Edward Arnold.

Colorado State Scenic and Historic Byways Program (1995) *Colorado Byways Resource Manual*, Denver: Shalkey Walker Associates, Inc.

Dean, K., Perry, R. and Shaw, D. (1984) 'The conceptualisation of counterurbanisation', *Area* 16(1): 9–16.

Economic Research Associates and the University of Missouri, (1989), *National Policy Study on Rural Tourism and Small Business Development Final Report*, Washington, DC: United States Travel and Tourism Administration.

Fridgen, J. (1991) *Dimensions of Tourism*, East Lansing, MI: Educational Institute of the American Hotel and Motel Association.

Hobbs, D. (1987), 'Why Save Rural America', S. Baugher and A. Somersan (eds) *Proceedings of A New Agenda for Rural America*

Conference, Universities of Minnesota and Wisconsin: Cooperative Extension Service.

Kampgrounds of America, Inc. (1996) *Information Bulletin*, Billings, MT: KOA Executive Offices.

Keinath, W. (1982) 'The decentralisation of American economic life: an economic evaluation', *Economic Geography* 58: 343–57.

National Rural Tourism Foundation, (1996), *Information Packet*, Boulder, Colorado: Tourism Management Programme, College of Business, University of Colorado at Boulder.

Nuckolls, J., Moss, J., Long, P. and Tucker, D. (1993) *Peak to Peak Highway Region Tourism Business Study*, Boulder, Colorado: Tourism Management Program, College of Business, University of Colorado at Boulder.

Pearce, D. G. (1992) *Tourist Organisations*, London: Longman.

Robinson, G. (1990) *Conflict and Change in the Countryside*, London: Belhaven.

Tourism Policy and Export Promotion Act of 1992. Public Law 102–372 September 30, 1992, Washington, DC.

USDA (1995) *Understanding Rural America*, Agriculture Information Bulletin No. 710 Washington, DC: Economic Research Service.

Rural tourism in Canada: the Saskatchewan vacation farm operator as entrepreneur

D. Weaver and D. Fennell

INTRODUCTION

Vacation farms constitute a significant and growing component of the rural tourism product of many industrialized countries. This chapter focuses upon the vacation farm operator as entrepreneur and describes the experience of one particular owner based in the Canadian province of Saskatchewan, as obtained through a self-administered questionnaire and a subsequent in-depth personal interview. Such an avenue of investigation assumes that valuable experiential data may be derived from contact with a select 'grassroots' component and that the resultant information usefully augments the macro-level data obtained through sector-wide surveys. The chapter opens with a brief overview of the vacation farm industry as an international phenomenon, then outlines the Saskatchewan rural tourism context. Following a discussion of the methodology, the results of the questionnaire survey and personal interview are presented and analysed in the context of the appropriate international vacation farm literature.

THE INTERNATIONAL VACATION FARM EXPERIENCE

The vacation farm phenomenon, while relatively recent in North America, is one that has been available on a large scale for quite some time in many European countries (see Chapter 6). For example, both Dernoi (1983) and Embacher (1994) reported the existence of over 20,000 vacation farms in Austria, although such farms had decreased in number by about 5,000 between 1970 and 1990 (see also Hummelbrunner and Miglbauer 1994; and Pevetz 1991 for descriptions of the Austrian vacation farm industry). Dernoi (1983) reported on the extent of vacation farms in Ireland, Finland, and (former) West Germany, with 500, 2,000, and 25,000 units in operation in those countries, respectively. Several authors have also investigated the vacation farm industry in the United Kingdom (Dower 1973; Frater 1983; Neate 1987; Winter 1987; Greenwood 1994), while Murphy (1985) discussed the changes over time in the vacation farms of France.

While the literature has been based on research in Europe, where vacation farm numbers have declined significantly, in other areas recent growth trends are evident. Australia, for example, had approximately 1,500 vacation farms in 1988, compared with only 300 units in 1978 (Hall 1995). The sector is relatively more important in New Zealand, where Pearce (1990) reported the existence of approximately 1,000 vacation farms during the late 1980s, representing 3 per cent of all farm units. The USA had only about 2,000 vacation farms in 1969 (Vogeler 1977), while Shaw and Williams (1994) attributed 700 vacation farms to Canada. North America is thus clearly the underachiever among the more developed regions with respect to the vacation farm sector. On a per capita basis, even Namibia's 54 vacation farms indicate a far superior participation rate (Shackley 1993). It is partly in recognition of this low participation rate, and of the lack of Canadian-based vacation farm research, that the current study was undertaken.

The increased level of research into the vacation farm sector, at least beyond Canada, reflects not only growth in the sector, but also the growing interest in alternative forms of tourism, especially in rural areas (e.g. Smith and Eadington 1992; Aronsson 1994; Bramwell 1994; Lane 1994; Fennell and Weaver, in press). This paradigm emphasizes small-scale, locally owned and operated enterprises, such as vacation farms, which are already integrated into the local economy (e.g. vacation farms are by consensus also working farms), and which usually provide a place-distinct, personal tourism experience for a clientele consciously seeking to avoid a conventional, impersonal 'mass' tourism product. But despite the fact that the research output is increasing, there is still a dearth of comprehensive micro-scale analyses available to assess the grassroots experience of operating a vacation farm; yet it is just on such an experiential basis that sound knowledge may be derived toward achieving a sustainable rural tourism sector. The in-depth personal interviews by Pearce (1990) with the operators of thirteen New Zealand vacation farms is one of the few examples of this micro-scale level of enquiry, although the emphasis in the latter was more on the sociological context of the tourist experience than on the entrepreneurial element.

RURAL TOURISM IN SASKATCHEWAN

Concepts such as rural tourism and vacation farming are particularly relevant to Saskatchewan given that province's essentially rural character. Agriculture, for example, employs just 3 per cent of the Canadian labour force, but 16 per cent in Saskatchewan (Statistics Canada 1994). Farms, along with communities of less than 1,000 persons and other 'rural' categories, account for 37 per cent of the population, and even the largest urban entity (Saskatoon) does not exceed 200,000 residents

(Saskatchewan Health 1996). The provincial population of just over 1 million people represents only 4.0 per cent of Canada's population, while the total area of 652,330 sq. km accounts for 6.5 per cent of Canada's land and fresh water base. The population density of 1.7 people/sq. km (Matthews and Morrow 1985) therefore reveals a sparse and widely dispersed settlement pattern. In comparison, Great Britain, at approximately 37 per cent the size of Saskatchewan, contains some 57 million inhabitants, or a population density of about 233 people/sq. km (*The Canadian World Almanac and Book of Facts* 1989).

This rural emphasis, evident throughout its post-settlement history, has made Saskatchewan especially vulnerable to the vagaries of the unstable modern farm economy, and has contributed to a pattern of virtual population stagnation through chronic out-migration. The 1991 population of 989,000, for example, represented only a marginal increase over the 1931 population of 922,000, when Saskatchewan boasted the number-three rank in resident numbers among the provinces (Statistics Canada 1992). While the farming sector has been particularly hard hit, declining from 101,000 units in 1914 (Richards and Fung 1969) to 61,000 in 1991, the associated deterioration of smaller communities within the province's central place hierarchy is also a well-documented phenomenon (Stabler et al. 1992).

Attempts to diversify beyond the primary sector, while long acknowledged as a desirable strategy for stabilizing the provincial economy, are hampered by the very economic and demographic characteristics outlined above. Potential manufacturers who seek to attain critical economies of scale in production and distribution are dissuaded by the lack of major urban centres and by the sparsely populated urban hinterlands. For similar reasons, though with one critical exception, the potential for expansion within the tertiary or service sector is also severely constrained. The exception alluded to is the tourism industry, which currently accounts for approximately 4 per cent of gross provincial product (Saskatchewan Economic Development 1991). Large urban centres host most of this sector, and will likely continue to do so by merit of their gateway status, concentration of accommodation and site attractions, major event schedules and the recent development of gambling casinos. However, several manifestations of the tourism industry are highly suited to a sparsely populated rural milieu, and thus may constitute the critical if not exclusive components of a realistic diversification strategy for non-urban Saskatchewan.

Paramount among these discrete components is the publicly controlled Provincial Park network, which accommodated 1,964,000 visits during the 1993 high season (April to September) (Saskatchewan Economic Development 1994). Of secondary importance is the network of National Parks and National Historic Sites, which hosted 182,600 and 89,000 visitors, respectively, in 1993 (Canadian Heritage 1995). Among the prominent private providers of rural tourism are lodges and outfitters, some 300 of which are located mainly in the central and northern portions of the province (Saskatchewan Tourism Authority 1995a). In contrast, the vacation farm sector is much smaller, accounting for seventy-six operations and about 6,500 visitor nights in 1993, entirely within the southern and central regions of Saskatchewan (Saskatchewan Economic Development 1994) (see Figure 4.1). With respect to potential growth, the provincial park visiting trend has been one of stagnation, related in part to the stability of the provincial population, from which most visits are derived. A scenario of consolidation and contraction is most likely as a cost-saving measure, and therefore this sector is not likely to contribute any more proportionally to the rural economy of the south. (There may be marginal increases in benefits in the north resulting from the anticipated establishment of wilderness provincial parks accommodating eco-tourism and adventure tourism.) The lodges and outfitters, for their part, are constrained by a dependence on activities which are well chronicled as being in decline within North America. A major longitudinal study of recreational behaviour among adults in the USA, for example, identified hunting as the pursuit which experienced by far the greatest decline during the period 1982 to 1995 (Cordell et al. 1995). Future growth will thus likely

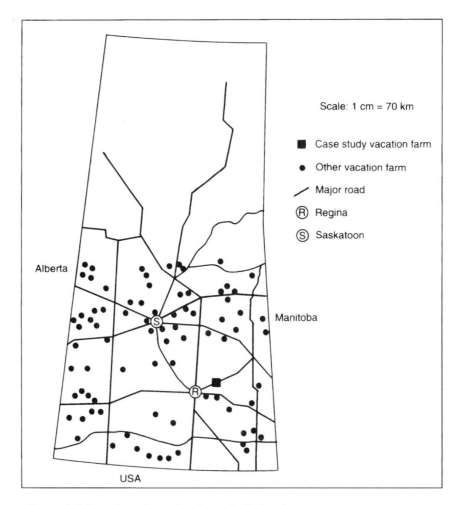

Figure 4.1 Location of vacation farms in Saskatchewan.

be influenced by the extent to which these operators facilitate the transition to eco-tourism activities such as birdwatching, which was identified as by far the fastest growing pursuit in the same study, and in a speculative Canadian analysis (Foot 1990).

The vacation farm sector in Saskatchewan merits attention because of its growth potential, as assessed from both the demand and supply perspectives. Regarding the latter, the current contingent of operators represents a mere 0.1 per cent of all farm units in the province. While Austrian-type participation levels of approximately 6 per cent (Pevetz 1991) are probably unrealistic in the short term given the smaller accessible market base, the attainment of a 1–2 per cent participation rate (i. e. 600–1200 units) by 2005 should not be considered unreasonable, as much of the necessary infrastructure and superstructure is already available in the farm residence (e.g. accommodation) and on the farm property. This would visibly contribute to the goals of a diversified rural economy and possibly provide a critical mass for an even larger sector in future. As suggested earlier, vacation farms are, from a demand perspective, ideally suited to meet the demand for alternative and more sustainable rural tourism opportunities (Bramwell 1994). Furthermore, while many vacation farms do cater for a hunter and angler clientele, it was wildlife viewing which was identified by operators in a recent survey as constituting the most important visitor activity within the provincial sector (Fennell and Weaver, in press).

METHODOLOGY

This study follows from a 1995 survey (Fennell and Weaver, in press) of Saskatchewan's eighty vacation farms, as listed in the province's official vacation guide (Saskatchewan Tourism Authority 1995b). The aforementioned survey provided a macro-scale description of the salient characteristics, strengths and weaknesses in this sector, and offered recommendations for its enhancement. Subsequent to this, in order to generate data on the vacation farm operator as entrepreneur, one vacation farm among the forty which participated in the survey was selected on a non-probability, judgemental basis and approached for an in-depth interview. The particular case study featured in this chapter was selected because it was thought to be representative, apart from its smaller size, of the Saskatchewan vacation farm experience. Furthermore, the completed questionnaire submitted by this operation in the broader survey was characterized by exceptional clarity, depth and breadth of response, and by the indicated willingness of the operator to offer further assistance.

One member of the research team travelled to the site in May 1996 to conduct the interview. After some ten or fifteen minutes of conversation with both the male and female operators, a one-hour interview ensued with the female operator only. The interview was conducted using an interview guide technique. Patton described the characteristics, strengths and weaknesses of this technique as follows:

1 *Characteristics*. Topics and issues to be covered are specified in advance, in outline form; interviewer decides sequence and wording of questions in the course of the interview.
2 *Strengths*. The outline increases the comprehensiveness of the data and makes data collection somewhat systematic. Logical gaps in data can be anticipated and closed. Interviews remain fairly conversational and situational.
3 *Weaknesses*. Important and salient topics may be inadvertently omitted. Interviewer flexibility in sequencing and wording questions can result in substantially different responses, thus reducing the comparability of responses.

(Patton 1987:116)

This process provided enough flexibility to permit the exploration of key ideas and thoughts, both central and tangential to the main objectives set forth prior to the meeting. The interview was taped with the consent of the interviewee. In this chapter information about this case study, obtained from both the questionnaire data and the in-depth interview, will be compared directly to the aggregate results of the provincial vacation farm study and to the relevant international research.

THE VACATION FARM OPERATOR AS ENTREPRENEUR

Open year round. Fish farmers, trap shooting, 2 double rooms. Couples invited for a quiet rest. Beaches and riding nearby. Bird watching, hiking, nature walks and cross country skiing. Teahouse open Thursday, Friday and Saturday afternoons July and August or upon request. Rates: bed and breakfast $25 S, $27 D (2 persons, 1 double bed). Lunch and supper extra. Prices subject to change. Please write or phone ahead. In-House Accommodation, Camping Available, Bus Tours Accepted, Packed Lunches, Meals on Request, Bed and Breakfast.

(Saskatchewan Tourism Authority 1995b)

Such is the advertisement of the case study vacation farm explored in detail in this chapter. The diversity of options offered in this advertisement as a means of securing income indicates a classic example of rural 'entrepreneurialism'. The operators consider themselves as 'hobbyists', who carve a living out of their involvement in a series of activities that are found to be personally rewarding and enriching. Similar economic behaviour was observed by one of the authors in the Shetland Islands of Scotland, where both the male and female heads of household became involved in a series of seasonally dependent enterprises that enabled them to sustain themselves over the course of the year. Examples of such enterprises included bed and breakfast (B&B) tourism, fish farming, knitting, handicrafts, crofting or fishing (Fennell 1994).

The case study vacation farm is situated near the town of Fort Qu'Appelle in the Qu'Appelle valley region of the province of Saskatchewan, Canada, and northeast of the capital city of Regina (see Figure 4.1). Parts of the Qu'Appelle valley represent somewhat of an anomaly in the broader context of the prairie region of Saskatchewan in which it is found, especially with reference to Fort Qu'Appelle. Here, dramatic changes in elevation associated with the glacial trough environment are coupled with a series of small lakes and a predominance of deciduous forest, including aspen, elm, birch and ash. This 'oasis effect' provides a stark contrast to the surrounding prairie regions. Due to the physiography of the area, Fort Qu'Appelle, in addition to its function as a service centre for the surrounding rural area, has status as a small resort centre catering to the needs of nearby population concentrations (Regina, under one hour's drive; Saskatoon, about 2½ hours by car). The popularity of the area is aided by the existence of Echo Valley Provincial Park, which provides visitors with the opportunity of participating in a variety of water- and land-based activities.

The vacation farm operation

The vacation farm experience in Saskatchewan is a relatively recent phenomenon, with the first operation starting in 1971. The case study in this chapter is the second longest-running operation of this sort in the province (it commenced operation in 1972). Its operation started slowly, and very personally, with the operator accommodating a Music Teachers' Association in Fort Qu'Appelle each year for six weeks at $60 per week (room and board). The operator reflected on the past, saying that 'four girls' came for 'a few summers' and stayed for six weeks at a time. Consequently it was discovered that 'there is a real need for the provision of accommodation for those wanting a quiet rest away from the hotels and motels, and for those in search of a unique experience'. In his New Zealand study, Pearce (1990) also noted that the desire to avoid conventional tourist accommodation was a major motivation for vacation farm patrons.

The farm unit is 23 acres in size, and this contrasts with the data of the overall provincial sample that indicated an average farm land base of 1,161 acres (see Table 4.1). Table 4.1 also illustrates that the case study vacation farm has 3 beds, accommodating three or four individuals (one

Table 4.1 Selected Saskatchewan vacation farm data: case study and sample comparisons

Variable	Case study	Sample of farms
Size of land base (acres)	23	1,161
Number of bed spaces	3	6
Number of staff employed		
full time	0	0.2
part time	0	0.3
seasonal	0	0.3

Note: The case study involves one farm selected from the vacation farm study sample. The sample is of forty farms drawn from the Saskatchewan vacation farm population.

double bed and two singles in two bedrooms). Conversely, the sample, on average, had 6.2 bed spaces. The accommodation options at the case study site were also more restricted than those found in the general sample. There were basically two options available to the tourists at the study vacation farm: two bedrooms in the main house, or the opportunity to camp on the premises.

There was a separate budget established for the vacation farm, due to the need for accountability of the farm operation, and also due to the fact that the husband had a partner in the other businesses. Due to the small nature of the operation, the case study employed no one throughout the year to help with the vacation farm. This finding was also evident in the aggregate data provided by the sample, who, on average, reported 0.2 full-time employees, 0.3 part-time employees and 0.3 seasonal employees (see Table 4.1).

For the case study operation, 10 per cent of income was derived from the vacation farm (see Table 4.1). Due to the low return from the enterprise, the operator was clear in suggesting that 'One has to enjoy it to work in this business, and not worry about the dollars and cents'. Clearly there is an element of intrinsic motivation associated with the farm operation: 'If you don't enjoy what you are doing, than forget it.' In absolute terms, it was also discovered that the vacation farm contributed less than $10,000 to the 1994 annual gross income, leading the operator to suggest that 'There is no salary, the profit is the salary'. This finding compares with the sample average, wherein the vacation farm component contributed 18 per cent, or $14,333, to the total gross income. In other research, Oppermannn (1995) discovered that for 53 per cent of German respondents, tourism contributed less than 10 per cent of gross earnings, while Winter (1987) surveyed 106 vacation farms in peripheral parts of England and Wales and found that for 72 per cent of respondents, tourism contributed 0–5 per cent of gross income. While no explicit financial details were solicited, Pearce (1990) found that revenues constituted a significant secondary goal, but never the primary goal, of New Zealand operators.

Tourists and tourist activities

The interview proved to be very rewarding both in terms of gaining an appreciation of the lifestyle of the farm operator and in obtaining a more complete package of data. A theme that was evident throughout the conversation was the very personal relationship between tourist and host. The operator had emphasized that 'the visitors that we get are real successful people, from Canada and all around the world. These people are very down to earth.' For example, the operator related a very telling story that illustrates the importance of the tourist–host relationship. During the 1980s the operator was having some difficulty raising pheasants. (It was not mentioned whether such pheasants were to be raised for aesthetic or utilitarian purposes, but we suspect the latter.) Evidently the operator had shown his hobby to a visitor from England, with a full explanation of the troubles being encountered. A number of months later the operator was pleasantly surprised to have been sent a wonderfully descriptive book on the raising of pheasants. This clearly was a very significant event in the mind of the operator, and one that reinforced the belief that personal interaction was a driving force behind deciding to operate a vacation farm.

In other research, Pearce (1990) cited the desire for interesting company as the major motivation among the surveyed operators for entering the New Zealand vacation farm sector. In contrast, Winter (1987) illustrated that the main motivation for sampled British operators to become involved in tourism was the need to utilize an existing vacant building, which was more important than income generation. As such, the upkeep of these buildings is better assured, as is therefore the probability of keeping them under family control, should a family member ever want to live there. In comparison, Frater (1983) lists the motives of Herefordshire operators as:

- 35 per cent to increase annual income;
- 25 per cent to enjoy the company of the tourists;
- 20 per cent to offset falling agricultural income;
- 16 per cent to utilize a disused resource.

Twenty-four activities were listed on the questionnaire in order to understand the types of activity provided and their relative importance to the vacation farm tourist (using a five-point scale ranging from 'very important' to 'not at all important'). Only four of these were recorded as 'very important' at the case study farm: camping, casual and professional photography, and wildlife viewing. Specifically, 25 per cent of the visitors to this operation were primarily motivated by wildlife viewing, as per the advertisement. Comparatively, each of the four 'very important' activities identified by the case study were also ranked highly by the sample: wildlife viewing was ranked first; casual photography, second; camping, sixth; and professional photography, seventh. There was a shared lack of importance in activities such as barn dancing, boating, canoeing, cultural tourism, snowmobiling, and study or research.

Birdwatching was found to be the favourite specific activity of tourists who visit the Fort Qu'Appelle operation. Saskatchewan in general is well regarded for its bird habitat for all sorts of migratory and non-migratory species (Richards and Fung 1969; Poston et al. 1990); however, the Fort Qu'Appelle region is especially rich in this regard, due to its variable physiography. The operator conducts mini nature tours at the farm and in the surrounding area. One cited constraint which interfered with client enjoyment was the wood ticks, which are abundant until about mid-July.

Seventy per cent of all visits to the operation were Canadian in origin, while 30 per cent overall were from Saskatchewan; 10 per cent were from the USA, while 20 per cent of visitors came from Europe. Comparatively, for the sample of vacation farms, most visitors came from within Saskatchewan (41 per cent), with 36 per cent of visitors coming from other areas of Canada. The USA was the source of 15 per cent of visits, while Europe was far less important to the overall sample (7 per cent) compared to the case study.

The statistics on numbers of visitors given in Table 4.1 indicate a significant difference in the volume of visits between the sample and the case study. This is due to the fact that one vacation farm in the study caters for up to 7,000 people per year. Other studies (Pizam and Pokela 1980) divided vacation farms on the basis of volume. These authors excluded vacation farms catering to more than forty guests at any one time in defining their sample. This leads to the question of whether or not capacity figures should define the vacation farm experience. From the perspective of the case study operator:

> Some larger farm vacation operations are reported to cater to up to over 200 people at a time. There is no doubt that these are rural experiences, but they are a different type of experience than the smaller-scale ones. These bigger operations are more like a resort.

A corroborative finding by Pearce (1990) was that a number of New Zealand operators felt constrained from expanding their annual intake beyond 100 guests because of the stress involved in maintaining the continuous friendly attitude expected by patrons, when a threshold of this magnitude is exceeded. Both the case study and sample findings indicate a variability in the numbers of visitors over the five years presented. The case study illustrates a significant increase in visits in 1994 over previous years. However, the interview revealed that visits again dropped in 1995 to twenty-six tourists. When asked about this trend, the operator indicated that 'it is impossible to project how many tourists you will get'. Ninety per cent of visits to the case study farm were by first-time visitors, while 75 per cent were first-timers in the sample.

Tourists typically stayed for one night (90 per cent) at the case study farm, with only 10 per cent staying for two or three nights (see Table 4.1). Nearly half (47 per cent) of all visits to the sample of vacation farms were for a period of one night. The contrast may be due in part to the proximity of the case study to Regina, a city of 180,000 residents one hour's drive away. Twenty per cent of visitors stayed for a period of two or three nights, with a similar number staying for day trips and four or more nights (14 per cent and 15 per cent, respectively). Business was split evenly between the weekend and weekday for the case study, while 58 per cent of business fell on the weekends as indicated by the overall sample, which led the operators to suggest that:

> A number of tourists are from Saskatoon, who are on their way to other parts of the province and country. A lot of single people come for a quiet rest and know that their motorbike or car is safe and secure.

The case study farm will cater for organized groups only on request. The operators have enjoyed catering for campfire groups (for teenagers), coffee stops, elementary school tours and the cubs.

Barriers and opportunities

The operators of the vacation farm felt that, overall, there were not too many natural-environment barriers, aside from the ticks, to the operation of their tourism enterprise. Conversely, the natural environment does benefit the operation as a habitat for birds. This has a direct bearing on the number of tourists visiting the farm throughout the year. There were no explicit reports of cultural or economic barriers and opportunities, and few reported governmental/political barriers or opportunities. Apart from the relationship with Tourism Saskatchewan, and their guides and brochures, the operators indicated that they had no other government assistance:

> You get more help from people who are doing the same thing. There is a network of people who help out. The Country Vacation Farm people get together each year for a meeting. The government [Departments of Agriculture and Tourism] helped start the Association in 1972, that's about it.

The operator has been a member of the Country Vacations Association (CVA) since its establishment in 1972. The main motivations for joining the CVA included the added insurance offered and market exposure through the *Country Vacations Guide*. Also, the CVA sends representatives to trade shows to help market the vacation farm product. In 1995 it cost the operator $200 to join the Association, up from $100 in previous years. The operator did not know why there was such an increase and thought that the fee was 'a bit much'. Although this levy was readjusted to $100 in 1997, there is an added fee of $110 for e-mail advertising, which was also perceived to be rather expensive. The operators also had their own bonded household insurance, which was thought to be adequate given that they had no swimming pool or horseback riding, both of which are higher-risk activities.

OTHER TYPES OF ECONOMIC ACTIVITY

The main industry on the farm was the fish-farming component, started in 1973, and which operates steadily for two months of the year (May and June). Pevetz (1991) observed that tourism may seem to compete with other forms of land use (e.g. agriculture) as both enterprises reach their peak at the same time of the year. This seems to be the case here, with the operators having elected to diminish this competition by restricting the vacation farm season to July and August. This is perhaps wise, since, as Oppermann (1995) has reported in a recent analysis of vacation farms in Bavaria, occupancy rates approach 100 per cent in July and August, and diminish throughout the year to almost nothing in winter, except in areas adjacent to major ski resorts.

The operators, it was explained, act as middlemen in the distribution of rainbow trout, from their supplier in South Dakota, to farmers of the province. They receive approximately four shipments of some 40,000 fish per year, and sell them as 6 in. and 4 in. fish. Other farmers in the area purchase the trout to stock their dugouts and use them primarily for their own purposes. The fish sell for 80 cents each, plus a $3 added expense for boxes, plastic and oxygen, or a total of $23 for a box of twenty-five fish.

Eight boxes of twenty-five fish, which seemed to be a normal order for farmers, would cost the consumer $160. The operators wanted to build a 'fish-out' pond that would enable visitors to catch fish to take away with them. This was not feasible, though, as the soil was found to be too silty and unable to hold water like a conventional dugout.

It was observed that the female partner assumes most of the responsibility for the operation of the vacation farm. She also contributes her time to the fish operation and to the other many sources of income mentioned elsewhere. It was emphasized, though, that both operators regard their involvement in the vacation farm industry highly. However, it was not mentioned how involved the male operator was, and it is suspected that his involvement is more peripheral, that he acts more in a frontline interpersonal capacity with the tourists. This female emphasis appears to be a prevalent phenomenon in the vacation farm sector, having been cited in studies of the United Kingdom (Frater 1983), Austria (Pevetz 1991) and the Isles of Scilly in the UK (Neate 1987). Frater's comment that 'but for the farmer's wife's interest and determination, few tourism enterprises would exist' (Frater 1983: 168) is especially telling. Other sources of income included the wife's involvement as a driving instructor, the husband's expertise as a woodworker and mechanic, and the wife's work with a number of different crafts that are sold regularly at a farmers' market (deer-horn buttons, leather belts, vases, work with bulrushes). They also sell fishing nets throughout the year. The operator was reluctant to put yearly figures to these enterprises due to the difficulty of making accurate projections. They both remain, in the wife's opinion, very busy. Such occupational diversity, as in the Shetlands, appears to be quite typical of related small-scale tourism enterprises within Canada's western provinces. Weaver et al. (1995), for example, reported in a sample of small-scale rural ecotourism enterprises in the adjacent province of Manitoba that operators were usually involved in several tourism-related and non-tourism options.

PLANS FOR THE FUTURE

There were definite plans to expand the operation within the subsequent five years. In particular, the operator was very enthusiastic about the development of lawn bowling as an added feature of the farm. There are plans for the construction of four lanes, accommodating up to thirty-two bowlers at a time. It was mentioned that bowling lanes in Saskatchewan were presently restricted to only a couple in Regina and Saskatoon. The cost to put in the lanes would be approximately $6,000 ($1,500 per lane). However, there would be other costs for the bowls ($125 a pair; eight pairs needed). The idea would be to attract tourists over the course of the day, as the operator would not be able to accommodate them overnight. The operator would supply coffee, doughnuts and other sustenance for them, with the added opportunity of purchasing memberships and thus creating the impetus for more involvement in the activity. The operator said she had done some research on the lawn-bowling option by visiting Regina and asking participants if they would be interested in travelling to Fort Qu'Appelle to participate in such an event.

The operator mentioned that she would like to be involved in the vacation farm business forever, but acknowledged that obviously this was not possible (the couple appear to be in their sixties). It was mentioned that she would like to develop a situation whereby the vacation farm would be carried on in the family after they were gone, or when they could no longer cope (however, there was an acknowledgement that this might not be as a much of a priority to her children). Furthermore, there was the possibility of starting a small lodge of about eight units, and of she and her husband staying in one of them while maintaining a tie with the operation. She warned that the government would 'take everything' if she and her husband didn't soon pre-plan the transfer of ownership of the property to her loved ones. When the operator was asked if she would like to join a small business club to help bolster the vacation farm or other enterprises on the farm, there was very little support for the idea. It was felt that such an endeavour would do very little to further the enterprise.

CONCLUSIONS

The case study approach adopted in this chapter yielded idiosyncratic data which could be compared with the sample of Saskatchewan vacation farms and other international research, toward the enhancement and managed expansion of this sector in the province and within similar jurisdictions. In particular, the interview brought a very personal perspective on the operation of a vacation farm, which otherwise would not have been possible using the aggregate survey data.

The operator was found to be involved in a variety of economic activities (e.g. fish, vacation farm and crafts) which apparently provided sufficient sustenance throughout the year. This suggests the need for a diverse rather than specialized economic base for the small-scale operator. A key motivation for the establishment of the tourism component of the farm seemed to be the operator's desire for human interaction. In this sense the tourist was indeed a person, and not simply a number or dollar-value. The operator gave the distinct impression that her role was one of facilitator or catalyst to the overall tourist experience, perhaps even as part of the base of attractions, for the purpose of strengthening this tourist–host relationship. In this sense, the operator is at least subconsciously projecting a basic attribute of the 'alternative' tourism paradigm which is being increasingly sought by the tourist market. However, one should not be trapped into believing that such an operation exists primarily for non-economic reasons – it is clearly an economic enterprise; yet there was an overwhelming feeling that prosperity had something other than a strictly economic bottom line. We suspect that this is due to the nature of the business and the people who run it, but also perhaps because of the variability (and therefore safety) of the other enterprises engaged in throughout the year. For example, fluctuating yearly visit levels (sometimes varying by as much as half or two-thirds on the previous year) were accepted by the operator and considered as minor inconveniences that did not 'make or break' the operator's fiscal year. Conversely, if the same fluctuations were to occur to a larger tourism operation it would likely not last for very long. Although this element of safety cannot be proven here, future research might wish to explore this avenue further. Future researchers might also wish to include an analysis of more than one case study, from the interview perspective, for the purposes of comparison. Two or three cases may be identified – similarly by a purposive/judgemental sampling approach – that are different according to a number of factors:

1 geography, with reference to those close and those further away from major markets;
2 time, from the perspective of operations that are younger against those that are older;
3 success, however defined, which would include those that are economically viable over those that are not;
4 scope, which includes a comparison of very large operations (from the perspective of visit levels or facilities and attractions) and those that are smaller.

REFERENCES

Aronsson, L. (1994) 'Sustainable tourism systems: the example of sustainable rural tourism in Sweden', *Journal of Sustainable Tourism* 2: 77–92.

Bramwell, B. (1994) 'Rural tourism and sustainable rural tourism', *Journal of Sustainable Tourism*, 2: 1–6.

Canadian Heritage (1995) *National Historic Sites: Person Visits* , Ottawa: Ministry of Supply and Services.

The Canadian World Almanac and Book of Facts (1989) Toronto: Global Press.

Cordell, H., Lewis, B. and MacDonald, B. (1995) 'Long-term outdoor recreation participation trends', in J. Thompson (ed.) *Proceedings of the Fourth International Outdoor Recreation and Tourism Trends Symposium and the 1995 National Recreation Resource Planning Conference*, University of Minnesota, Minneapolis, USA.

Davidoff, G., Davidoff, S. and Eyre, J. D. (1988) *Tourism Geography*, New York: National Publishers.

Dernoi, L. (1983) 'Farm tourism in Europe', *Tourism Management* 4(3): 155–66.

Dower, M. (1973) 'Recreation, tourism and the farmer', *Journal of Agricultural Economics* 24: 465–77.

Embacher, H. (1994) 'Marketing for agri-tourism in Austria: strategy and realisation in a highly developed tourist destination', *Journal of Sustainable Tourism* 2: 61–76.

Fennell, A. (1994) 'The space–time characteristics of tourist group movement in the Shetland Islands, Scotland', unpublished doctoral dissertation, University of Western Ontario, Canada.

Fennell, D. and Weaver, D. B. (1995) *The Vacation Farm Industry of Saskatchewan: A Profile of Operations*, Regina, Saskatchewan: Saskatchewan Tourism Authority.

—— (in press) 'Vacation farms and ecotourism in Saskatchewan, Canada', *Journal of Rural Studies*.

Foot, D. (1990) 'The age of outdoor recreation in Canada', *Recreation Canada* 48: 16–22.

Frater, J. (1983) 'Farm tourism in England: planning, funding, promotion, and some lessons from Europe', *Tourism Management* 4(3): 167–79.

Greenwood, J. (1994) 'Dartmoor area tourism initiative – a case study of visitor management in and around a national park', in A. Seaton (ed.) *Tourism: The State of the Art*, Chichester: John Wiley.

Hall, C. M. (1995) *Introduction to Tourism in Australia*, 2nd edn, Melbourne: Longman.

Hummelbrunner, R. and Miglbauer, E. (1994) 'Tourism promotion and potential in peripheral areas: the Austrian case', *Journal of Sustainable Tourism* 2: 41–50.

Lane, B. (1994) 'Sustainable rural tourism strategies: a tool for development and conservation', *Journal of Sustainable Tourism* 2: 102–11.

Matthews, G. J. and Morrow, R. Jr. (1985) *Canada and the World*, Scarborough: Prentice-Hall.

Murphy, P. (1985) *Tourism: A Community Approach*, New York: Methuen.

Neate, S. (1987) 'The role of tourism in sustaining farm structures and communities on the Isle of Scilly', in M. Bouquet and M. Winter (eds) *Who From Their Labours Rest? Conflict and Practice in Rural Tourism*, Aldershot: Avebury.

Oppermann, M. (1995) 'Holidays on the farm: a case study of German hosts and guests', *Journal of Travel Research* 34: 63–7.

Patton, M. Q. (1987) *How to Use Qualitative Methods in Evaluation*, Newbury Park, NJ: Sage.

Pearce, P. L. (1990) 'Farm tourism in New Zealand: a social situation analysis', *Annals of Tourism Research* 17: 337–52.

Pevetz, W. (1991) 'Agriculture and tourism in Austria', *Tourism Recreation Research* 16: 57–60.

Pizam, A. and Pokela, J. (1980) 'The vacation farm: a new form of tourism destination', in D. Hawkins, E. Shafer and J. Rovelstad (eds) *Tourism Marketing and Management Issues*, Washington, DC: George Washington Press.

Poston, B., Ealey, D., Taylor, P. and McKeating, G. (1990) *Priority Migratory Bird Habitats of Canada's Prairie Provinces*, Edmonton, Canada: Canadian Wildlife Service.

Richards, J. and Fung, K. (1969) *Atlas of Saskatchewan*, Saskatoon, Canada: University of Saskatchewan.

Saskatchewan Economic Development (1991) *A Tourism Strategy for Saskatchewan*, Regina, Canada: Department of Economic Development.

—— (1994) *Tourism Saskatchewan Indicators Report 1993*, Regina,

Canada: Department of Economic Development, Tourism Information Unit.

Saskatchewan Health (1996) *Covered Population 1995*, Regina, Canada: Health Insurance Registration File.

Saskatchewan Tourism Authority (1995a) *Saskatchewan Outdoor Adventure 1995*, Regina, Canada: Saskatchewan Tourism Authority.

—— (1995b) *Saskatchewan Vacation Guide*, Regina, Canada: Saskatchewan Tourism Authority.

Shackley, M. (1993) 'Guest farms in Namibia: an emerging accommodation sector in Africa's hottest destination', *International Journal of Hospitality Management*, 12: 253–65.

Shaw, G. and Williams, A. (1994) *Critical Issues in Tourism: A Geographical Perspective*, Oxford: Blackwell.

Smith, V. and Eadington, W. (eds) (1992) *Tourism Alternatives: Potentials and Problems in the Development of Tourism*, Philadelphia: University of Pennsylvania Press.

Stabler, J., Olfert, M. and Fulton, M. (1992) *The Changing Role of Rural Communities in an Urbanising World: Saskatchewan 1961–1990*, Regina, Canada: Canadian Plains Research Centre, University of Regina.

Statistics Canada (1992) *Canadian Population and Census Data*, Ottawa: Ministry of Supply and Services.

—— (1994) *Canadian Labour Statistics*, Ottawa: Ministry of Supply and Services.

Vogeler, I. (1977) 'Farm and ranch vacationing', *Journal of Leisure Research* 9: 291–300.

Weaver, D., Glenn, C. and Rounds, R. (1995) *Ecotourism in Manitoba*, Report Series 1995–5 Brandon, Canada: Rural Development Institute.

Winter, M. (1987) 'Private tourism in the English and Welsh Uplands: farming, visitors and property', in M. Bouquet and M. Winter (eds) *Who From Their Labours Rest? Conflict and Practice in Rural Tourism*, Aldershot: Avebury.

Rural tourism in Canada: issues, opportunities and entrepreneurship in aboriginal tourism in Alberta

5

D. Getz and W. Jamieson

INTRODUCTION

Visitor interest in authentic aboriginal experiences and cultural contacts is a growing segment of the heritage tourism business. Campbell (1994: 43) referred to an Angus Reid survey which revealed that 66 per cent of the North American travelling population had some level of interest in aboriginal tourism products. Of that large group, 25 per cent identified aboriginal attractions as the main reason for a trip. Much of aboriginal tourism is situated in rural areas because of two factors: the existence of large reservations or other forms of traditional land occupation; and the fact that most cultures which have remained traditional have done so because of some degree of physical isolation from urban centres. In this chapter we examine the nature of aboriginal tourism, together with the nature of aboriginal tourism products and businesses located in Canada; a case study of a Southern Alberta aboriginal tourism enterprise is also discussed.

ABORIGINAL TOURISM

Aboriginal and traditional cultures have often been exploited through tourism development, and until the early 1990s there were few examples of aboriginal people acting as entrepreneurs or owners of tourism enterprises. There are a number of complications which arise when attempting to develop or market aboriginal cultural tourism: the need for cross-cultural consultations; concern about negative cultural impacts; the issues of land claims and preserving traditional resource uses; and perhaps the need for special educational and training programmes to help groups reach the tourism development's potential. Evidence of exploitation is global. For example, Crystal (1989) reported how rapid mass-tourism growth impacted on the Taraja of Sarawak, Indonesia, causing commercialization of rituals and the looting of antiquities. Smith (1989) showed how tourism on Boracay in the Philippines had resulted in pollution, modernization, inflation and the sudden adoption of a wage economy. However, the rural residents did want infrastructure and income improvements. McGregor and McMath (1993: 47) noted how New Zealand's aboriginal people, the Maori, were 'romanticized as historical noble savages' while at the same time being deprived of their land in tourism areas like Rotorua. For over a hundred years following the formalization of tourism in the 1870s, Maori were marginalized and remained peripheral to tourism developments, despite being the object of tourist interest. Today Maori are active in tourism developments and businesses, although there is controversy within the community over the image being portrayed and therefore the very nature of the product. Gordon (1990) showed how Kalihari Bushmen in Namibia had been reduced to 'side-show attractions', while Daltabuit and Pi-Sunyer (1990) noted that the Maya in Mexico had lost lands to the unilateral formation of parks and received only menial jobs in return.

Specific benefits can arise from what Smith (1989: 4) has called 'ethnic tourism', mainly a rejuvenation of arts, crafts and other customs. Smith refers to 'ethnic tourism' as being typically in remote places with limited numbers of visitors, although it is clear that global travel is bringing more tourists to more remote places all the time. On the other hand, aboriginal people have often found out very quickly how to exploit tourism for cash and other benefits, although the resultant exchange process is typically unbalanced. In Smith's (1989) seminal study *Hosts and Guests: The Anthropology of Tourism* a number of examples of the management of impacts and the securing of direct involvement in tourism are given. The term 'indigenous tourism' is used by Swain to describe the Kuna Indians of Panama, who internally control their involvement through cooperatives, with both ethnic and ecological dimensions stressed (Swain 1990: 85). McKean demonstrated how the Balinese found cultural identity through tourism, and managed impacts by keeping some rituals off limits to visitors (McKean 1989: 132). Deitch concluded that American Indians of the Southwest had responded to tourism demand for arts and crafts by increasing their productivity and reviving old traditions (Deitch 1989: 235). One consequence was mass-produced junk, but innovation and revival also followed.

Browne and Nolan (1989) surveyed reservations in the western USA to determine aboriginal tourism initiatives and attitudes. Many aboriginal people felt that tourism is culturally beneficial, leading hopefully to better understanding of and respect for contemporary aboriginal culture. Increased friendship and sympathy among peoples was a stated goal. However, opposition to tourism initiatives exists in some aboriginal communities. According to Browne and Nolan, reservation-based tourism has gone through an evolution involving much trial and error, beginning in the 1960s. Declining government funding has meant that aboriginal communities must strive for self-sufficiency.

Aboriginal tourism products and businesses

Campbell has argued that ownership is not the determining factor when defining aboriginal tourism products or businesses (Campbell 1994: 41). The connection with aboriginal culture and values is seen as critical, with the ideal product encompassing history, lifestyle, customs and entertainment, spiritual values, arts and crafts, and a connection to the land. Products, and related businesses, could be classified on the basis of these criteria, although detailed examination from the perspective of both aboriginal people and tourists would be necessary. Browne and Nolan (1989) documented many examples of aboriginal-produced events as tourist attractions:

> Many of those [reservations] surveyed focus primarily on special event tourism, welcoming most of their visitors during periods of celebration such as dance festivals, rodeos, or historical pageants. . . . In ten cases, most of which were small Indian settlements, the only tourism attraction mentioned was a special event.
>
> (Browne and Nolan 1989: 365 and 368)

For example, the Southern Ute Reservation in Utah has horse races, bingo, an annual Bear Dance in May and Sun Dance in July, and a fair in the autumn (Browne and Nolan 1989: 366). A very pertinent issue is deciding which rituals and ceremonies to perform for the public and which to preserve from public view. Also in the USA, Sweet (1990) noted that 'adventure tourism' on aboriginal lands was expanding. This type of tour emphasized personal contacts with aboriginal communities, which placed pressures on the hosts. In response to both planned tourist visits and other encroachments on aboriginal lands, some communities have placed limits on access to sites or ceremonies. Rules of behaviour for visitors are enforced on some reserves, while in some ceremonies a ritual clown seeks to influence visitor behaviour. Many tourists, according to Sweet, feel that such limitations are worthwhile in order to preserve authentic experiences. Similarly, Klieger (1990) noted that the government of Bhutan places tight restrictions on visitors seeking contact with tribal peoples.

The State of South Dakota has been developing markets for aboriginal products and collaborating with aboriginal people to organize packages from their point of view. The US Bureau of Indian Affairs is providing encouragement and support to tribes that identify a tourism opportunity, such as Wounded Knee monument, or scenic and historic byways which cross aboriginal land. In Queensland, Australia, *A Guide to Experiencing Aboriginal and Torres Strait Islander Culture* provides basic information as well as advice on issues of cultural sensitivity: can I take photographs? Do I need permission? Specific aboriginal tourism products are listed: galleries and shops; celebrations and festivals; cultural centres; parks (rock paintings and other sites); commercial attractions with cultural exhibits and theatre; guided tours (to rock paintings) and package tours with accommodation. The guide also distinguishes between aboriginal and non-aboriginal tour operators. A failed aboriginal tourism initiative was discussed by Chapin (1990), who examined the Kuna Ecotourism project in Panama. Its lack of success was attributed to a combination of factors, including lack of government interest, remoteness and poor roads, and failure to form arrangements with the tourism industry. Table 5.1 summarizes a range of aboriginal tourism businesses and types of development. Personal service businesses provide direct host–guest contact, while manufacturing and retailing do not necessarily bring tourists into contact with the producers. Passive aboriginal and traditional tourism occurs when aboriginal lands, communities or artifacts are made accessible to view, sometimes without permission and based on a fee paid to the community. More recently, as revealed in the Alberta example, more intensive forms of tourism development have occurred, including museums, interpretive centres, resorts and restaurants, with the emphasis on authentic aboriginal experiences. Many forms of non-traditional developments, such as casinos and bingo halls, have also occurred on reservations in North America.

Table 5.1 Forms of aboriginal tourism businesses

Personal service (direct contact with visitors)	guided tours: ecotours, adventure tours, sightseeing
	outfitting and guiding, hunting and fishing, recreation activities and expeditions
	interpretation and demonstrations ('living history'), cultural performances (powwows and dances, festivals and rituals, rodeos, roundups, fairs, historical pageants and dinner theatres)
	traditional food service
	storytelling and legend-telling ('speakers')
	teaching (educational programmes concerning aboriginal culture)
	home-stays or shared camping
Manufacturing and retailing (on-site or for export)	handicrafts and art
	manufactured 'aboriginal' products
Passive	permission for sightseeing or external tours to visit monuments and archaeological digs on display
	provision of trails or observation points
Intensive development	museums, cultural centres and interpretive facilities
	aboriginal-cuisine restaurants
	aboriginal art and craft shops and galleries
	transportation services
Non-traditional	bingo halls and casinos
	commercial accommodation of all types
	golf courses and other recreational facilities
	resorts

While these developments might present little in the way of a traditional experience, they are viewed by many aboriginal people as legitimate business ventures that can provide greater economic benefits and perhaps open doors to other forms of aboriginal tourism enterprise.

Aboriginal Tourism in Canada

The Canadian National Aboriginal Tourism Association (CNATA) was established in 1990 to promote, protect and preserve the integrity of aboriginal tourism (CNATA, no date). Although CNATA estimated there were 1,300 aboriginal tourism businesses in the country (mostly small operators), the organization noted several reasons why aboriginal tourism products were not more available in Canada:

- lack of awareness or knowledge of tourism potential (among aboriginal people);
- lack of education or training (skills);
- lack of participation by aboriginal people in tourism organizations;
- lack of pertinent market research;
- concern by aboriginal people about the potential loss of cultural identity that tourism might engender.

CNATA (no date) produced a document entitled *For the Love of Nature: Nature Based Tourism for Aboriginal Peoples*. Nature tours are viewed as a way of sharing aboriginal culture, as are other aboriginal tourism products: arts, crafts, exhibitions, fashion, festivals, interpretive centres with guides, markets, monuments and museums, and restaurants featuring aboriginal cuisine. Several cases of aboriginal tourism were documented, one of which is the Haida initiative in the Queen Charlotte Islands. There, 'watchmen' have been employed to protect aboriginal cultural sites while also interpreting them for visitors. Slow growth and a minimum of facilities are preferred by the Haida, and some types of tourism – notably sports fishing – are considered to be threatening because of the type of tourist attracted.

A second case featured Mountain River Outfitters, a Dene aboriginal family business in the Northwest Territories which provides guiding and outfitting services to tourists, plus contract work for other non-aboriginal outfitters. A third case documented the entrepreneurial activity of Solomon Suganaques, who was developing an attraction in Northern Ontario. The idea was to create a remote meeting place with wigwams, living accommodation, and the 'living and doing' of traditional aboriginal crafts. Funding and advice had been received from the Aboriginal Business Development Programme and provincial ministries. The Northern Ontario Aboriginal Tourism Association does training and provides services to this type of business venture. In 1995 CNATA, with support from the Aboriginal Economic Programmes of Industry Canada, launched a new video aimed specifically at encouraging aboriginal communities to evaluate potential tourism developments and to advise them on the process and challenges. Entitled *The Stranger, the Aboriginal and the*

Land, this highly professional video stresses nature-based products, but also covers the cultural components. A major theme of the video is environmental and cultural responsibility, encompassing the costs and benefits of tourism.

Treaty Seven Nations of Southern Alberta

The 'Treaty Seven' First Nations of Southern Alberta, namely Siksika, Blood, Peigan, Tsuu T'ina and Stoney, are well positioned in relation to Calgary and the Rocky Mountain parks to capture a portion of the rapidly expanding tourism industry (see Figure 5.1). A number of existing tourist-

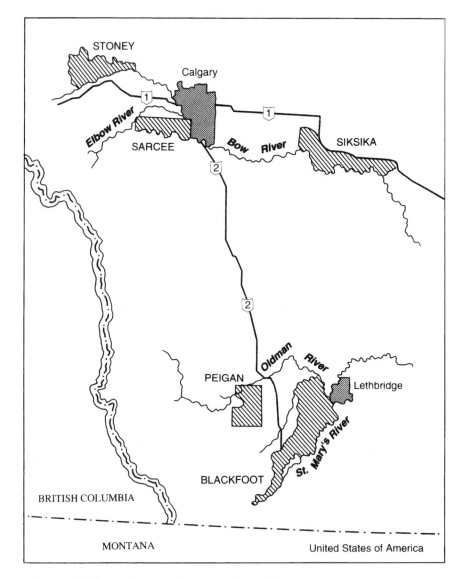

Figure 5.1 Treaty Seven nations in southern Alberta.

oriented products are available on aboriginal lands, and there are dance groups which do performances at other attractions and events in the region. The extent of development to date is relatively minor, but major new developments are being pursued. The potential seems considerable, but a number of obstacles must be overcome. An overview of the current situation and major proposals sets the scene for a more specific case study of one aboriginal entrepreneur who is engaged in the tourism industry. Located west of Calgary along the Trans-Canada Highway, which is the main approach to Banff National Park, the Stoney lands have considerable potential to attract tourists. The Chief Chiniki service centre and restaurant is a longstanding landmark along the highway, and there is a campground facility. Nakoda Lodge on Chief Hector Lake functions as a learning and conference centre and contains a guest lodge with fifty rooms. Proposals have been developed to add a museum, art and interpretive centre to the complex. A remote camp was created to accommodate horse pack tours. The Stoney are involved with other bands in a broadbased group called the Buffalo Nations Cultural Society, which is devoted to inter-band cooperation. The society owns and manages the Luxton Museum in the town of Banff. This society has an ambitious plan to develop a major attraction on provincially owned land just off the Trans-Canada Highway as it approaches the Rocky Mountains.

Buffalo Nations Cultural Park

The aim of the Cultural Park is to present and interpret the lore and unique histories of North American aboriginal bands. The original idea was conceived by Stan Cowley, owner of nearby Rafter Six Ranch, who had proposed a cultural centre adjacent to the property. Buffalo Nations Cultural Society is now proceeding with this idea, in cooperation with Mr Cowley. Its foundation will be a Medicine-Wheel design that is meant to represent the four great elements: air, earth, fire and water. Aboriginal symbols such as the hearth, bison, the whale and the eagle are to be incorporated into the site's physical layout. The first phase would be the reconstruction of a long-vanished Royal Northwest Mounted Police facility called Bow Fort, with an attached teepee village and museum showing the progression of settlement and development. Stages would be located around the fort for aboriginal dance and musical performances. Additional phases would include representative habitations of North American aboriginal peoples: Chiquotian, Eastern Six Nations, Haida, Hopi Pueblo, Inuit, Kasan, Mandan, Northern Cree, Plains Indians and Salish. The employment generated by this scheme could be as high as 1,500 full-time jobs, plus additional spin-off entrepreneurial activities (cultural performers, suppliers and crafts). The society hope the site could operate all year round as a convention and educational facility. It is estimated that this project will take four years to complete, at a cost of $100 million, with funding to be provided by government bodies or foundations and corporate investors. A convention hotel and restaurants will eventually be added. Siksika Nation currently has limited tourism infrastructure and products. An on-site pottery studio produces tourist-oriented goods, and some land has been leased to a private development which includes a golf course and second homes. A major proposal called Blackfoot Crossing Historical Park is being pursued, with a video and promotional material being distributed widely to attract support and investment resources. The Blackfoot Crossing site is of major historical significance as it is a traditional camp site and focal point of trade. Here, in 1877, Treaty Seven was signed by the Dominion of Canada and the Blackfoot Confederacy. The crossing is designated a National Heritage Site and has been considered for designation as a World Heritage Site. The area is scenically beautiful and relatively unspoiled, lying within the Bow River Valley about one hour's drive west of Calgary. A development plan, prepared with lengthy community input and professional advice, calls for a 'world class tourist centre' featuring a major interpretive/cultural centre, teepee village sites, trail system, and access to various historical and archaeological sites. Annual events are also proposed.

Peigan

In March 1989 the Peigan Nation developed a vision to restore and strengthen the community's traditions. This vision was a concept of cultural renewal entitled Keep Our Circle Strong. The stated intent was to renew Peigan culture through the interpretation of the Nation's heritage, using traditional community development, management and participation processes. A desired consequence was to increase awareness and understanding of Plains culture among all visitors and to develop a broader appreciation of the rich traditions of Canada's First Peoples. A focal part of this endeavour was the development of a Cultural Renewal Centre in Brocket. With the assistance of the directors of the Oldman River Cultural Centre, programmes related to the facility, training and employment, research, cultural presentation and tourism were developed. Financial support was provided by the province and Communications Canada's Museum Assistance Programme to complete a Facility Programme for the Centre's physical design and layout. The structure was completed in 1995. To diversify this cultural renewal process, traditional crafts such as moccasin-making have been reintroduced.

Tsuu T'ina

Of the Treaty Seven nations, Tsuu T'ina is the most influenced by urban conditions. Situated adjacent to Calgary, the community (often called the Sarcee) has ready access to urban amenities yet remains predominantly rural in appearance and function. Facilities such as administration and schools, and most housing, are dispersed. A small museum is situated within the community recreation facility, and the nation also operates a facility in the foothills near the village of Bragg Creek for an annual rodeo and powwow. They are planning to build a golf course and business-park complex; for them to do this, lands have to be 'designated' by majority vote of the band in order to obtain financing and city services.

This development will act as a buffer against city expansion. Other tourism-related plans include the upgrading of facilities for recreational vehicles and banquets at the powwow/rodeo site. In early 1996 the elders announced plans to construct a major casino/resort complex on the reservation, adjacent to a built-up part of Calgary. Like all casino proposals in Alberta, the plans are controversial and require provincial enabling legislation.

EagleStar Tours Ltd

Origins and philosophy of the business

When Hal Eagle Tail first approached Tsuu T'ina elders with the proposal of allowing bus tours to come on to the reserve to visit historical sites, he was surprised to hear that it was about time tourism development occurred! This eventuality had been prophesied as far back as 1883 when a Medicine Warrior named Eagle Ribs had envisioned boxes surrounding newly acquired aboriginal lands, providing a good opportunity to gainfully co-exist with the new arrivals. The expansion of Calgary in the postwar period has meant that the built environment has now reached right up to the reservation boundary and tours are now available on the reserve through EagleStar Tours Ltd. The goal of this private enterprise is to provide domestic and international visitors with an historical perspective on the Tsuu T'ina Nation and how the people and traditions have evolved to the present day. The community views tourism as an opportunity to correct misperceptions about aboriginal people while generating income and creating jobs. According to Hal, only aboriginal people can rectify centuries of misperceptions, and developing a positive self-image is a key. Hal Eagle Tail's philosophy for the venture, and for aboriginal tourism in general, has been stated as follows:

> We are Tsuu T'ina, Cree, Blackfoot. We all have a different culture and evolution. This is one thing that you have to set straight. You don't want to be setting precedents or stereotypes in tourism, and in regard to aboriginal people as a whole, this is important because we are not going to be too much better if we are to address ourselves as this is how aboriginal people are in Canada or the United States. It is more important to talk about who you are and what your cultural background is.

This enterprise began as a partnership between two families, but as of January 1996 Hal assumed full control of EagleStar Tours, with the new emphasis being placed on eco- and adventure tours. The Starlight family, headed by Bruce Starlight, will be contracting services to EagleStar Tours under the aegis of Spotted Elk Catering Ltd. This reflects a trend in the band of having a loose consortium of individual family-owned businesses based on tour operators, crafts, amenity and food provision.

Community relations

When Hal Eagle Tail first prepared a feasibility study and developed a business and marketing plan, the idea was to create a community-based enterprise. But after securing approval and tangible support and operating tours at a financial loss for a year or so, the elders decided it would be better to have a private company do the tourism work for the nation. Tsuu T'ina does not have a designated Tourism Officer. The band itself, however, has decided to support tourism marketing and employment efforts, based on the elders' view of maintaining cultural identity and the need to develop employment skills. Some early reluctance to see the encouragement of tourists on the reservation has been overcome and Hal now feels there is no opposition. Because the company is separate from community business affairs it can move more quickly and avoid red tape. This does not mean, however, that consultation is unnecessary. Hal now has the ability to programme tours a year in advance, which is essential for dealing with foreign tour operators. Tsuu T'ina's cultural and historic resources are located across the reserve's wide expanse. Consequently, the band elders mandated that traffic flow had to be controlled. This was done by limiting access to groups of tourists arriving in vans or on buses. EagleStar provides a trained guide, and passengers are restricted from leaving the proximity of their vehicles. This helps conserve the historical sites and avoids invasion of privacy.

Products and services

EagleStar Ltd functions as a receptive tour operator, providing aboriginal-themed products and services to visitors – both local and international. The basic service is a tour of the Tsuu T'ina lands and facilities, but increasingly the emphasis is on adventure camps and ecotours. Other services can be arranged through tie-ins with other community-based enterprises such as Spotted Elk Catering. There are ten trained tour guides available on Sarcee to support this business. A typical tour itinerary begins at the Sarcee People's Museum, developed in 1983 as part of the Sportsplex, located at the northeast corner of the reserve and adjacent to Calgary residential areas. Sarcee history and legend is provided through a display of artefacts, legend-telling and interpretation by the guide. The past is intertwined with the present in this structure, where occasional clamour from the adjoining revenue-generating hockey rink can be heard in the background. The tour then goes on to show present and future aboriginal businesses, such as a gravel pit and planned golf course. A stop at Bull Head's House (1909), built for the first chiefs, is followed by interpretation at a prominent monument called the Rock Cairn, which was dedicated by Prince Charles in 1977. A visit to see murals painted on the side of new aboriginal-run schools ensues. The murals reflect retention of the Nation's cultural symbols and traditions as the band is modernized. The tour concludes with a trip to the buffalo paddock, where a herd of over 200 are kept for spiritual reasons and occasional feasts. Customized tours can also be offered in conjunction with neighbouring bands. Performances, banquets, overnights in teepees and trail rides are all part of the repertoire offered. In turn, these tours generate tourism dollars for a broad range of band members – the people who perform traditional dances, aboriginal-cuisine cooks, tour guides, and local arts and crafts people.

Good coverage in magazines has been received for the adventure camps. In a typical programme teepees are set up collectively, under the guides' instructions. Different sites on and off the reserve are used, depending on whether the clients want soft or hard adventure. Wilderness camping imposes more risks, while a camp-site near the Sportsplex allows use of the indoor plumbing facilities. When the camp is assembled an opening ceremony is conducted by a tribal elder and some rules are set. Kids' programmes might feature animal tracking. Sarcee hunters will bring a fresh kill into the camp to demonstrate skinning and meal preparation. Horse trail rides are popular. Cultural performances are a highlight of the aboriginal adventure camp, and feature authentic costumes and dances. The guides stay in the camp, and a cook tent provides a focal point. As a special treat, buffalo steaks might be served (using an off-reserve supply). EagleStar also provides wardrobe and horses for movies, arranges dinner theatre and trail rides. The company acts as an agent for all Treaty Seven reserves. Plans include greeting ceremonies at the airport.

Marketing

A considerable amount of the tour business to Sarcee is local, but the European and Asian markets are growing. Hal believes there is major growth potential for adventure camps, especially aimed at European visitors. There is no real competition for his services and he is definitely ahead of the other Treaty Seven communities when it comes to a deliverable product. In February 1996 Hal travelled to Switzerland with a Tsuu T'ina dance troupe on a tour organized by the Calgary-based Creative Western Tour Company. They participated in a western fair in Zurich, and promoted the band's tourism businesses at a booth sponsored by Air Canada. The partnership with Creative Western Tour Company was thought by Hal to represent the best potential for growth, as neither he nor the community would otherwise have the means to develop foreign markets. Packages are assembled and sold through wholesalers, with a typical western Canada tour incorporating a variety of aboriginal sites and experiences. They are setting up an Internet page to advertise their services. If the casino is built it will present many new opportunities for entrepreneurial activity among the Sarcee, including performances, supplies and access to many potential tour or camp consumers.

CONCLUSIONS

The experiences of Treaty Seven Nations and the case study of EagleStar Tours reveal a number of issues relating to contemporary aboriginal tourism development in Alberta. Although the resource base is impressive, both for eco/adventure tours and for historical interpretation, other resources are lacking. The nations have inadequate financial means to fulfil their ambitious plans for major facilities, and certain legal obstacles exist related to the prohibition against selling or mortgaging reservation lands. Few entrepreneurs have come forward and most are operating without much capital. Although Sarcee boasts ten trained tour guides, little in the way of tourism training has been available for aboriginal communities. Interest in developing tourism among the aboriginal communities is very high, but it has become clear that external partnerships are required in order to realize both the grand dreams of major new facilities and the more modest ambitions of entrepreneurs. Major corporate sponsors and government grants are needed to create the attractions, while marketing expertise and clout can be provided by mainstream tour companies. The emphasis, in the short term at least, must be on providing more deliverable products like EagleStar Tours, while, in the longer run, major attractions – if realized – will present many more opportunities.

Individual aboriginal entrepreneurs must still work within a community context. Typically, social goals will take precedence over private motivations. Tourism is looked upon as a way to generate employment and income, but also as a way to improve perceptions of aboriginal people and enhance self-image. The entrepreneur is also likely to be part of a family

Table 5.2 Major challenges facing aboriginal tourism businesses and entrepreneurs in Alberta

Ownership	land is communal and therefore cannot be sold or mortgaged
	private businesses must have approval to use communal resources
	social and cultural goals tend to take precedence over profit
	the community must guard against externalized costs from private business ventures
Finances	it is difficult to obtain major financing for communal projects
	there is a lack of personal capital to fund business ventures
	grants and corporate sponsors are required
	it is necessary to guard against loss of control
Training	there is a lack of aboriginal tourism training opportunites
	business management skills are required
Product	few First Nations presently have deliverable tour products and services
	how many large aboriginal attractions can the province support?
	will these cultural/interpretative centres be competitive or complementary to each other?
	it is vital to develop all-season attractions
Marketing	there is a need to join regional, provincial and national tourism organizations to extend and reach new business
	partnerships with tour companies are vital

business, and perhaps also to have strong band relationships within the tribe, thereby complicating business but also extending her or his reach. Major challenges facing the aboriginal tourism business, and the entrepreneur in particular, have been summarized in Table 5.2. The future of aboriginal tourism in southern Alberta appears to be highly promising yet uncertain. Given the growing demand, the existing resource base and strong interest on the part of the Treaty Seven nations, success should be assured. While rural tourism enterprises in general face many problems, the aboriginal communities have additional challenges stemming from their historically isolated position in the economic mainstream, as well as a lack of capital and training. In this context, the effort required of both communities and entrepreneurs is extraordinary.

REFERENCES

Aboriginal Council of Canada (1987) *An Inventory of Metis and Non-Status Indian Tourism Opportunities*, Ottawa: Aboriginal Council of Canada.

Altman, J. (1989) 'Tourism dilemmas for aboriginal Australians', *Annals of Tourism Research* 16(4): 456–76.

Blundell, V. (1993) 'Aboriginal empowerment and the souvenir trade in Canada', *Annals of Tourism Research* 20(1): 64–87.

Brayley, R. (1992) 'Tourism and sacred sites: balancing the need for authenticity with the limits of culture', in L. J. Reid (ed.) *Community and Cultural Tourism: Conference Proceedings*, Regina, Canada: Travel Industry Association of Canada.

Browne, R. and Nolan, M. (1989) 'Western Indian reservation tourism development', *Annals of Tourism Research* 16(3): 360–76.

Campbell, B. (1994) 'Aboriginal cultural tourism: the market' *ICOMOS Canada Bulletin* 3(3).

Canadian National Aboriginal Tourism Association (CNATA) (no date) *For the Love of Nature: Nature Based Tourism for Aboriginal Peoples*, Ottawa: CNATA.

Chapin, M. (1990) 'The silent jungle: ecotourism among the Kuna Indians of Panama', *Cultural Survival Quarterly* 14(1): 42–45.

Cohen, E. (1992) 'The study of touristic images of aboriginal people: mitigating the stereotype of a stereotype', in D. Pearce and R. Butler (eds) *Tourism Research: Critiques and Challenges*, New York: Routledge.

Contours (1989) 'Tourism and aboriginal peoples', *Contours* 4(4).

Crystal, E. (1989) 'Tourism in Toraja (Sulawesi Indonesia)', in V. Smith (ed.) *Hosts and Guests: The Anthropology of Tourism*, Philadelphia: University of Pennsylvannia Press.

Csargo, L. (1988) *Indian Tourism Overview*, Ottawa: Policy Development Branch, Economic Development Sector, Indian and Northern Affairs Canada.

Daltabuit, M. and Pi-Sunyer, O. (1990) 'Tourism development in Quintana Roo, Mexico', *Cultural Survival Quarterly* 14(1): 9–13.

Deitch, L. (1989) 'The impact of tourism on the arts and crafts of the Indians of the Southwestern United States', in V. Smith (ed.) *Hosts and Guests: The Anthropology of Tourism*, 2nd edn, Philadelphia: University of Pennsylvania Press.

Evans-Pritchard, D. (1989) 'How they see us: aboriginal American images of tourists, *Annals of Tourism Research* 16(1): 89–105.

Goering, P. (1990) 'The response to tourism in Ladakh', *Cultural Survival Quarterly* 14(1): 20–5.

Gordon, R. (1990) 'The prospects for anthropological tourism in Bushmanland', *Cultural Survival Quarterly* 14(1): 6–8.

Government of the Northwest Territories (1988) *The Northern Lure*, Yellowknife: Economic Development and Tourism.

Hinch, T. (1992) 'Planning for changing tourism markets: the case of aboriginal communities in Alberta', in L. Reid (ed.) *Community and Cultural Tourism: Conference Proceedings*, Regina, Canada: Travel Industry Association of Canada.

Hinch, T. and Delamere T. (1993) 'Aboriginal festivals as tourism attractions: a community challenge', *Journal of Applied Recreation Research* 18(2).

Hollingshead, K. (1992) 'White gaze, red people – shadow visions: the disidentification of "Indians" in cultural tourism', *Leisure Studies* 11(1): 43–64.

Klieger, C. (1990) 'Close encounters: "intimate" tourism in Tibet', *Cultural Survival Quarterly* 14(2): 38–42.

Laxson, J. (1991) 'How we see them: tourism and aboriginal Americans', *Annals of Tourism Research* 18(3): 365–91.

Lujan, C. (1993) 'A sociological view of tourism in an American Indian community: maintaining cultural integrity at Taos Pueblo', *American Indian Culture and Research Journal* 17(3).

McGregor, H. and McMath, M. (1993) 'Leisure: a Maori and a Mangaian perspective', H. Perkins and S. Cushman (eds) *Leisure, Recreation and Tourism*, 1st edn, Auckland: Longman.

McKean, P. (1989) 'Towards a theoretical analysis of tourism: economic dualism and cultural involution in Bali', in V. Smith (ed.) *Hosts and Guests: The Anthropology of Tourism*, 2nd edn, Philadelphia: University of Pennsylvania Press.

Martinez, A. (1992) 'Roadways to North America: aboriginal peoples', *The Journal of the Heard Museum* 6(1).

Parker, B. (1992) 'Aboriginal tourism: from perception to reality', in L. Reid (ed.) *Community and Cultural Tourism : Conference Proceedings*, Regina, Canada: Travel Industry Association of Canada.

Pierce, D. (1995) 'Edu-tourism in Montana's Indian country', *Winds of Change: A Magazine for American Indians* 10(2).

Queensland Tourist and Travel Corporation (no date) *A Guide to Experiencing Aboriginal and Torres Islander Culture*, Brisbane: Queensland Tourist and Travel Carparatia.

Smith, V. (ed.) (1989) *Hosts and Guests: The Anthropology of Tourism*, Philadelphia: University of Pennsylvania Press.

Sofield, T. (1991) 'Sustainable ethnic tourism in the South Pacific: some principles', *Journal of Tourism Studies* 1(3): 56–72.

—— (1993) 'Indigenous tourism development', *Annals of Tourism Research* 20(4): 729–50.

Stainton, M. (1990) 'Tourism, aboriginal people and land rights', *Contours* 4(5).

Swain, M. (1990) 'Commoditizing ethnicity in southwest China', *Cultural Survival Quarterly* 14(1): 26–9.

Sweet, J. (1990) 'The portals of tradition: tourism in the American Southwest', *Cultural Survival Quarterly* 14(2): 6–8.

—— (1991) 'Let 'em loose: Pueblo Indian management of tourism', *American Indian Culture and Research Journal* 15(4).

Tourism Canada (1989) *The Aboriginal Tourism Product: A Position Paper* Ottawa: Tourism Canada Products and Services Division.

Val, E. (1993) *Tourism Initiatives in Canada's Northwest Territories: The Pangnirtung Experience – A Partnership for Sustainable Development*, paper presented at the World Conference on Tourism Development and the Environment, Canary Islands, Spain.

Walle, A. (1993) 'Tourism and traditional people: forging equitable strategies', *Journal of Travel Research* 31(3): 14–19.

White, D. (1993) 'Tourism as economic development for aboriginal people living in the shadow of a protected area: a North American case study', *Society and Natural Resources* 6(4).

Wolfe-Keddie, J. (1993) 'Tourism in the Eastern Arctic: Coping with "dangerous children"', *Journal of Applied Recreation Research* 18(2.1).

6 Rural tourism in Germany: farm and rural tourism operators

M. Oppermann

INTRODUCTION

The importance of tourism in Germany is often not recognized, despite an accommodation capacity of more than 2 million beds in 1 million rooms (in accommodation with nine or more beds). With tourism constituting at least 5 per cent of total employment (Statisches Bundesamt 1995), and 15 million international tourist arrivals spending more than US$11 billion (World Tourism Organization 1994), the political infrastructure is at best rudimentary, especially when compared to agriculture. There is no tourism ministry at federal or state level, nor any other bureaucratic structure in charge of this important but overlooked economic activity. This is even more amazing considering that Germany is, by any measure, the world leader in tourist generation (Hudman and Davis 1994; Oppermann and Chon 1995) and that, as a number of studies have shown, domestic tourism still outnumbers international tourism by Germans (e.g. Aderhold and Lohmann 1995; StfT 1992) or is of similar importance (Statisches Bundesamt 1995).

FARM AND RURAL TOURISM

Rural tourism in Germany dates back more than 150 years (Schöppner 1988). Ever since the introduction of paid holidays for civil servants in 1873 and for white-collar workers in 1914 (Knebel 1960) tourism has been a part of life for the middle classes. In the early years, holidays were spent in inexpensive accommodation in villages close to the city, often in the hillier areas. Accommodation was in the form of small hotels or privately let rooms on farms (Löschburg 1977). The establishment of alpine clubs in the middle of the nineteenth century introduced similar trends into the European Alps, particularly in neighbouring Austria (Staudacher 1984).

A major problem in analysing rural tourism is data availability (Dernoi 1991). In Germany, for example, overnight stays and accommodation supply are nowadays registered only when the operator has nine or more beds. Yet many operators in rural areas remain below this threshold and are therefore not recorded. Hence, in regions with a large number of small operators official statistics may deviate considerably from the actual supply or demand, possibly up to 50 per cent or more (RVO 1992a).

TYPES OF RURAL TOURISM

Farm tourism, bed and breakfast places or apartments to let by operators other than farmers, rural hotels or guest houses, camping and second homes constitute the wide range of accommodation facilities in rural tourism. The wide variety of rural accommodation with respect to size and type further diffuses the clarity of what constitutes rural tourism. In an attempt to eliminate the lack of consistency surrounding the notion of rural, non-urban and farm tourism, Oppermann proposed a model of rural tourism (Figure 6.1). In line with Dernoi (1991), it distinguishes between rural tourism and tourism in other non-urban areas. Thus, rural tourism is defined as tourism in a 'non-urban territory where human (land related economic) activity is going on, primarily agriculture; a permanent human presence seems a qualifying requirement' (Dernoi 1991: 4).

The accommodation spectrum in rural tourism ranges from camp-grounds, self-catering and bed and breakfast (B&B) to full-catering establishments. It also includes hotels/motels in rural communities. Farm tourism is a part of rural tourism, the location of the accommodation on a part-time or full-time farm being the distinguishing criterion. Although farm tourism can cover the whole accommodation spectrum, the emphasis is usually on self-catering and bed and breakfast establishments.

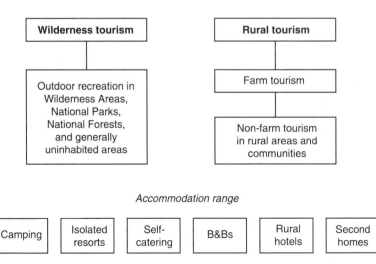

Figure 6.1 Model of non-urban tourism.

Although the definition of what constitutes a larger urban centre may be ambiguous, it seems important to exclude tourism in urban centres because tourists purposely choose 'urban comfort' and immediate access to urban amenities.

For them, rural areas surrounding the town or resort constitute just an attraction and perhaps a place for day activities such as hiking. But they do not want to forego the urban infrastructure provided only in larger urban centres. The definition is intentionally based on the accommodation used, because the stay in a rural area is what distinguishes rural tourists from rural excursionists. The latter are travellers who remain in the countryside for less than 24 hours. Similarly, recreation activities by rural residents not involving a stay away from home are excluded.

THE CURRENT DISTRIBUTION PATTERNS OF RURAL TOURISM ACCOMMODATION IN GERMANY

Tourist accommodation is not equally distributed in Germany today. The eastern states are characterized by a relatively small number of accommodations (see Figure 6.2). The two southern states Bavaria (24.9 per cent) and Baden-Württemberg (13.2 per cent) account for the largest number of registered beds. Attractions such as the Alps, Lake Constance and the Black Forest are the major explanatory factors.

In a laudable attempt to shed some light on farm tourism, Schöppner (1988) devoted her doctoral dissertation to this topic. Using a number of different measures, she portrayed the importance, forms, and price structure of farm tourism for the whole of former West Germany. Figure 6.3 graphically illustrates the varying importance of farm tourism in various parts of Germany. Mountainous and coastal areas stand out as having high numbers of farms offering accommodation. Another area is the famous Mosel Valley, a wine-growing area.

Farm and rural tourism development in southern Germany

The study area is located in Southern Germany in the state of Baden-Württemberg, within a region called Oberschwaben-Allgäu (see Figure 6.3; for a more detailed map, see Oppermann 1996). The area may be roughly delineated by Lake Constance to the west, the river Danube to the north and the Baden-Württemberg–Bavaria state border to the east and south. The region's landscape is largely the result of the last three ice ages. The advancing and retreating glaciers left a hilly area with generally higher relief in the southern parts closer to the Alps. Several large lakes were formed between successive terminal moraines, and a multitude of smaller ones in the rest of the area. Eventually, the growing and decomposing vegetation transformed many shallow lakes into moorland. The resulting 'mud' has been used for several centuries for heating purposes, as fertilizer and for health treatment in the region's four mud baths. The numerous lakes not only add to the region's land-

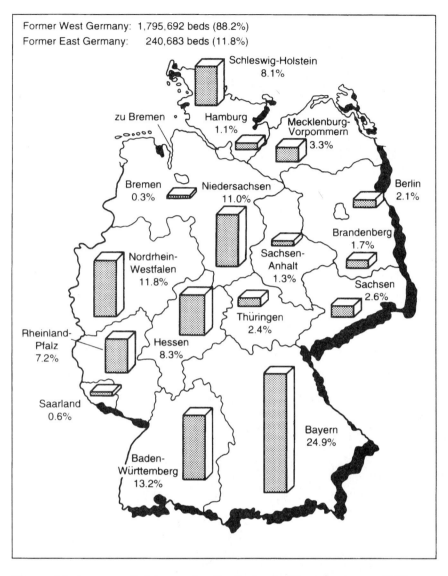

Former West Germany: 1,795,692 beds (88.2%)
Former East Germany: 240,683 beds (11.8%)

Schleswig-Holstein
8.1%

zu Bremen
Hamburg
1.1%

Mecklenburg-
Vorpommern
3.3%

Bremen
0.3%
Niedersachsen
11.0%

Berlin
2.1%

Nordrhein-
Westfalen
11.8%

Sachsen-
Anhalt
1.3%

Brandenberg
1.7%

Sachsen
2.6%

Thüringen
2.4%

Rheinland-
Pfalz
7.2%
Hessen
8.3%

Saarland
0.6%

Bayern
24.9%

Baden-
Württemberg
13.2%

Figure 6.2 Accommodation capacity distribution in Germany, August 1993.

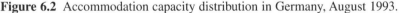

scape attractiveness, but are also utilized for all sorts of water sport activities.

The study area is an economically backward region that has been identified by state planners as structurally disadvantaged. It is agriculturally oriented, with some of the highest primary-sector employment in the state of Baden-Württemberg (Statistisches Landesamt 1991). Owing to differences in elevation, relief and soil type, the mainstay of most farmers changes from that of mostly crop farming in the north towards dairying in the south. Relatively low yields – due to natural factors, the introduction of milk quotas for each farm, limited expansion possibilities, and stagnant prices for agricultural products but increasing production costs – have

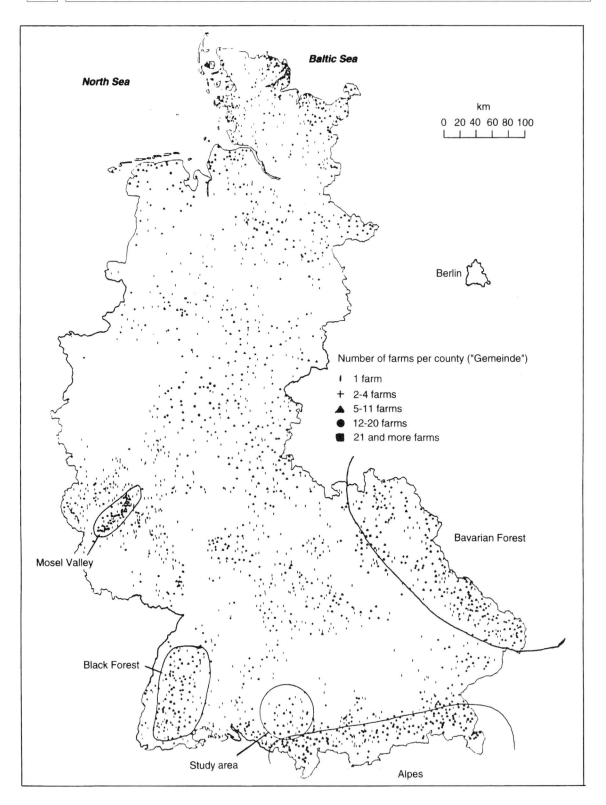

Figure 6.3 Spatial distribution of farm tourism operators in Germany.

resulted in a decreasing number of farms each year. Between 1960 and 1987, primary-sector employment in the study area dropped from 35 per cent to 10 per cent. However, the study area is still characterized by above-average importance of the primary sector. Only a few producing industries have located there because infrastructure is lacking. It has been identified as the area in Germany with the worst access (RVO 1992b). Only a minor railroad crosses from north to south, and the area still does not feature an *Autobahn* (motorway). Only in the very south, Wangen has gained good access to neighbouring Austria and Switzerland through the new *Autobahn* to Lake Constance. In the rural areas surrounding the health resorts, one out of six workers is still employed in agriculture. Thus, economic alternatives are badly needed to provide either additional incomes to the farmers or new full-time job opportunities.

Methodology

Drawing on accommodation directories provided by the health resorts, all rural tourist operators in the study area were identified. The main sources were catalogues from local tourist bureaux, the Fremdenverkehrsverband Oberschwaben-Allgäu (Regional Tourist Association), and the state-wide organization Urlaub auf dem Bauernhof (holidays on the farm). Only operators in the hinterland were extracted, not those in the health resorts themselves. Hence, large spa hotels and other urban accommodation were not included. Although this sampling is far from perfect and a few operators were probably missed, it was considered an acceptable approach in view of the lack of complete official directories. Schöppner (1988) disclosed that in some areas the number of establishments in catalogues may represent only 50 per cent of the actual supply. Owing to the very comprehensive coverage of the Fremdenverkehrsverband Oberschwaben-Allgäu, however, only a few unlisted operators were 'discovered' during fieldwork. These were added to the inventory. The total list included 506 rural tourism operators, although not all were in existence during the whole study period (1991–93). It is a very dynamic field, with several operators starting each year, while others disappear for various reasons. In the process of the larger project (see Oppermann 1996), some 268 operators were interviewed, 119 of whom offered 'holidays on the farm' and 40 of which were other B&B operators. The rest of the sample was made up of other private operators and 32 small hotels in the villages.

Rural and farm tourism operators

Most of the operators interviewed had started their business within the preceding twenty to thirty years. Farm operators started on average slightly earlier than did the B&B operators (Table 6.1). They were also slightly larger (6.7 beds vs 5.4 beds) although this may be a function of their longer involvement in tourism (Oppermann 1995a). Very few B&B operations had more than 8 beds, whereas almost one out of five farm operators was in this category. Although farm operators tended to have a

Table 6.1 Development of farm tourism, 1971–91

	1971 (former West Germany)	1979 (former West Germany)	1991 (former West Germany)	1991 (unified Germany)
Farms	1,145,316	947,317	748,405	770,836
Farms with tourist accommodation	24,491	21,198	9,982	10,151
Tourist nights per farm	307	384	438	435

Source: extracted from Statisches Bundesamt (1995).

slightly higher annual occupancy rate (158 *vs* 145 nights), it contributed less to their net income. Reasons for the higher occupancy rate may include the longer average stay of their guests and the higher repeat visitor rate. Almost 75 per cent of the farm operators indicated that the average length of stay of their guests was two weeks or longer. This compares to 65 per cent for the B&Bs. Nonetheless, both figures illustrate that rural tourism in Germany usually means long-stay tourism where the whole holiday is spent at one location. In most cases, these single-destination holidays are of the base-camp type, and excursions (on average six days) are undertaken to attractions in the proximity (Oppermann 1995b). The long average length of stay was confirmed by the guests (Oppermann 1996) and stands in contrast to the average length of all holiday trips by Germans, only about 17 per cent of which last two weeks or longer (Statisches Bundesamt 1995).

It is possible to convince repeat visitors to come in the shoulder season, which helps to extend the tourist season and also improves occupancy in the slower months. With respect to the guests' origins, there are only minor differences. Notable is the lower share of Bavarian guests in farms; Bavaria features a very similar landscape, so the main reasons for spending holidays on a farm (i.e. to show the children farm life, to experience something different) are less relevant to them. The importance of the family market is well documented in this study – families with children had a share of total demand for farm holidays almost three times higher than that for B&Bs (Table 6.2).

The following two examples of a farm and B&B operator were chosen for their representativeness. Yet they are both unique in some ways, illustrating innovative and adaptive ideas and approaches. Since all operators were promised anonymity, the names are invented.

A life history of a rural bed and breakfast operator

Mrs Maier (a fictional name) runs this small B&B operation all on her own; her husband died many years ago. The B&B is just outside one of the smaller spas in the region and is located in a small settlement of a dozen houses, several of them being farms. It is a very quiet neighbourhood, since it is well away from any major road. It is a very hilly and tranquil area with forests dominating the immediate surroundings of the

Table 6.2 Comparative characteristics of farm and B&B operators

Variable	Farm operators (N = 119)	Rural B&B operators (N = 40)
Average years of operation	15 years	12 years
Number of beds	6.7 beds	5.4 beds
Tourist income as % of total net income	17%	22%
Annual occupancy	158 nights	145 nights
Seasonality of occupancy (%)		
January–March	13	15
April–June	49	43
July–September	84	80
October–December	21	17
Guests' average length of stay	14 nights	12 nights
Number of repeat visitors*	42%	35%
Guests' origin (%)		
Foreign	4	3
Germany	96	97
Former East Germany	18	22
In-state (Baden-Wurtemburg)	31	31
Bavaria	3	10
Families with children (% of total)	74%	28%

Note: * For the purpose of the study, defined as those who visited the same operator three or more times.

settlement. After high school Mrs Maier went on to a vocational school for three years to study home economics. Soon afterwards she married and became a housewife. Yet she was always interested in hospitality. This dream came closer to reality when she visited an agricultural/home-improvement trade exhibition in 1974. On display at one of the stands was a portable shower unit that could be easily installed. While this may sound banal today, the reader should be aware that they were something very new at the time. Most households had bathrooms equipped with a bathtub only, and not a shower unit. In the small accommodation units, and even some small hotels in the study region, hardly any bedroom was equipped with en-suite bathroom facilities. Bathrooms and toilets were usually shared by all guests.

Realizing the potential of such showers, as they needed much less room, she convinced her husband to invest in tourism. They converted their attic into two bedrooms with two beds each and provided shower and toilet facilities for both. Operations started in 1975, which places Mrs Maier's B&B among the early entrants into this type of operation in the area, and particularly among those not on a farm. At the time of the interview, she is in her mid-fifties. After her husband died several years earlier, she had to find employment since the small size of the B&B did not (and still does not) provide enough profit for a living. Several days a week she cleans houses in the neighbourhood, mostly in the nearby spa town.

The B&B has essentially remained the same for the last twenty years. It still consists of four beds in two bedrooms and shower/toilet facilities on the floor. Guests are charged less than DM 20 per night (US$12) which includes a rich and varied breakfast. While this is about average for the region (Oppermann 1995a, 1996), the price is a contributory factor to the low profitability of Mrs Maier's B&B. After German unification, she experienced a major demand shift, so that in the early 1990s the majority of her guests (70 per cent) were from the former East Germany, with people from the former West Germany (25 per cent) and foreigners (5 per cent) being less important. This change, albeit less drastically, has affected the whole area (Oppermann 1996). A large portion (30 per cent) of her guests are repeat visitors (three or more visits), despite the fact that she has had a huge influx of 'new' customers in recent years. On average, her guests stay for one week. During the winter months she has a lot of demand from temporary workers or salespeople who are in the area. This facilitates a relatively high occupancy rate of 210 nights per annum. She is fully booked throughout the summer from June to September, with demand easing off from autumn to spring. Yet a rough estimate of the income derived from the two bedrooms shows a profit of about DM 8,000 (US$5,000) per annum, not accounting for her labour – too little to earn a living despite the high occupancy rate, which is far above average (Table 6.2).

Noteworthy in Mrs Maier's career are two points. First was her innovativeness some twenty years ago when she realized the potential of portable shower units in providing modern facilities to the customers within given space limitations. Second, for whatever reasons, she did not build upon this. While she may have realized the change in demand towards self-contained units and en-suite bathroom facilities, she did not change her B&B. She still attracts a large number of guests, but is helped in this by the strong influx of tourists from former East Germany and their demand for low-cost accommodation. Mrs Maier is also rather disillusioned with tourism. When asked what she would do if she won DM 100,000 in a lottery, she unequivocally declared that it would not be in tourism. However, she did not want to disclose the actual source of her disenchantment.

A life history of a farm operator

The farmers Mr and Mrs Werner (a fictional name) operate a small accommodation unit in addition to their mid-sized farm. The farm is situated in the midst of the grazing area almost at the foothills of the European Alps. Dairy farming and cattle breeding are the farm's mainstay, as they are for most other farms in the neighbourhood. The farm is in a somewhat atypical location (for Germany, but not for this region); its nearest neighbour lives a couple of kilometres away. It is about 10 km outside a popular and touristy spa town. Mrs Werner, who is mostly in charge of the tourists, is in her late thirties and she is already the second generation looking after guests in her family. After school she also went on to a school for vocational study (technical institute) to study agricultural sciences. The Werner's farm started to offer accommodation to tourists on a commercial basis in 1970 while Mr Werner's parents were still running the operation. At that time, they offered bed and breakfast only, as did most farmers involved in tourism (Oppermann 1995a). In the early 1980s Mr and Mrs Werner married and took over the farm side of the business while the parents retained the accommodation element. In 1985, however, Mrs Werner assumed responsibility for what was then still a B&B operation.

Having realized that demand from tourists was changing towards more self-contained units (apartments) and modern facilities, and not being very happy with the amount of time required for a B&B operation, she convinced her husband to modernize and change the operation. They reorganized the rooms so that they could be rented out as an apartment and modernized the bathroom facilities by adding an en-suite shower unit. Today they have the option of letting rooms on a B&B basis or as a self-contained unit. They prefer the latter option, as it releases Mrs Werner from a lot of daily chores. In contrast to the previous Werner generation, they only accommodate tourists from May until September in order to have the farm to themselves and their children during the winter months, when tourist demand would normally be relatively low. Obviously, they do not rely on tourism as their mainstay. About 10 per cent of their net income is derived from the existing six beds, which see an occupancy of about 90 nights per annum. The charges for the rooms are about average for the region: DM 18 (US$12) per person on a B&B basis and DM 40 (US$25) for the whole apartment, excluding cleaning fees. To guests who cook the meals themselves they sell milk and eggs if so desired.

The majority of their guests are from northern Germany (50 per cent) and come to southern Germany for the different scenery, hiking, and the opportunity for visits to Switzerland and Austria. Their guests stay on average 2.5 weeks and spend more than 10 days on their day excursions to Lake Constance, Bavaria, Austria and Switzerland. They intentionally have few repeat visitors. An often-mentioned problem with repeat visitors in such farm settings is that after a few stays the guests presume to take greater liberties. They see themselves almost as part of the family and appear in the private quarters of the hosts at almost all hours. Consequently, the hosts are placed in a situation where they would like to tell their guests to back off, but feel obliged not to. This actual or perceived infringement of their private life is a major reason for not having guests during the winter months from October to April. To avoid such situations, Mrs Werner often advises former guests that she is fully booked at the times desired, when indeed she is not. Since demand during their months of operation is generally very strong, they can easily do this. In 1991 the Werner's counted more than 100 enquiries for their apartment for the months of July and August when they can take only about five groups during the whole two months. Nonetheless, it appears that this uneasiness with potential host–guest conflict situations led Mrs Werner to state, when asked where they would invest DM 100,000 if they won it in a lottery, 'My husband would prefer to invest it into the farm (not accommodation); I would like to spend it on ourselves, for example, in the form of a long holiday.'

CONCLUSIONS

Rural and farm tourism enterprises in southern Germany are often run by women. Frequently the operation provides them with social contacts outside their immediate environment, and these are highly valued. Otherwise, it can increase self-esteem and provide the feeling of financial independence. Commentators have argued that at a certain stage rural and farm operators continue more for these social contacts than for the monetary aspects (Oppermann 1996). The two cases presented above are very characteristic of the situation in southern Germany, yet they are also very distinctive. Common characteristics are that women tend to run the operation and often have to convince their husbands before embarking on such a venture. Despite the availability of financial and management advice from the agricultural bureaucracy and some regional planning institutions, most operators seem to pick up the trade themselves without receiving advice or financial assistance.

The case studies also illustrate how innovativeness and adaptability are key issues for successful entrepreneurship. They also show the limitations of such enterprises in the existing price structure. Unlike in North America or New Zealand, B&B and farm tourism are relatively inexpensive forms of accommodation in Germany. Even with high occupancy rates, only small profits can be realized. And as Oppermann (1996) has pointed out, the legal and regulatory limits imposed on expansion in the study area effectively force most operators to remain small (i.e. below nine beds or two apartments). Hence, farm tourism has only a limited potential as an economic alternative. It can even be argued that state and federal governments should either stop promoting farm tourism as an economic alternative or do away with the legal and regulatory barriers.

REFERENCES

Aderhold, P. and Lohmann, M. (1995) *Urlaub + Reisen 1994 – Kurzfassung*, Hamburg: Forschungsgemeinschaft Urlaub und Reisen.

Dernoi, L. (1991) 'About rural and farm tourism', *Tourism Recreation Research* 16(1): 3–6.

Hudman, L. and Davis, J. (1994) 'World tourism markets', *Proceedings 25th TTRA Conference 1994*, Bal Harbour, Florida, June.

Knebel, H. (1960) *Soziologische Strukturwandlungen im modernen Tourismus*, Stuttgart: Enke Verlag.

Löschburg, W. (1977) *Von Reiselust und Reiseleid. Eine Kulturgeschichte*, Frankfurt: Insel Verlag.

Oppermann, M. (1995a) 'Holidays on the farm: a case study of German hosts and guests', *Journal of Travel Research* 34(1): 63–7.

—— (1995b) 'A model of travel itineraries', *Journal of Travel Research* 33(4): 57–61.

—— (1996) 'Rural tourism in Southern Germany', *Annals of Tourism Research* 23: 86–102.

Oppermann, M. and Chon, K. S. (1995) 'German outbound tourism', *Journal of Vacation Marketing* 2(1): 39–52.

RVO (Regionalverband Oberschwaben) (1992a) *Entwicklungskonzept Fremdenverkehr-Region Bodensee-Oberschwaben*, Ravensburg: RVO.

—— (1992b) *Verkehrsuntersuchung West-Ost-Verbindung. Vorstudie 1992*, Ravensburg: RVO.

Schöppner, A. (1988) *Urlaub auf dem Bauernhof. Eine fremdenverkehrs-geographische Untersuchung*, Bochumer Materialien zur Raumordnung 36, Bochum: University of Bochum.

Statisches Bundesamt (SBA) (1981) *Statistisches Jahrbuch für die Bundesrepublik Deutschland 1981*, Wiesbaden: Statisches Bundesamt.

—— (1995) *Tourismus in Zahlen 1994*, Stuttgart: Metzler Poeschel.

Statisches Landesamt Baden-Württemberg (1991) *Regionalstruktur Baden-Württemberg 1987. Gemeinde- und Kreisdaten der Volks- und Berufszählungen 1961, 1970 und 1987*, Stuttgart: Statisches Landesamt.

Staudacher, C. (1984) 'Invention, Diffusion und Adoption der Betriebsinnovation "Urlaub auf dem Bauernhof"', Beispiel Niederösterreich. *Zeitschrift für Agrargeographie* 2: 14–35.

StfT (Studienkreis für Tourismus) (1992). *Urlaubsreisen 1991. Kurzfassung der Reiseanalyse 1991*, Starnberg: StfT.

World Tourism Organization (WTO) (1994) *Yearbook of Tourism Statistics*, Madrid: WTO.

7 Rural tourism in China: development issues in perspective

T. Sofield and F. Li

INTRODUCTION

Influenced by the xenophobia of the Maoist years, from 1949 to 1976, the outside world vision of China was obscured by the bamboo curtain which was drawn across its landscape for those (nearly) three decades. The result is that Westerners tend to think of tourism in China as a new phenomenon. This may be so in terms of world tourism. But in domestic terms, the traveller in rural China has a recorded history extending back for more than three thousand years. Thus, to understand rural tourism in China in the 1990s one needs an appreciation of the historical place of rural landscapes in the dynastic travels and tours of its emperors, philosophers and scholars.

This chapter traces the history of tourism and the centrality of the pilgrimage in ancient China through to the travel undertaken by Confucian, Daoist and Buddhist philosophers, poets and scholars until the demise of the imperial dynasties in 1911–12 brought them to a halt. The next section briefly outlines the vicissitudes of twentieth-century unrest which engulfed China until the communist revolution of 1949. This prolonged unrest militated against any resumption of either domestic or overseas travel. This was followed by almost three decades under Mao Zedong in which the imposition of rigid controls over movement internally and the closed-border policy prevented the development of a mature tourism sector. Finally, the socio-economic reforms instituted by Deng Xiaoping from 1978 are examined, especially the consequences of the policies of 'household responsibility for production', de-collectivization, the 'open-door' policy and approval of private enterprise (albeit it within a socialist system) for the development of rural tourism in China. These reforms resulted in a virtual explosion in tourism numbers, both in domestic and international tourism, and this expansion is traced from 1978 to the present day. Several examples of rural tourism enterprises are outlined, and the characteristics of much Chinese domestic tourism to sites of natural and cultural significance are detailed.

THE PLACE OF TRAVEL IN CHINA'S HERITAGE: THE DEVELOPMENT OF A RURAL TRAVEL ETHOS

For its first 6,000 years China developed its civilization independently from the rest of the world. Isolated from its neighbours by the vast deserts of central Asia and the Tibetan plateau to the west, by tropical forests to the south and by the Pacific Ocean to the east, it evolved with minimal contact with the other great civilizations of the Asian continent (Figure 7.1). Indeed, it called itself Zhongguo, the 'Central Kingdom', superior to all other civilizations and therefore needing no interaction in any substantial way with others. A strong xenophobic thread runs consistently through China's history from the ancient kingdoms to the communist party rule of Mao Zedong. Only in the last two hundred years has China,

Figure 7.1 Chinese provinces and government area.

however unwillingly, become part of the global community (Ogden 1992).

For more than three thousand years China was ruled by powerful dynasties. The emperor stood at the apex of a religious and political hierarchy in which ancestral gods and animistic spirits resided in mountains, rivers, lakes and other biophysical features. These other worldly beings required regular propitiation if the rule of an emperor was to flourish. In an unbroken chain from the beginning of the Shang dynasty (*c.*1350–1050 BC) to the final demise of the emperors with the fall of the Quing dynasty and the declaration of a Republic in 1912, each successive emperor and his court paid homage to the gods. Nine revered sites of particular significance evolved over the centuries – five sacred *shan*, or mountains: the eastern Tai-shan, the southern Heng Shan ('Balanced/Harmony mountain'), the western Hua-shan, the northern Heng-shan ('Eternal Mountain') and the central Song-shan; and four sacred *shui* or rivers: the Chang Jian (Yangtze), the Huang He (Yellow River), the Huai Shui and the Ji Shui.

The first Shang king is recorded as travelling each year to worship the spirits at Tai-shan, which became established as the paramount sacred mountain. Propitiation became so important that the imperial courts appointed a minister with responsibility to ensure that pilgrimages were also made each year by senior members of the royal household to other sacred sites. The sites multiplied over the centuries, with each province and district evolving its own local pantheon of gods and spirits, some of which became part of the national ethos. Many shrines were constructed, often with accommodation facilities. As Buddhism later became established and many more sacred sites were added, temples provided accommodation. Thus much of the ancient rural travel was pilgrimage travel, embedded in the beliefs of the god-kings.

Under the Zhou dynasty, which supplanted the Shang dynasty in the eleventh century BC, Confucianism emerged as central to the Chinese tradition. From this era evolved the institution of the Mandarins, a scholarly class who assumed a central role in the administration of the state for the emperors. For much of the past three millennia, social status in China was achieved by receiving an education and then serving in the bureaucracy: it was more worthy to be a scholar than to be wealthy, to be born into an aristocratic family or to possess military prowess.

It became an accepted lifestyle for mandarins to spend several years, perhaps even their entire lifetime, touring the various sacred sites in pursuit of greater wisdom and knowledge. Their creative talents went into poetry, painting and calligraphy inspired by the rural landscapes. The Confucian ethic implored them to seek the ultimate truth in the landscape (Ge 1991; cited in Petersen 1995). The courtier/poet as traveller became a familiar figure throughout China and his philosophical interpretations of the Chinese landscape became part of Chinese 'common knowledge' (Petersen 1995: 143). Under the prevailing feudal system, peasants and commoners were forbidden from visiting most of the sacred places – and in any case their economic circumstances were hardly conducive to leisure – so that this travel was restricted to the elite classes and their entourages.

Nevertheless, as the Chinese poet Li Bai illustrates, travel in China was a socially sanctioned way of life for thousands of its scholars and creative artists. The biographical note about Li Bai in *Illustrated History of China's 5000 Years* (Anon. 1994: 259) records that this renowned poet from the court of the Tang dynasty Emperor Li Long Kaië 'travelled around all the most famous mountains and rivers of China, and his poetry stands as testimony to his passion for the landscapes of China and the daily life of the people'(Anon. 1994:259). The works of Li Bai and other Tang dynasty poets and artists such as Wang Wei (701–761AD) have influenced generations of Chinese. They continue to be taught in Chinese schools today and are instantly familiar to millions of Chinese, both in China and overseas. Indeed, in some respects poetry has taken on the function of religion and the Chinese have come to worship Li Bai in temples as 'the God of the poets' (Lin 1935: 241).

Twentieth-century turmoil

With the advent of Sun Yat Sen's Republic in 1912, pilgrimage travel in China largely ceased. It was at this time that tourism in its modern form was beginning in Europe and the Americas. Tourism, however, was simply irrelevant to China, a poor and struggling nation confronted internally with 'warlordism', and externally by a hostile Japan and unfriendly colonial Western powers which had carved out trading enclaves in China's territory.

The onset of the First World War in 1914 led to the cessation of all tourism globally. Even after the end of the war in 1918, as the lights in Europe again began to glitter and travel to the continent became 'fashionable', China remained xenophobic, wracked by internal strife as the warlords and politicians battled for supremacy, with a Japanese occupying force in Shandong. China had neither the inclination nor the capacity to engage in the development of facilities and attractions.

The formation of the Communist Party of China in 1921 added more unrest to endemic warlordism, and this turmoil was compounded after the Japanese invasion of Manchuria in 1931. For a brief period from 1923–26 several travel agencies were established in Shanghai to handle both inbound and outbound travel (Yang and Jiang 1983), but these ventures were short-lived due to the turbulence of the times. Hostilities against the external aggressor continued until the defeat of Japan in 1945, only to be replaced by civil warfare between the nationalists and the communists. This had the Kuomintang under Chiang Kai Shek pitted against the Communist Party under Mao Zedong for control of China.

Mao Zedong and 'non-tourism' 1948–78

In 1949, with the Communist Party victorious, the doors of the bamboo curtain swung shut. They were to remain closed to all but a handful of overseas visitors for the subsequent thirty years. At a time when much of the world was embarking on rapid expansion of infrastructure and facilities to embrace mass tourism, China locked itself away. The communist regimes in China from 1949 until 1978 were dismissive of tourism as an appropriate form of economic activity. Both domestic and international tourism were almost non-existent (Chow 1988; Hudman and Hawkins 1989; C. M. Hall 1994). Entry for overseas visitors was strictly controlled and tourism activity was held tightly in the hands of the state machinery. The little foreign tourism which existed was sanctioned on the grounds that the successes of communism could be paraded before a selected international audience. Tour guides accompanied foreign tourists at all times and were able 'quickly and proficiently [to] report the great strides society and the economy had made under socialism' (Hudman and Hawkins 1989: 178). Access was restricted to 'showcase' attractions, and contact between tourists and locals was strictly regulated (D. Hall 1984). Segregation in hotels according to the categories of foreign tourists, overseas Chinese, Hong Kong and Macau Chinese, and locals was rigidly enforced (Chow 1988). From 1954 to 1978 the China International Travel Service (set up to arrange visits by 'foreign friends') played host to only 125,000 visitors (Richter 1989). Internal travel was suppressed even more rigidly, with a permit system required for any travel outside one's local district. 'Tourism' was not an approved reason for travel.

Deng Xiaoping and Socio-Economic Reform after 1978

In 1978 China's leadership rejected the politics of the Cultural Revolution at the Third Plenum of the 11th Central Committee and embraced the goal of economic modernization with the adoption of the so-called 'open-door' policy. Under Deng Xiaoping, China embarked upon a multi-faceted modernization programme in agriculture, industry, national defence, and science and technology (the 'four modernizations'). The tourism industry gained new acceptance as part of this programme, its foreign-exchange earnings recognized as being able to make a significant contribution to financing the four modernizations. The 'bamboo curtain' was pulled aside and the Chinese door opened to world tourism in a comprehensive way. The first national conference on tourism was held in that year to formulate guidelines and organizational structures for its development (Gao and Zhang 1982). Politically, tourism as an acceptable industry was justified in socialist terms because:

- it would advance economic reforms and the policy of opening the country to the outside world;
- it would further friendship and mutual understanding between the Chinese proletariat and other peoples of the world;
- it would contribute to world peace (Li and Sofield 1994).

In three different speeches in 1979 Deng Xiaoping stated the need for the swift growth and development of tourism (*Tourism Tribune*, December 1992).

The decision to embrace the tourism industry was not reached lightly, because international tourism was recognized by the Chinese government as a vehicle which inevitably promoted the penetration of Western values and Western culture. According to Ogden:

> the Chinese leadership developed a far greater tolerance for market forces of supply and demand which challenge socialism, than for Western values that might pollute Chinese culture: the government was more willing to sacrifice socialist values than Chinese cultural values in the pursuit of economic development.
>
> (Ogden 1992: 6)

In this context, tourism was to be developed around Chinese heritage; most tourism was to be 'cultural' and 'sightseeing' in character. Funds were provided for the restoration of cultural sites such as the Ming Tombs, the Xi'an terracotta army of warriors and horses, and repairs to the Great Wall. Famous landscapes were automatically included in the pantheon of attractions for tourism (Petersen 1995). In the same way, the opening of ethnic minority areas to tourists was a deliberate policy designed to demonstrate to the world the diversity of Chinese culture and to show how well integrated the minorities were (Matthews and Richter 1991).

In domestic terms, the growing labour needs of industries in towns and cities resulted in a relaxation of the strict control over internal movement. Millions of rural dwellers relocated to urban areas. Domestic tourism, particularly at times of cultural significance in the Chinese calendar, has seen millions of Chinese travel for family reunions and celebrations. Therefore, from being virtually non-existent in China as recently as 1979, tourism in China has rapidly become one of its largest sectors. Following the 'open-door' policy, its growth has been nothing short of spectacular. In 1978 a total of 1.81 million tourists visited China, 1.6 million of them from Hong Kong. In 1979 that figure expanded to 4.2 million (3.8 million of them from Hong Kong), an increase of 232 per cent. By 1993 the total of overseas visitors had reached 41.5 million and international receipts had climbed from US$263 million in 1978 to US$5.1 billion. The number of domestic Chinese tourists was estimated at 406 million by the National Tourism Administration of the People's Republic of China (NTA) (1993). It was estimated by the NTA that in 1994 there were 430 million domestic tourists and more than 44 million international visitors, constituting – at least in sheer numbers – one of the most dynamic tourism industries in the world (National China Tourism Administration 1990, 1991, 1992, 1993, 1994).

There are a number of special, almost unique, features of this rapidly expanding industry, such as the role played by overseas Chinese (numbering more than 55 million) in high rates of annual visitation to mainland China, and the very high levels of visiting friends and relatives (VFR) participation in major festival events in the Chinese calendar, such as the Chinese Lunar New Year. For example, in 1995 more than 79 million Chinese made reunion visits to families during the two-week period of the Lunar New Year in February and more than 1 million overseas Chinese made the trip to China for the festival. There is no other country which experiences such massive movements on a repeated, annual scale. The logistics of transporting so many millions over a short span of time is a management nightmare, and shortcomings in the transportation system remain one of the most serious problems for the further development of tourism in China (Gormsen 1995a).

POLICIES AS DETERMINANTS OF RURAL TOURISM DEVELOPMENT

Government policy towards tourism became a fruitful area for research in the mid-1990s (see Hall and Jenkins 1995). The new policy of 'socialism with Chinese characteristics' which was pursued with the 'open-door' policies of 1979 and 1984 gradually moved China away from a centrally administered command economy to a more decentralized, market-oriented system. A socialist state remained the distant goal, but capitalism was accepted as being a necessary interim stage to create the wealth to build the base for socialism (Li and Sofield 1994).

In the early 1980s a series of reforms to implement these policies changed the whole face of rural China. A central feature of the economic reforms was the localization of the economy and approval of private enterprise. The centralized, hierarchically organized bureaucracies led by communist cadres were replaced by decentralized decision-making between individual enterprises and economic units. Decollectivization of the rural communes which had been formed by combining small villages during Mao's Great Leap Forward in the 1950s, and which Mao described as 'the main pillar of socialism' (Kwan Ha Yim 1991: 204), began in October 1983. By mid-1985 the nation's 56,000 communes had been replaced by more than 92,000 townships in which economic and administrative functions were separated. Under the monolithic centralized authority of the Communist Party, both tasks had been controlled by production brigades run by communist cadres. But with the reforms individual households were given responsibility for meeting production targets, and the brigades were replaced by 820,000 elected villagers' committees. The 'household contract responsibility system' returned land to the peasants under fifteen- or thirty-year 'assignments'. This preserved the communist notion of the state owning the land, although as the reforms gathered momentum 'assignment' in practice took on the features of leasehold, with, for example, the right to pass on usury rights, to inherit the plots from current generations and to sell assignments of parcels of land.

One of the consequences of the rural reforms was that households found that from the limited farmland they were contracted to work 'a massive workforce could be released for other lucrative propositions. In consequence, village and town-run enterprises have blossomed everywhere in the countryside. It can be said that rural village and town industry is the off-spring of the combination of surplus labour and new means of production and objects of labour' (Fei Xiatong 1989: 46). Chen Ximen, Director of the Department of Rural Development at the Development Research Centre of the State Council, speaking at a conference on rural reform (*South China Morning Post*, 4 December 1993) stated that the rural workforce numbered 430 million out of a total rural population of 900 million; that 330 million worked on the country's 100 million hectares of farmland, while the other 100 million worked in rurally based enterprises; and that those 330 million had work for only one-third of the year. Non-agricultural rural enterprises had absorbed 12.6 million workers per year between 1984–88; but from 1989 modernization, with investment in plant and equipment, resulted in only 2.6 million new jobs each year, leaving millions in the rural areas unemployed or under employed. Chen proposed that 100 million should move off the land to live permanently in China's 10,000 towns and small cities to work in factories and service industries such as tourism.

The State Bureau of Statistics (SBS) estimated in 1993 that there were more than 22 million village- and township-owned cooperative enterprises. They employed anything from a handful of people to several thousand. There were also hundreds of thousands of individually owned private businesses, often very small and operating at an informal level. They proliferated as labour became available in the rural areas and peasants were encouraged to use the surplus labour for local economic development. The SBS estimated that in 1993 village and township enterprises registered a gross output of 2.7 trillion yuan, accounting for 33.6 per cent of the country's total industrial output. They employed 118 million people in the rural areas (Chen 1993). Thousands of tourism sites and thousands of tourism-related businesses were developed by local interests. 'Having the peasants leave the land without leaving the village to participate actively in village- and town-run enterprises was acknowledged as a guiding principle of national strategic importance' (Fei Xiatong 1989: 50).

In a study of four counties in Guandong Province, Xu Xueqiang and Zhang Wenxian (1989) found that in 1978 there were only nine towns in the four counties but by end 1984 there were sixty-four. The town populations in 1978 totalled 275,303 (10.3 per cent of the total population of the four counties); by 1984 town populations totalled 434,508 (15.8 per cent of the total population of the four counties). Xu and Zhang examined tourism visitation as one variable in the swiftly changing economic structure of the counties. The number of overseas Chinese and other foreign visitors was recorded as 167,000 in 1978. The situation was largely stagnant to the end of 1983 with only 170,000. But by the end of 1984, there was a 20 per cent leap in the number of recorded visits, to 200,000. The development of numerous non-state-owned facilities in the new towns following decollectivization to service the industry had accelerated the rate of tourism (Xu and Zhang 1989: 50).

Rural tourism enterprises

It has not been possible to determine just how many private enterprises are engaged in rural tourism and the provision of tourism-related services in the rural areas because there is insufficient disaggregation of national statistics and many operate outside the formal sector. Given the number of China's tourist visits it is not unreasonable to suppose that there are perhaps as many as 2 million tourist-related enterprises in the rural areas. Gormsen attempted a national survey of hotels in 1991 and arrived at a total of 98,686 accommodation units (Gormsen 1995a). They were not broken down into rural/urban locations but were disaggregated into those which were domestically owned and those which involved foreign investment. Of the total, only 2,130 were classified as 'international tourist accommodations', of which only 421 were foreign joint ventures or cooperatives.

Gormsen noted that inexpensive hotels and hostels exist throughout China for domestic travellers and that foreign visitors are generally not permitted to stay in them (Gormsen 1995a: 81). However, the capacity of these state- and collective-owned establishments is insufficient to handle the burgeoning numbers of domestic tourists, and during the peak periods local government and collective buildings such as schools, public bath houses and even underground shelters may be pressed into service (Gormsen 1995a). At the ancestral village of one of the present authors (Li), the village collective of Sun Ming Ting in Zhongshan County, Guangdong Province, obtained compensation for agricultural land which was sold to the government for a new highway between Zhuhai and Guangzhou. This was combined with significant financial inputs from overseas relatives in Hong Kong and elsewhere and invested in a small hotel (100 rooms), constructed in 1993. The hotel was built specifically because of the absence of commercial accommodation near the village to handle VFR traffic. The new road also opened the village to domestic tour bus companies, which now use the hotel regularly. Lew (1995) has analysed the role of compatriot Chinese in investment in China's tourism industry and noted a propensity to invest in ventures in their home villages.

In the 1990s private houses in some rural cities and towns have also been opened up for use by domestic tourists. Gormsen (1995a) provides the example of a special 'tourist village' south of the city of Xi'an in which the government not only provided new apartments for ninety-four families resettled there under an urban renewal programme, but gave them a small one-family house as well. 'This building can be set up as a privately-owned guest house using their own funds and state credit. One family reported that in 1986 their 20 beds were occupied every night for nine months and that, consequently, they vacationed in Southern China during the winter on their profits' (Gormsen 1995a: 81).

Any attempt to compile an estimate of the number of rural tourism businesses is confounded by the proliferation of businesses outside the formal economy. To give but one example, on a tour from the southern Guandong city of Zhaoqing to the scenic caves at Ling Xiao (described as 'the primary attraction in southern China' (Shing Pao 1993), the tour buses all stop at a small village about half-way, where the entrepreneurial village cooperative has built a public toilet. This sits over the water of the village-owned cooperative fish ponds. The toilet is basic – four walls and a roof, two compartments, a bench seat in each compartment with a hole straight through to the water beneath. Chinese visitors are

Figure 7.2 Itinerant stallholder, Jade River caves, Guandong, China (T. Sofield).

charged 50 cents to use the facility; foreign tourists are charged 5 yuan. Since more than 2 million tourists visit the caves each year and the toilet is the only such facility along the 150 km, it is possible that this simple facility generates as much as 1 million yuan each year. Along the road verge on either side of the toilet are a shop and several itinerant stallholders (sixteen at the time of the authors' visit) selling a variety of items such as oranges, drinks, souvenirs (clay teapots) and basketware (see Figure 7.2). It is virtually certain that the village fish ponds and shop are registered with the government authorities, but it is highly doubtful that the toilet is – and the itinerant hawkers certainly will not be.

At the Ling Xiao caves complex itself (see Figure 7.3), a similar mix of formal and informal enterprises operates. The main caves complex consists of a quite extensive formal structure financed largely by the state-run China Development Bank and owned and operated by Yang Chun County trading as the Ling Xiao Scenic Region Management Company (Li and Sofield 1994). It is adjacent to the village of Yu Leung Hang and comprises a small hotel (sixty rooms, built in 1993), a restaurant capable of seating 200 guests, two souvenir shops, management offices, a manager's house, a small warehouse, a picnic area at the entrance to the caves with twenty tables and eighty stools of reinforced concrete, three bridges over the small Jade River, which runs through the caves, three small boats, internal stairs throughout the caves system, a power house with a 40 KVA generator supplying lighting for the caves, a water tower, a large car park (very few cars, but capacity for thirty tour buses) and a toilet block (with flushing WCs) adjoining the restaurant. Total investment by the company at the end of 1993 was approximately 9.8 million yuan (US$2.9 million), which included a new loan in 1993 to build the hotel with a two–three star rating for international guests to replace an older inn.

At Yu Xi village, about 10 km downstream, where the Jade River runs through three mountains and the caves are accessed by boat, the company has constructed a small dam about 10 m high across the entrance to Middle Cave to allow use of the river all year round. Boats are flat-bottomed, with a single 15 hp outboard motor each and a carrying capacity of fifty. Infrastructure, which cost about 1 million yuan, includes a car park for tour buses and other vehicles, a 250 m-long concrete path and steps constructed down to the dam site, a landing and jetty, a souvenir shop, manager's quarters and public toilets, all built in a single complex beside the dam wall in 1985. Management stated that in 1992 and 1993 total revenue for the company amounted to around 4 million yuan (US$0.5 million) per year, generated by more than 2 million visitors per year (Li and Sofield 1994). Differential entry prices are charged for local Chinese (free, 1–2 yuan); compatriot Chinese (10 yuan) and foreign visitors (20 yuan). This kind of price structure is fairly standard throughout China.

At both sites, the villagers of Yu Leung Hang and Yu Xi have established numerous side line businesses. These include stalls selling fruit, drinks, postcards, souvenirs and so forth. The services they provide include personalized calligraphy and pony rides. The company manage-

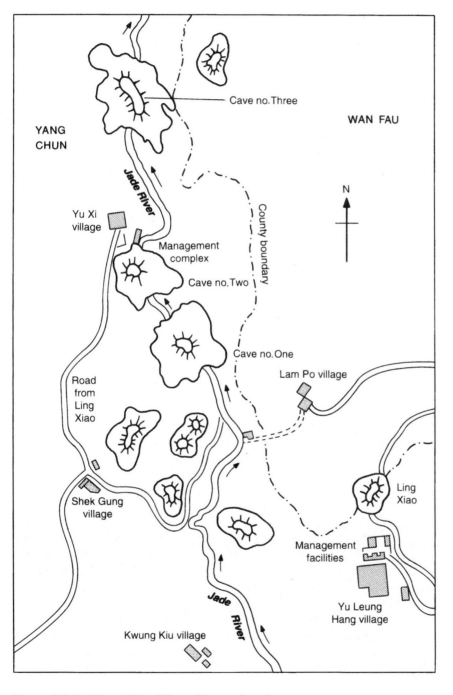

Figure 7.3 Yu Xi and Ling Xiao with cave locations.

ment estimate that these businesses generate about 1.5 million yuan (US$150,000) each year (Li and Sofield 1994).

This pattern of formal and informal enterprises is repeated at literally thousands of sites throughout China. Swain (1993) recorded the participation of women of the Sani Yi minority in numerous craft enterprises, both formal and informal, in Yunnan. Oakes (1992) stated that in 1988 in Guizhou Province, sixty-three township and village enterprises had established ethnic textiles and handicraft factories with formal outlets as far distant as coastal Shenzhen, but that most selling of ethnic handicrafts in the Province was actually carried out informally at tourist sites. Gormsen stated that there were more than 6,600 beds for foreign tourists in the Huang Shan region of Anhui Province in predominantly state-owned hotels, and 729 small employers with 1,266 employees in small tourism businesses, with many opportunities for private accommodation as well (Gormsen 1995b: 134).

Liu (1992) provides one of the few case studies of tourism development in rural China with an analysis of the impacts of tourism in the Yesanpuo Scenic Area in Hebei Province. While relatively close to Beijing, this mountainous region had been isolated for several centuries and from the beginning of the Ming Dynasty (1368AD) the villagers were exempted from providing men and produce to the imperial authorities. In the Ch'ing Dynasty, by virtue of historical practice the Emperor's officials could not enter the region. After the 1911 revolution, the area remained as a virtually autonomous enclave. During the Sino–Japanese War in the 1930s it was a refuge for the People's Liberation Army, and even in 1985 some remote villages were apparently unaware that the Japanese had been defeated four decades earlier. To this day some villagers still follow Ming Dynasty customs and wear clothing styled on the fashions of that era.

Tourism development began in 1985 with the declaration of the 460 sq. km Yesanpuo Scenic Area by the Hubei Province Government (subsequently upgraded to 'a scenic area of national importance' in the China-wide inventory of tourism resources undertaken by the NTA in 1988). The Provincial Government provided basic infrastructure (e.g. access roads to supplement the first railway line, which had been constructed through the area in the mid-1970s). The County formed a company to construct several small hotels and open scenic spots. As Liu argues, 'Tourism opened the door of Yesanpuo, which had been closed for 500 years' (Liu 1992: 52). Significant numbers of tourists first arrived in 1985 but commercial accommodation proved inadequate. Officials embarked on a programme to persuade the conservative villagers to open up their houses to meet the demand. Some villagers finally agreed but initially resisted payment: local custom demanded that guests in their own homes be treated as relatives, and to charge a fee would have resulted in loss of face. It took a few years for the business principle of profit to replace tradition. As more villagers became involved and competition increased, sideline businesses were undertaken. These included horse-and-cart rides, pony rides, air mattresses for river 'rafting', hiring guns for hunting and even charging for use of their dogs for photographic opportunities (Liu 1992: 53).

Table 7.1 1990 income statistics (in yuan) for three villages, Yesanpuo National Scenic Area, Hubei Province

Village	Average annual family income	Average family size	Average annual per capita income	Annual tourism income	Percentage of total income per family
A	Y 1326.47	4.29	Y 309.20	Y 52.94	3.99%
B	Y 1170.49	3.63	Y 322.45	Y 117.07	10.01%
C	Y 3026.11	3.58	Y 845.28	Y 1797.22	59.39%

Source: Liu Zhenli (1992).

By 1991 tourism was firmly entrenched as a major industry within the scenic area. Before 1984 it was impoverished, with an average annual per capita income of only 70 yuen (US$15). By 1991 some families were earning more than 3,000 yuen per year (US$400). Liu compared the incomes of three villages, where there was a range from very little to major involvement in tourism (Table 7.1). Village A was least involved; it had no proper access road, very few tourists could get there and less than 4 per cent of family income was derived from tourism. Village B (medium involvement) was some distance from the scenic spots but a few individual families provided accommodation and about 10 per cent of family income was earned from tourism. Village C was highly involved; it was located close to the region's scenic 'hot spots', and 80 per cent of the families were directly involved in providing various services and accommodation, and about 60 per cent of family income was attributed to tourism.

Liu provided no figures on total tourism earnings for the Yesanpuo Scenic Area, nor total annual visitation. However, his analysis of this once remote region reveals the same dualism of government-owned tourism businesses and private enterprise which developed throughout rural China after 1984. The rapid development also demonstrates the entrepreneurship of China's rural population once 'business consciousness' was allowed to flourish.

MOTIVATION OF THE CHINESE MARKET SEGMENT FOR RURAL TRAVEL

In examining rural tourist visitation in China, it is important to recognize that the motivation for much domestic tourism lies in the traditions established 3,000 years ago and now firmly entrenched in the Chinese psyche. Millions of Chinese each year visit sites immortalized by their poets and artists. The five mountains, the four rivers, places such as Yellow Crane Terrace, which was commemorated in a poem by Li Bai, are all favourite destinations. They feature in such 'lists' as the State Council's (1988) *State Level Scenic Wonders and Historical Sites* and a survey undertaken in 1991 by the China Travel Service of the top forty most favoured tourist spots (*Special Zones Herald 1992*). Gormsen (1995b) recorded that in 1987, the most recent year for which figures on domestic tourists are available, the mountains of Huang Shan in Anhui Province played host to 1.6 million visitors, of which only 15,000 (fewer than 1 per cent) were overseas tourists. The attraction of Huang Shan resided in the 'amazing landscape of bizarre granite rocks, ancient pine trees, and always changing clouds, as well as being a traditional place of Buddhist pilgrimage' (Gormsen 1995b: 134). Splendid China Miniature Scenic Spots, Shenzhen, which consists of 100 sites built in 1989 on scales of 1:15 or 1:9, includes the most famous of the sacred mountains, rivers and other landscapes and is visited by more than 3 million Chinese each year, who are seeking out a postmodern expression of their traditional images.

As Petersen stated:

> To the Chinese people, visiting a scenic spot or a historical place is always attached to sentimental expectations. In order to watch the sun rising over Mt Tai, for example, many old and young Chinese wait in the chilly darkness for hours. What they are really looking for is not simply the scene of the sun rising from the clouds but the experiences and reflections which have been memorialised again and again in Chinese poetry.
>
> When western tourists look at the Yangtze they see a river, the Chinese see a poem replete with philosophical ideals. Part of the common knowledge of Chinese-ness is to recognize representations of the picturesque hills of Guilin, the sea clouds of Wu-shan, the Three Gorges of the Yangtze River, the waterfalls of Mt Lu, the elegant gardens of Suzhou.
>
> These images bring spiritual unity even if the people have never visited them; but when they do visit the importance of these images is reinforced.
>
> (Petersen 1995: 149)

Petersen has suggested that Chinese domestic tourism to such places constitutes 'a voluntary cultural decision more akin to a pilgrimage to historical, cultural and political centres' made in order 'to validate the poetic knowledge of places such as the gardens of Suzhou' (Petersen 1995: 150). Without having been nurtured in the Chinese cultural milieu it is difficult for foreign visitors to enter Chinese places with the same experiential understanding.

REGIONAL INEQUALITY IN RURAL TOURISM

Wen and Tisdell (1996) examined regional inequality and the decentralization of China's tourism industry with a sophisticated analysis of several demand and supply-side indicators for international visitation to twelve coastal regions (Beijing, Tianjin, Hebei, Liaoning, Shanghai, Jiangsu, Zhejian, Fujian, Shandong, Guangdong, Guanxi and Hainan). These provinces, which in 1992 supported 40 per cent of China's population and produced about 57 per cent of its national income on 14 per cent of the country's total land area, captured 84 per cent of China's international visitors and received 90 per cent of the nation's international tourism receipts. The disproportionate share of tourists, tourism facilities and tourism receipts is due not to a richness of natural tourism resources but to the status of the twelve coastal regions as Special Economic Zones. This provides them with access to development finance and foreign investment which is not available to the interior regions and more isolated rural areas.

This analysis is of interest because of the details it reveals about the coastal regions as a whole – many parts of which are, of course, rural. Guilin in Guanggxi Province (see Figure 7.4), for example, is situated some 500 km northwest of Macau and is the base for tours of the surrounding lakes and mountains, whose picturesque qualities have been extolled in Chinese literature and paintings for several thousand years. There would be very few tourists who visited Guilin for its urban attractions. The capital cities of the twelve coastal provinces attract large numbers of tourists in their own right (Beijing, with the Forbidden Palace, the Great Wall and other major cultural attractions, is a favoured destination), but a large part of their visitation may be attributed to their roles as gateways to the rural hinterland and to the access they provide to transportation links to other parts of the country.

The rich symbolism, philosophical affinity and traditional relationship which most Chinese have with their rural landscapes, with many of the most famous sites dispersed throughout the interior regions, may, as domestic tourism becomes an ever greater force, help to reduce some of the disparity between the eastern coastal regions and the interior. Wen and

Figure 7.4 Roadside private enterprise in rural China near Guilin (T. Sofield).

Tisdell (1996) note that China established its first nature reserve in 1956 and that by the end of the 1980s there were some 59 nature reserves and 20 national parks, 19 of the latter being located in the interior regions. China's biodiversity ranks eighth in the world (it is ranked first in the northern hemisphere), with many diverse ecosystems (Herath 1996). Gormsen (1995b) observed that many more Westerners than Chinese visit the peripheral regions of the ethnic minorities because of a preference for the exotic. Toops (1995) provided details of international tourism to the isolated cities of Xinjiang Uygur Autonomous Region, in which the culture of the people constitutes the major attraction and where foreign tourists greatly outnumber domestic visitors. Oakes (1995) also noted that international visitors and compatriot and overseas Chinese formed the majority of tourists to experience the Miao minority culture of Guizhou Province. The tourism industry in this isolated and economically depressed Province has been constructed almost solely around the Miao, and this 'represesents an interesting twist on tourism as "modernization", since ethnic sites are promoted as exotically unmodern' (Oakes 1995: 210).

Tourism in China's interior may thus be expected to grow significantly, especially as new international entry points are opened up. The recently opened Kunming airport in Yunnan Province (famous for its petrified forest at Shilin, its tropical rainforest and the cultural attractions of the Sani Yi minority; Swain 1993), with direct services from Bangkok, is a case in point.

CONCLUSIONS

The business of rural tourism in China transects both the formal and informal sectors, with this duality characterized by integration of the services each provides (tour bus companies utilizing wayside toilet facilities, for example, and itinerant hawkers providing supplementary services such as pony rides at major attractions). An understanding of the dynamics of the development of rural tourism in China requires an exploration both of culture and traditions and of contemporary politics. While pilgrimage tourism and cultural tourism were extant several thousand years ago and endured through almost three millennia, the communist regime of 1949 brought virtually all tourism in China to a grinding halt. Both restrictions on international access to China and the strict control of all internal movement by its people saw China bypass the development of tourism at a time when many countries were actively pursuing its expansion. Only after 1978, when major economic reforms were introduced, did China embrace tourism as an accepted form of economic development.

The enunciation of market principles within the bounds of socialist policy by the communist regimes since 1978 has given a particular form and structure to rural tourism business in three major ways:

1 Thousands of previously undeveloped sites have been opened to tourism;

2 Millions of peasants have been released from farming and established hundreds of thousands of tourism-related businesses in rural areas;

3 Chinese people have found the freedom to explore their own country in their many millions.

This freedom may be perceived in two ways: as a freedom from the bureaucratic strictures preventing independent internal movement by people; and as freedom from penury, with rising levels of income which have allowed travel to become affordable. The result has been domestic visitation by millions to the sites of inculcated images of rural China. The 'open-door' policy of Deng Xiaoping heralded a dramatic shift away from centuries of xenophobia and directed China along a path of increasing international contact, of which international tourism is a major component. This has found expression in the further development of rural tourism, particularly for the peripheral regions, because the exotic cultures of China's ethnic minorities have proved a primary attraction for overseas visitors. Tourism development has also been aided by relaxations on foreign investment, and a feature of much of the resultant activity has been the willingness of compatriot Chinese to invest in their homeland. Their rural ancestral villages have often been the beneficiaries, adding a different element of joint ownership to rural tourism businesses in places which may have no particular tourism resources and which have been outside the scope of state, provincial and county tourism development plans.

The sheer volume of numbers involved in rural tourism in China, with the certainty that these numbers will grow, is likely to add to pressure for improved facilities and environmental management. For hundreds of years visitation to many natural areas was restricted by the social exclusivity of the imperial dynasties coupled with sacred 'zones of exclusion', so that environmental impacts would have been slight. Following the overthrow of the Qing dynasty in 1911, for seventy years little visitation to many of these sites took place. Obviously some destruction occurred through acts of war, misguided industrial development and the ravages of the Cultural Revolution; but very little could be attributed to tourism and recreation. Now, however, the explosion in travel since the reforms of 1978, especially as millions of Chinese seek to experience for themselves the icons of their rich heritage, are imposing extreme pressure on some sites. Planning for ecologically sustainable development is not at the forefront of rural tourism activity in China. The challenge confronting the authorities is of a magnitude which, it is suggested, is faced by no other country in the world.

REFERENCES

Anon. (1994) *Illustrated History of China's 5000 Years*, Shanghai.

Asia Research Centre, Murdoch University (1992) *Southern China in Transition. The New Regionalism and Australia*, Canberra: Australian Government Publishing Service.

Chen, K. (1993) 'The Pearl River Delta', *South China Morning Post*, (20 December).

Chow, W. S. (1988) 'Open door policy and tourism between Guangdong and Hong Kong', *Annals of Tourism Research* 15(2): 205–18.

Fei Xiatong (1989) 'Small towns: a re-exploration', *Chinese Sociology and Anthropology* 22(1): 42–58.

Gao Di-chen and Zhang Guang-ri (1982) 'China's tourism: policy and practice', *Tourism Management* 4(2): 75–84.

Gormsen, E. (1995a) 'International tourism in China: its organization and socio-economic impact', in A. Lew and L. Yu (eds) *Tourism in China. Geographic, Political and Economic Perspectives*, Boulder, Colorado: Westview Press.

—— (1995b) 'Travel behaviour and the impacts of domestic tourism in China', in A. Lew and L. Yu (eds) *Tourism in China. Geographic, Political and Economic Perspectives*, Boulder, Colorado: Westview Press.

Hall, C. M. (1994) *Tourism in the Pacific Rim: Development, Impacts and Planning*, Melbourne: Longman Cheshire.

Hall, C. M. and Jenkins, J. (1995) *Tourism and Public Policy*, London: Routledge.

Hall, D. (1984) 'Foreign tourism under socialism: the Albanian "Stalinist model"', *Annals of Tourism Research* 11(4):539–55.

Herath, G. (1996) 'Ecotourism in Asia and the Pacific: potential, problems and an integrated planning model', in G. Prosser (ed.) *Tourism and Hospitality Research. Australian and International Perspectives*, Proceedings of the Australian Tourism and Hospitality Research Conference 1996, February, Canberra: Bureau of Tourism Research.

Hudman, L. and Hawkins, D. (1989) *Tourism in Contemporary Society*, Englewood Cliffs, NJ: Prentice-Hall.

Kwan Ha Yim (1991) (ed.) *China Under Deng*, New York: Facts on File, Inc.

Lew, A. (1992) 'Perceptions of tourists and tour guides in Singapore', *Journal of Cultural Geography* 12(1): 45–52.

—— (1995) 'Overseas Chinese and compatriots in China's tourism development', in A. Lew and L. Yu (eds) *Tourism in China. Geographic, Political and Economic Perspectives*, Boulder, Colorado: Westview Press.

Lew, A. and Yu, L. (eds) *Tourism in China. Geographic, Political and Economic Perspectives*, Boulder, Colorado: Westview Press.

Li, Fung Mei Sarah and Sofield, T. (1994) 'Tourism development and socio-cultural change in rural China', in A. Seaton (ed.) *Tourism. The State of the Art*, Chichester: John Wiley.

Lin, Yu-Tang (1935) *My Country My People*, New York: John Day Company.

Liu, Zhenli (1992) 'The social impact of tourism on destination areas: problems and solutions', *Tourism Tribune* 7(3): 52–5.

Matthews, H. G. and Richter, L. K. (1991) 'Political science and tourism', *Annals of Tourism Research* 18(1): 120–35.

Meisner, M. (1986) *Mao's China and After. A History of the People's Republic*, London: Collier Macmillan.

National Tourism Administration of the People's Republic of China (1990) *The Yearbook of China Tourism Statistics*, Beijing: NTA.

—— (1991) *The Yearbook of China Tourism Statistics*, Beijing: NTA.

—— (1992) *The Yearbook of China Tourism Statistics*, Beijing: NTA.

—— (1993) *The Yearbook of China Tourism Statistics*, Beijing: NTA.

—— (1994) *The Yearbook of China Tourism Statistics*, Beijing: NTA.

Oakes, T. S. (1992) 'Cultural geography and Chinese ethnic tourism', *Journal of Cultural Geography*, 12(2): 3–17.

—— (1995) 'Tourism in Guizhou: The legacy of internal colonialism', in A. Lew and L. Yu (eds) *Tourism in China. Geographic, Political and Economic Perspectives*, Boulder, Colorado: Westview Press.

Ogden, S. (1992) *China's Unresolved Issues. Politics, Development and Culture*, 2nd edn, Englewood Cliffs, NJ: Prentice-Hall.

Petersen, Ying Yang (1995) 'The Chinese landscape as a tourist attraction: image and reality', in A. Lew and L. Yu (eds) *Tourism in China. Geographic, Political and Economic Perspectives*, Boulder, Colorado: Westview Press.

Qiao, Yuxia (1995) 'Domestic tourism in China: policies and development', in A. Lew and L. Yu (eds) *Tourism in China. Geographic, Political and Economic Perspectives*, Boulder, Colorado: Westview Press.

Richter, L. (1989) *The Politics of Tourism in Asia*, Honolulu: University of Hawaii Press.

Shing Pao (1993) 'Because of a boundary dispute a tourist attraction was damaged', South China Morning Post (8 February).

Swain, M. (1993) 'Women producers of ethnic arts', *Annals of Tourism Research* 20(1): 32–51.

Toops, S. (1995) 'Tourism in Xingjiang: practice and place', in A. Lew and L. Yu (eds) *Tourism in China. Geographic, Political and Economic Perspectives*, Boulder, Colorado: Westview Press.

Tourism Tribune 7(6), (1992)(December).

Wen, Jie and Tisdell, C. (1996) 'Regional inequality and decentralisation of China's tourism industry', in G. Prosser (ed.) *Tourism and Hospitality Research. Australian and International Perspectives*, Proceedings of the Australian Tourism and Hospitality Research Conference 1996, Canberra: Bureau of Tourism Research.

Xu Xueqiang and Zhang Wenxian (1989) 'A preliminary study of the driving force behind rural urbanization in areas open to the outside world. A case study of four Guandong counties', *Chinese Sociology and Anthropology* 21(2): 35–51.

Yang, Shijin and Jiang, Xinmao (1983) *Introduction to Travel and Tourism*, Beijing: China Travel and Tourism Press.

Zhang Guangrui (1995) 'China's tourism development since 1978: policies, experiences and lessons learned', in A. Lew and L. Yu (eds) *Tourism in China. Geographic, Political and Economic Perspectives*, Boulder, Colorado: Westview Press.

International case studies in the southern hemisphere

PART 3

Rural tourism in Australia: the Undara Experience

T. Sofield and D. Getz

8

INTRODUCTION

This chapter examines the development and management of a unique Australian attraction and resort – the Undara Experience in outback Queensland. Owing to its remoteness and dependence on a sensitive resource within a national park, Undara Experience faces a number of special management, marketing and environmental challenges. The chapter begins with a review of rural tourism in Australia and the issue of ecotourism to provide a context for the analysis of the Undara Experience as a rural tourism business, emphasizing the nature of the attraction, accessibility, the type of tourist experience being promoted, the role of guides and the attraction's development, followed by management issues and prospects for the future.

The lava tubes which constitute the core attraction are situated in Undara Volcanic National Park, and the tours provided by Undara Experience through the Savannah Guides are a world-class eco-experience. Lava Lodge, lying just outside the park boundaries, is a wilderness/outback resort with considerable potential for expansion, yet its financial success is by no means assured. Other eco-attractions and resorts in rural areas will face similar problems and it is hoped that the findings presented in this chapter can help other eco-attractions and businesses to learn from issues examined in the Undara Experience.

RURAL TOURISM IN AUSTRALIA: ECOTOURISM AND THE RURAL ENVIRONMENT

Much of Australia's land area is rural and remote from urban areas. The 'Outback', as the remoter rural areas are commonly called, while being more a state of mind than a region, contains enormous tourism potential which is being increasingly exploited through the establishment of eco- and adventure tours and new accommodation in the form of lodges or small, exclusive resorts. According to Hall, the Commonwealth Department of Tourism defined rural tourism as a 'multi-facted activity that takes place in an environment outside urban areas and represents to the traveller the essence of country life' (Hall 1995: 280). Hall also argues that the activities and experiences deemed important by the Commonwealth Department of Tourism in a rural context include agriculture/country life, nature-based activities, Aboriginal heritage, cultural aspects of rural areas, sports activities in rural areas, adventures activities located in rural areas, and beach activities, of which the Outback has a considerable potential in relation to eco-development. Yet a critical relationship exists in such environments between tourism and the symbiotic relationship to the environment it is based in (Romeril 1989). Hall examines this critical relationship in the context of ecotourism development in Australia in terms of the distinct management, policy, planning and development problems it presents:

> ecotourism is 'green' or 'nature-based', which is essentially a form of special interest tourism and refers to a specific market segment and the products generated for that segment; and, ecotourism as any form of tourism development which is regarded as environmentally friendly.
>
> (Hall 1995: 286).

In this respect, ecotourism has become propagandized in Hall's (1995) view, being deemed good or desirable, though Berle adds a note of caution in that 'Ecotourism is big business. It can provide foreign exchange and economic reward for the preservation of natural systems and wildlife. But ecotourism also threatens to destroy the resources on which it depends' (Berle 1990: 6). To retain some degree of sensitivity to the nature of fragile tourism environments, the Ecotourism Association of Australia has developed a code of conduct to reduce negative impacts, as Table 8.1 shows. In fact Valentine (1992) has suggested that conservation needs to be incorporated into any conceptual understanding of ecotourism so that the symbiotic relationship between tourism and the environment can be more clearly understood. In Australia, the Australian Tourism Commission and the various state tourism commissions have embraced ecotourism as a promotional mechanism for the development of new tourism products (see Hall 1995 for more detail). Furthermore, the Commonwealth Department of Tourism's (1992) national tourism strategy and subsequent ecotourism strategy (Commonwealth Department of Tourism 1994a) has meant that the eco-potential of Australia's rural areas has become a marketable commodity. As the ecotourism strategy observes, ecotourism is defined as 'nature-based tourism that involves education and interpretation of the natural environment and is managed to be ecologically sustainable' (Commonwealth Department of Tourism 1994a: 3). Thus between 1993/1994 and 1996/1997, $10 million was targeted at nature-based tourism programmes in terms of industry accreditation, market profiles and research, energy and waste minimization practices, infrastructure projects, ecotourism education, baseline studies and monitoring, integrated regional planning, business development, conferences and workshops (Hall 1995: 288). Thus, for small businesses operating in a rural environment there are many issues to be considered in terms of government policy, planning and the minimization of the environmental impact of tourism. As ecotourism development continues, questions regarding economic viability and environmental impact are certain to become more important.

Despite the growth of interest in ecotourism as a form of rural tourism business development, the National Rural Tourism Strategy noted that 'rural tourism has been relatively unacknowledged as a tourism market sector, yet estimates of domestic and international visitation to rural areas are substantial' (Commonwealth Department of Tourism 1994b: 10). In addition to the development of government policy towards ecotourism development in rural Australia, a A$42 million package of regional tourism development initiatives was announced in the 1993/94 budget, including some A$4 million over four years for a Rural Tourism Programme. This money has been directed towards development of industry leadership, education in sales and marketing, customer service training, international marketing of rural tourism and demonstration projects which have a regional emphasis (see Jenkins 1996 for more detail on this programme). The Strategy guides funding over the remaining years of the programme.

Stakeholder input to the strategy revealed a number of key issues:

- the need for increased focus on product and enterprise development, particularly featuring regional integration;
- a need for appropriate accreditation and industry standards;
- education and training opportunities for new and inexperienced rural tourism operators;
- innovative and cooperative marketing, both domestically and internationally;
- market analysis to assist policy, planning, development and target marketing, and strong and informed industry leadership;
- transport and infrastructure improvements;
- recognition of the important role of local authorities.

From a business perspective, the strategy concluded that a lack of profitability was a problem in rural tourism and that many small enterprises fail. Stronger collaboration among stakeholders and joint marketing were thought to be possible solutions, though, as research by Curran and Storey observes (see Chapter 1, pp. 28–9), this is not a feature affecting only rural tourism businesses in Australia.

In the Queensland context, most tourism development to date has been coastal and on islands, with a mass-market orientation. A number of smaller-scale rainforest lodges have been established, and these are generally marketed as ecotourism opportunities. One of the least developed regions in the state is the dry savannah zone inland from the international resort of Cairns. In this setting, Undara Lava Lodge has a critical role to play.

Table 8.1 Ecotourism Association of Australia's guidelines for ecotourism

Before you go
Ensure that you prepare well for the trip by reading about the places you are about to visit. Choose your ecotours after asking the following questions:
● Does the ecotourism operator comply with the Ecotourism Association Code of Practice for Ecotourism Operators?
● Is a percentage of the economic benefit going back to or staying in the local community/environment?
● Does the tour operator have local guides and use local services and supplies when needed?

While you are away
Minimize the negative impacts of your visit:

Social impacts
● be culturally sensitive and respect local customs
● remember you are a guest
● try to allow enough time in each place

Environmental impacts
● leave an area cleaner than when you found it
● be efficient with natural resources
● travel by your own muscle power wherever possible
● stay on the trail
● take only pictures to remember the places visited
● be careful not to introduce exotic plants and animals
● do not exploit an area when food gathering
● respect animal escape distances
● familiarize yourself with local regulations
● do not use soaps or detergents in natural water bodies
● consider the implications of buying plant or animal products – ask if they are rare or endangered species, or taken from the wild.

Economic impacts
● when travelling spend money on local enterprises
● do not encourage illegal trade by buying products made from endangered species

When you return
Foster and generate a natural and cultural understanding of places you have visited.
Consider the environmental and cultural effects of your visit. Provide feedback to tour operators, you travel agent and government agencies (who manage the areas visited).

Source: Ecotourism Association of Australia (1993); cited in Hall (1995).

UNDARA: THE ATTRACTION

Savannah Guides lead small parties of ecotourists up a rough hill of sharp granitic rocks to tell the story of Undara. Across the broad, eucalyptus-dotted landscape which is Undara Volcanic National Park, they point to a series of low cones and ridges and interpret the scene. Their monologue describing the attraction goes something like this:

The lava from that one cone, Undara, flowed over a gently sloping plain and spilled into existing river valleys. It created this entire basaltic plain and formed the longest lava flow anywhere. Something quite unique was created when the lava following the rivers began to cool and solidify around the sides and top, while inside the molten rock continued to pour onwards. Eventually the eruption stopped and the lava drained out of the valleys leaving behind tunnels completely buried under hardened basalt. These tubes, sixty kilometres in length – possibly the longest in the world – would have remained buried forever, except that time and weather caused sections of the roof to erode and collapse. Where the roof caved in, pockets of vine thickets and miniature rainforests flourished, hiding the entrances to the dark tunnels. Only in very recent times have these been explored, and now we are able to experience in comfort and safety this unique geologic feature with its special vegetation and wildlife. Welcome to the Undara Experience.

In terms of the experience for visitors, nothing can prepare them for the descent into the lava tubes. Each depression is filled with huge boulders, thickets of vine and immense rainforest trees. What looks to be a shrub is actually the canopy of an ancient fig which has gained purchase on the rockfalls below. The air is cooler and damper. Scurrying noises mark the presence of shy wallabies, while bird sounds attract the visitors' attention upwards. Upon entering the caverns, their floors level with centuries of flood-deposited silt, visitors stare in silence and with awe. Each cavern is unique; some are small and arched, others long and seemingly endless. Bats dwell in the longest of the visitor caverns, and paper masks are donned to hold back the smell of ammonia.

When the tour ends, the guide steers the minibus back along dusty bush tracks while guests spot the abundant kangaroos and cockatoos. Arriving at Undara Lava Lodge, overnight visitors debate the merits of having a cool drink at the bar or heading straight for the showers. Some are staying in restored railway cars now used as accommodation, while others are using tents or their own recreational vehicles. After an outdoor dinner under a canopy or inside a dining car, guides tell tales around the campfire or lead a spotlighting troop into the dark bushland to search out nightlife. In the morning, guests walk a short distance to the base of a granite rise and enjoy a bushman's breakfast.

Accessibility

Once remote, but now within a daytrip of the international coastal resort of Cairns, Undara Lava Lodge is a very different kind of resort. Small, isolated and devoted to exploration of the lava tubes and other natural wonders, Undara Experience has great potential to attract international and domestic tourists. With the growth of adventure and ecotourism, this site beckons to travellers in pursuit of the world's dwindling natural places. It is becoming a must-see attraction alongside the reef and rainforest that have made northern Queensland famous.

There are a number of critical questions associated with this attraction:

1 How much tourism development can the area support ?
2 How many visitors can the lava tubes tolerate without serious deterioration of the attraction?
3 When the company's exclusive touring rights expire, will competition pose a threat?
4 What markets are there for longer stays and new tours to other outback attractions?
5 Can a tourist operation in such a remote place and based on a single core attraction be profitable?

As to the future, owner Gerry Collins has to temper his ambitious plans with concern for the natural environment. He is on record as saying: 'I was born and bred in this locality and, as I grew up, learned to love and appreciate the bush, and to recognise how precious it is. The Undara Experience was conceived as an endeavour to share this with everyone, and at the same time ensure reasonable protection of a potentially fragile area' (quoted in Jealous, no date).

The Outback theme and evolution of a heritage tourist experience

As well as the geological emphasis of the lava tubes and their lesser emphasis on associated wildlife there is another theme which may be described as belonging to the Outback ethos. The location of the lava tubes, embedded as they are in the savannah lands, means that they are intrinsically part of the Outback, and this theme finds expression in several different ways.

The Outback country lifestyle is manifested in several ways, including the bush breakfast and barbecue bush lunch, where the settings are out in the savannah eucalyptus forests, kilometres from the Lava Lodge, the meals are cooked over an open log fire, the seats and tables are simply logs on the ground, and kangaroos, kookaburras and goannas are interested onlookers. The menus – which include 'bush tucker' such as steak and eggs, 'damper' (dough baked in the open fire without yeast) and 'billy tea' (black tea boiled in a tin can over the open fire) – also reflect the same theme. The name Swag's Tent Village is evocative of the legendary itinerant bushman who walked the Outback with his 'swag' – camping gear rolled up in a blanket – over his shoulder. This figure has entered many bush ballads and songs. Campfire nights, where the guides tell stories, sing songs and recite bush ballads around a blazing log fire, also reflect the pioneer traditions.

Early transport in the Outback was by teams of horses or bullocks drawing wagons called drays. The Lava Lodge has a team of draught horses with a ten-seater dray which transports guests to a heritage hut. There are plans to construct a small 'Heritage Hut' (pioneer museum) situated out in the bush about 2 km from the Lava Lodge, tours to which would be by the teamster's dray. There are also possibilities for pony safaris through the savannah forests and grasslands to a natural rock pool about 12 miles from the Lava Lodge.

Railway history is also featured by way of the up-market accommodation at the Lava Lodge, which consists of a line of nineteenth-century railway carriages, beautifully restored and appointed, which sit beneath shady gum trees. The Fettler's Licensed Bistro also consists of several restored carriages placed around a central square ('fettlers' is the Australian name given to the railroad gangs who maintained the lines). The architecture of the service buildings – the restaurant, bar, administration centre, reception, shop and conference centre – mirrors the distinctive style of Australia's outback railway stations.

Early European exploration into the area is reflected, with some of the facilities named after pioneers – the Mitchell's Deck Bar, the Fettler's Bistro and the Leichhardt Conference Centre. The latter is named after the German explorer and naturalist Ludwig Leichhardt, who led several expeditions into the savannah lands in the 1840s and camped just 30 km away from Undara Lava Lodge in 1845.

Savannah Guides

Within the literature on heritage tourism (Hall and McArthur 1996), guiding is acknowledged as an important element in providing tourists with a better understanding of the attraction and environment they are visiting. The Savannah Guides are a system of professionals who both protect and interpret a range of unique parks and attractions across northern Australia. With specialist training and detailed local knowledge, guides offer access to some sites, like Undara, that cannot otherwise be visited. They play a major role in terms of direct visitor contact, park supervision and protection. Always dressed in uniforms reminiscent of ranger services the world over, the Savannah Guides help create the special Undara Experience. Savannah Guides have a contract with Undara Experience under which the number of guides to be stationed there is agreed (currently six). The resort provides accommodation and meals and pays their salaries. There are two 'Guide Schools' run by the Savannah Guides Association each year, and certified Savannah Guides must attend one of these. There is peer group assessment during the school but there is no external evaluation.

The development of Undara

The Collins family settled in Spring Creek in 1862, beginning the pastoral traditions that remain dominant today in the savannah lands. Locals knew about the tunnels early on, but access to them was limited by the remoteness and private ownership of the lands. After a Commonwealth geological survey of the region in the early 1960s, publicity was given to the tubes. In 1967 the Parks Association of Queensland proposed the establishment of a 221 sq. km national park to protect these unique features.

In 1987 a firm proposal was made by Gerry Collins to the State of Queensland Lands Department to construct a lodge near the tubes. It was also at this time that the tourism potential of the vast Gulf Savannahs was being studied by a Pacific Asia Tourism Association (PATA) taskforce, and the coastal resort of Cairns was booming. At the request of the Collins family, market research was conducted by the newly established James Cook University of North Queensland Chair of Travel and Tourism Studies, Townsville. This was completed in 1989, and repeated the following year. By June of 1990 the first refurbished railway carriages were on site and ready for use. The speed and efficiency with which development occurred reflects both the vision of the developer and the single ownership of the site and the company.

Undara Experience was immediately successful at the 1991 Northern Queensland Tourism Awards, winning three categories: Major Tourist Attraction, Tourist Development Project and Specialist Accommodation. It was a finalist in the state-wide tourism awards for Specialist Accommodation. In 1992 it won the Northern Queensland awards for Major Tourist Attraction and Environmental Tourism. In 1993 Undara Experience won the major Queensland Environmental Tourism Award. In 1992, the Undara National Park was established, accompanied by a joint statement (9 August 1992) from the Premier of Queensland, Wayne Goss, and the Minister for Environment and Heritage, Pat Comben, which declared, 'Undara National Park to Add to Booming Ecotourism':

> Mr. Goss said eco-tourism was one of Queensland's fastest growing industries with more and more people wanting to visit natural and environmentally significant areas. Last year more than 7,000 tourists visited Undara alone, representing a growth of more than about 200 percent during the peak winter period. . . . Mr. Goss also visited the neighbouring Undara Lava Lodge – a low-key, high standard resort operated by local grazier, Mr. Gerry Collins. The national park land was purchased from Mr. Collins. He commended Mr. Collins for recognising and supporting the benefits of the Undara National Park declaration. . . . Mr. Pat Comben said the declaration of the 17,600 hectare park . . . had the full support of the Gulf Local Authorities Development Association. . . . Undara will join the Great Barrier Reef, the Wet Tropics, Lawn Hill and Cape York Peninsula on the priority list of ecotourism destinations in Australia and the world.
>
> (Joint Statement 1992)

The Minister's previous visit to Undara, in April 1992, had inaugurated two important access links between Cairns and Undara: Flight West air tours and Australian Pacific coach tours.

Negotiations regarding the establishment of the national park had not always been smooth. When Gerry Collins first proposed his Lodge, the government responded by proposing a national park. Some doubts naturally arose regarding the impact park status would have on the tourism potential of the area, not to mention the question of public versus private ownership. In the end, an agreement was reached whereby the lands for the national park were deeded to the state in return for 'sole commercial operator' status for a ten-year period being assigned to Undara Experience Pty Ltd. The Department of Environment and Heritage administers the park, while only parties under the supervision of trained and licensed

Savannah Guides obtain access. In its press release of 8 April 1993, the Department said:

> The combination of Undara Experience and the Department of Environment and Heritage provides not only a high level of protection for its significant natural features but also a sophisticated tourist experience tailored to the particular environment . . . . The Department is committed to the concept of ecotourism in all its forms and considers the tourist programme offered by Undara Experience to be an excellent example of the interlinking of natural resource conservation and private sector business.

Financial issues: investment and attraction development

The total investment to date has reached A$2 million. Capital development has been accomplished without debt, owing to investment support and injections of capital from the parent company, Collins Brothers; Dutana Pty Ltd, the operating company; Undara Pty Ltd; and the actual service provider on the ground, Undara Experience. The mix of investment by the parent company (which has been based on cattle stations, real estate, transport and now tourism) has provided solidity. However, the operating costs of Undara Experience (Dutana Pty Ltd) have exceeded income from its inception and a change in strategy is required to generate increased income.

A new business plan in 1995 was aimed at increasing the average length of stay from one day or night to three nights (details are described under 'Problems, prospects and future planning', pp. 156–9.). This also involves a shift in accounting practices from a pastoral-based system to one more attuned to the exigencies of operating a seasonal resort (the current profile of Undara Lodge is outlined in Table 8.2).

Management issues associated with the Undara Project

Organizational Structure

Undara Experience is owned and operated as a family business, with three Collins brothers constituting the Board of Directors. Policy guidelines are set by the Board, and specific issues are also handled by them. One director, Gerry Collins, works hands-on with the professional Operations Manager at the Resort. The other partners tend to stay in the background. Headquarters are located on site, but the marketing function is located in Cairns and accounts in Townsville.

Working relations with the National Park

When it was established, Undara Volcanic National Park was given a twelve-member advisory committee comprising people from the local area, local authority, the Queensland Tourist and Travel Corporation,

Table 8.2 Profile of Undara Lava Lodge, 1996

Facilities
- accommodation (see below)
- dining facility and bar (see below)
- toilet facilities for camping areas
- reading car with reference material
- meeting lodge (completed 1994)
- shop (completed 1994)
- offices
- staff quarters
- workshops
- petrol
- telephones
- ice machine
- bush-breakfast area
- bush-lunch areas
- tour minibuses
- self-guided walking trails
- airstrip (length 1900 m, gravel)

Accommodation
- 14 restored railway sleeper cars; 25 rooms each with double bed (capacity 54 persons); each car has a toilet/shower shared among two units; the cars are interconnected by surrounding platforms and steps; and the collection contains a separate guest laundry car. Price (including three meals): A$96 adult, A$48 child.
- Swag's Tent Village: for the price-conscious traveller, 25 'igloo' tents are permanently mounted on platforms; each is provided with electric lighting and beds with mattresses; a central cooking and washing area is provided; washrooms with hot showers.
  - capacity: approximately 68 persons
  - prices
    tent plus three meals: A$56 adult, A$32 child
    tent only: A$14 adult, A$10 child, A$50 family
- Campground: 13 unserviced pitches; shared cooking and washroom facilities with Swag's Tent Village.
  - capacity approximately 80 persons.
  - prices: A$8 adult, A$4 child, A$19 family;
- Safari Bus Campground: a separate area is reserved for coach parties up to 40 persons.
- Caravan sites: up to 11 sites unserviced; shared facilities with Swag's tent village. A$10 per caravan or rental van.

Dining
Fettler's Bistro consists of two dining carriages plus a covered outdoor area: Mitchell's Deck Bar area; evening meals are from limited, standardized menus as guests seldom stay longer than two nights; food is described as 'healthy country fare complemented by a comprehensive selection of wine'; breakfast is served in the bush around campfires; tour lunches are served picnic-style in prepared bush sites.

Transport fleet
The resort operates a fleet of vehicles composed of four tour minibuses (capacity 19 each, plus driver/savannah guide), one smaller minibus (capacity 16 plus driver/guide), one four-wheel drive (small, capacity 6) and one Toyota High-ace 4-WD van (capacity 10 plus driver/guide).

Packages available out of Cairns (effective 1994–95)
- 4 days and 3 nights
- 3 days and 2 nights
  – the above include a full-day tour of lava tubes and a second full-day tour of Tallaroo Hot Mineral Springs; all meals
- 2 days and 1 night
- day tours (return coach: A$93; return by air: A$275)

Regular tour prices
- full-day tour (lunch and tea included): $70 adult, $35 child
- half-day tour (lunch included): $52 adult, $26 child
- Budget Tour: A$18 adult, A$12 child, A$50 family

Other tours
- sightseeing by air
- four-wheel-drive safaris

Seasonal Differences: from 1 October to 31 March (summer) only budget and half-day tours are offered.
Scheduled Bus Access: Cairns–Karumba Coachline runs three return trips weekly; Australia Pacific Tours runs trips seven days per week.

Aboriginal interests, Gerry Collins and the lava tube expert Anne Atkinson. A management plan was prepared to establish the operation of guided tours.

The joint management plan for Undara Experience is not particularly detailed and had to be drawn up on inadequate research and incomplete knowledge about impacts. For example, it was not possible to determine carrying capacity for visits to any one particular lava tube. At present the resort operates on a limit of 200 people per day to the park, but that is a self-imposed limit not based on any specific research. There is a concern that Queensland Department of Environment & Heritage (QDEH) could impose its own quota without consultation, although operations to date suggest that 200 per day is a conservative figure.

Management of the park impinges on resort operations to the extent that they are based on different premises. The legislation governing management of parks is based first and foremost upon protection and conservation, with natural values determining management planning responses. The resort, while itself pursuing the same values, must prove a commercial success or fail to be sustainable. While the present relationship with QDEH is reasonably harmonious, there is a lack of communication at times which can be destructive. An example occurred in May 1995 when QDEH, without consulting Undara Experience, applied for a grant to cover construction of concrete stairways, walkways and viewing platforms in the tubes. The first Undara Experience knew of the QDEH plan was when a bemused Gerry Collins was congratulated by the Minister for Tourism on being the recipient of A$80,000 under the Federal Government's Sites of National Significance Programme.

Uncertainty remains about the continuation of the exclusivity agreement which expires in 1997. Because of the Collins's landholdings another development could not occur near to the lava tubes, but other tour companies could gain access to the park.

Environmental practices

Ecologically sustainable development principles govern operations in the management of Undara Lava Lodge, and this fact is mentioned in promotional materials as 'Undara's environmental management plan'. Undara Experience contributes to the conservation of habitat and of sites which may be affected by tourism, and ensures that environmental assessment becomes an integral part of the ongoing operation of the facility. It fosters in both management and staff an awareness of environmental and conservation principles. Undara Experience enhances the appreciation and understanding by tourists of the environment by providing accurate information and appropriate interpretation. It supports the inclusion of professional conservation principles in tourism education, training and planning. These various principles are translated into practice as follows:

- there is a self-imposed daily limit of 200 people in the lava tubes (only seven caves are readily accessible), with tour groups limited in size to 20 people (including guides);
- no self-drive is permitted in the national park to the tube entrances – transport is only by minibus (or, if the group consists of fewer than five, by four-wheel drive);
- all visits to the tubes are controlled by the Savannah Guides, to ensure accuracy of information and minimization of inappropriate behaviour – not permitted are shouting, souvenir-taking, floodlighting the colonies of bats festooned from the ceilings of the tubes, and independent exploration;
- the main 'nursery' cave of the bats (Barker's tube) is closed for several months each year during the breeding season, when as many as 100,000 bats may inhabit the 905 m-long tunnel;
- most recently, hardened stairs have been constructed to provide secure access to the tubes, and some boardwalks within the tubes to reduce physical impacts;
- septic sewage systems have been installed, which process sewage so that (at least in theory) water of drinkable quality only is discharged;
- garbage and other wastes are disposed of in rock-lined areas well above the water table to minimize any degradation;
- an active re-vegetation scheme has been set up in degraded areas and all cattle have been removed from the area of operations;
- no horseback tours to the lava tubes are permitted because of the Australia-wide policy of removing all non-native species from national parks – the horse has been identified as a particular problem because exotic species of plants may be introduced into areas of pristine native vegetation through their droppings, and their hard hooves cause erosion;
- natural materials are used wherever possible in resort construction – e.g. most of the paths and roads are of compressed 'anthill' clay, and signage consists of carved timber beams and boards set between pillars of local stone;
- there is strong support for the Savannah Guides Association and a high quality of professional training and interpretation – for example, visi-

tors are provided with a booklet called *The Undara Experience* (Jealous, no date), which gives background information on geology, vegetation and wildlife, including a birdwatching checklist.

Staffing

The appointment of a new Operations Manager in early 1995 resulted in a revised approach to staffing. A survey in May 1995 revealed that of 25 staff 13 had been there for less than three months, and 5 had been there for less than eight months; 4 had been there for just over twelve months, 1 for two years, 1 for three years and only 1 for five years. Grounds staff comprised the only section to demonstrate longevity – of 4 staff, 1 had been there for five years, 1 for two years, 1 for seven months and 1 for five months. Of the 6 Savannah Guides stationed at Undara, 4 had been there for more than twelve months (2 for more than three years), and the other 2 had been recruited only four months previously. Originally, a majority of staff were recruited locally and there was less staff turnover. But as the resort expanded and a greater need for professionalism and training became apparent, the area of recruitment expanded. In May 1995 17 staff were not from the surrounding district. The isolation of the resort (the closest township – which has one pub, one cafe and one petrol station – is about 100 km or 1½ hours' drive away) in many ways equates to the isolation experienced on small island resorts, where rapid staff turnover is a continuing problem.

Marketing

Marketing is based in Cairns because it is the major gateway to northern Australia for both international and domestic air travellers. A reservations desk (sales) is located in Cairns as part of the marketing operations, although bookings can also be made through the Townsville (accounts) office and Undara Experience's own reception desk.

Although Cairns has a population of only 100,000 (April 1996) it is currently the fourth busiest airport in Australia, with more than ninety international flights each week. It is also the major destination for car travellers, more than 90 per cent of whom follow the coastal route and so pass 160 km to the east of Undara. The location of the marketing arm of Undara Experience at Cairns facilitates interaction with travel agents, airlines, tour companies and others with whom cross-promotions and cooperative advertising are undertaken. In addition, Cairns is the hub of efforts to promote the Far North Queensland Region, and Undara Experience, as a major attraction in the region, can key into this.

The marketing of Undara Experience is, however, a challenge. This is because there is a general lack of awareness of Undara and ignorance about lava tubes, and so marketing has to be preceded by education. The diversity of the Outback is both a strength and a weakness: a strength because there is a richness to the variety of outback experiences available through Undara, but a weakness because of the difficulty, in marketing terms, of providing a clear focus. Product diversity is also apparent in the market segments which make it difficult to target specific areas – self-drive, package tours, caravanners, campers, and the up-market carriage resort component.

The publication of articles about Undara has helped develop its profile as a unique ecotourism attraction. While these have generally highlighted the lava tubes and related ecosystem (e.g. Hill, 1991; Beeh 1994), the resort offers the only means to gain access to the natural attraction.

Understanding the visitor market: research on visitor patterns

The resort has used a visitor questionnaire since about 1990. However, it provides little information of use to the daily operations of the resort since it does not cover visitor satisfaction. It is mainly concerned with collecting visitor demographics for determining market segmentation, and is therefore analysed and used by the marketing manager.

There is a relative lack of detailed information about many aspects of visits to Undara. The average length of stay at Undara is one day and one night, which constitutes the major demand problem. No detailed per capita breakdown of visitor spending is available, but different segments have different levels of expenditure and the average is much lower than it could be if longer stays could be generated. Also, 60 per cent of visitors take the Budget Tour (1½ hours; price: A$18 adult, A$12 child, A$50 family). Only 20 per cent of guests take the one-day tour with bush barbecue lunch and dinner (price: A$70 adult, A$35 child), and the remaining 20 per cent take the half-day tour (lunch included; price: A$52 adult, A$26 child).

Most visitors (68 per cent), perhaps surprisingly given its remoteness, arrive by self-drive. Fly-in visitors are a small minority (perhaps 2 per cent), and the remainder arrive on tour buses, mostly from Cairns. As to types of visitors, school and youth groups constitute about 20 per cent of guests, and small tour groups (less than ten people) about 10 per cent. Large group tours make up less than 5 per cent of the total visitation.

A range of all-inclusive two-day, three-day and four-day tours are marketed; originally they included flights to and from Cairns (275 km away), accommodation in the railway carriages, guided tours of the lava tubes, all meals, evening campfire and activities; the price ranges from A$228 to A$688. By coach from Cairns the costs range from A$318 to A$518. Self-drive tour packages cost from A$148 to A$318. Day-tours out of Cairns range from A$92 both ways (by coach) to A$275 return(fly). These prices were valid up to 31 March 1996. As of April 1996, the flight packages were discontinued.

Problems, prospects and future planning issues for Undara

The short average length of stay of one day plus one night for about 90 per cent of visitors is a significant problem for the resort. A tour of two to four lava tubes provides most visitors with saturation, and general interest wanes after this time, perhaps because the differences between tubes are subtle. Technical geological explanations about different types of lava flows, as revealed in the slightly different patterns of the tube walls and floors, are of limited general interest and likely to enthral only students of geology. Visitors tend not to stay another day and night to see more lava tubes.

Undara Experience's management is therefore actively exploring alternative activities and attractions in an attempt to retain visitors for a longer period of time. These include:

1 Various ways of utilizing horses for visitor activities. The horse was an integral component of the pioneering effort which opened up the savannah lands for grazing and for droving vast herds of cattle with "drovers' or 'stockmen' (inter-changeable Australian names for 'cowboys'). The Collins family have now bred and used horses on their cattle stations (ranches) in the savannah country for five generations. However, the lava tubes cannot be visited on horseback because of the aforementioned exclusion of horses from national parks. It might be possible to use horses around the resort and the surrounding countryside, outside park boundaries. A recent innovation has been the introduction of a large horse-drawn dray to take people to the bush breakfast. While no visitor satisfaction survey has been undertaken since the introduction of this feature, the Operations Manager reports that it receives almost as many favourable comments as the lava tubes. Certainly guests queue to join the ride (there may be as many as 60 to 70 people for breakfast and most have to walk through the bush, itself a pleasant experience). The dray ride – under gum trees with the early morning sun filtering through the black and white trunks, past the lagoon and its water birds, the horses clip-clopping in front, the dray swaying slightly, kangaroos, wallabies, cockatoos and kookaburras quizzically surveying the dray as it passes, perhaps the thrill of a 2m snake whipping across the trail, and a breakfast of sizzling sausages and bacon at the end of the ride – provides a quintessentially Australian Outback experience that is highly sought after.

2 A small cultural centre/museum, paying tribute to the pioneering days, is to be constructed beyond the bush camp site and it is planned to extend the present limited use of the horses and dray as the mode of transport to the centre. As well as presenting the history of settlement in the district and displays of bush craft, the museum would develop a display of Aboriginal culture. It is anticipated that a visit to the museum would take about two hours and fill a morning or an afternoon.

3 In addition, Undara Experience's management has under consideration the introduction of one-day pony safaris to a natural waterhole about 12 miles from the Lodge. Again, the route would be outside the park boundaries, most of it through an adjoining cattle station. As a day-long activity it would be designed to 'capture' visitors for another night. Other horse-trail rides could also be designed for shorter periods.

4 A swimming pool has been constructed for the main resort, between natural rock walls adjacent to the tented camp site. Additional water supplies have been tapped.

5 Finally, the idea of drought-proofing one of the lagoons (by lining the bottom with clay) is being examined. Except in rare circumstances, the lagoons are seasonal, swiftly drying up after the annual 'Wet' ceases. Huge concentrations of birds are attracted to the water but disappear as the water dries up. A permanent lake would ensure a permanent water-bird population (magpie geese, pelicans, brolgas, herons, cranes, ibis, egrets, ducks and spoonbills). This additional attraction would be capable of 'holding' visitors for another half to one day.

Water resources

The resort has a water supply problem and is actively seeking additional sources. Until a new supply is accessed, the drought-proofing cannot proceed. Nor indeed, can any expansion of accommodation proceed beyond the preparation of several more caravan sites and camp sites. The latter is all that is planned for the foreseeable future.

Consumer resistance

Another characteristic of visitation which concerns the management is that more than 65 per cent of the tours sold are for its Budget Tour, which takes visitors to only two lava tubes. The resort has encountered significant customer resistance to its half-day and one-day tours because of price. At A$70 per adult for the full-day tour, adverse comparisons are drawn with tours through other parks and cave systems where the cost is less than A$25 per person. Comparisons are even made with entrance fees to theme parks like Sea World on the Gold Coast (southern Queensland), where the daily admission price of A$30 provides free rides on all the park's attractions. This is a completely artificial, 'built' environment and most visitors are aware that it cost its present owners more than A$100 million to build. They note this fact in querying why a visit to the lava tubes, where there is no capital cost in their 'construction', should cost two and a half times as much. The cost of support services (highly trained guides, a four-star resort, restaurants, own power generation, transport and services) is not 'visible' in the same way as the theme park facilities.

Operationalizing ecologically sustainable development and ecotourism

In effect, this raises the difficult issues of just how far an operation may go in operationalizing the principles of ecologically sustainable development (which incorporate additional costs to operations which 'cut corners' and do not employ a highly professional guide service), and of how much the visitor is prepared to pay for an experience enhanced by the application of those principles. The argument so often made is that there is a steadily increasing number of environmentally conscious travellers who are prepared to pay more for a true 'eco-experience'. But resorts like Undara Experience are finding it difficult to attract such travellers, which raises the question as to whether such travellers yet exist in sufficient numbers to make a truly ecotourism operation profitable. Management has in fact queried whether there is such a creature as an 'ecotourist'.

Access

Access to the park and resort along the final 20 km stretch of unsealed road is an increasing problem. The condition of the road draws more complaints by a factor of 100 than any other aspect of the Undara Experience. The maintenance of the road is the responsibility of Elthridge Shire Council, but the condition has deteriorated rapidly under the impact of greatly increased vehicle numbers since the early 1990s. Initially it was considered that the unsealed road was part of the outback experience; but it is proving a deterrent to visitors, and in any case the unformed tracks through the bush to the lava tubes by the resort buses and jeeps provide the same experience without risk to visitors' vehicles. Sealing the road is now seen as an option to be pursued.

Research

Discussions with management revealed a number of needs which could be met by a series of small research projects. These included the following:

- reinterpretation of the existing collection of visitor questionnaires and redesign of both the registration forms and visitor questionnaires for marketing and resort operations needs;
- measurement of visitor satisfaction levels with the current range of facilities and tours;
- a detailed survey of all potential attractions and activities in the property/national park, as the basis for forward development and planning;
- an impact assessment on lava tube visit numbers with the objective of setting carrying capacity;
- a review of current marketing strategy;
- a survey of backpacker interest, leading to target marketing;
- an independent review of guide interpretation and guiding;
- a transport survey regarding access and attraction capabilities;
- a strategy for the development of the heritage centre, focusing on pioneer history (interpretation), greater Aboriginal culture presentation and bush craft;
- a survey of the potential of agri-tourism out of Undara;
- design of a cost centre system.

The selection of an appropriate computerized system to maintain records for bookings, accounts, staff wages, stores inventories and visit numbers was installed after due research.

CONCLUSIONS

The Undara Experience is an innovative rural tourism development based on a unique natural resource. It demonstrates many of the opportunities and challenges facing rural tourism enterprises in general and ecotourism in particular. Such projects must be subjected to stringent environmental protection or enhancement criteria as well as achieving sustainable rates of return on investment.

Undara's natural attraction was revealed to be unique and highly appealing, but insufficient to generate adequate lengths of stay and visitor spending. To be economically successful the owners must develop additional attractions and infrastructure, all at great personal cost, and increasingly emphasizing the outback experience in addition to ecotourism. The alternative, from an environmental perspective, might be to rely purely on the national park status to attract visitors and to avoid permanent accommodation or resort-like development. This would have the effect of minimizing visitor numbers, especially given the remoteness of the site, and would fail to achieve explicit public goals for developing rural tourism potential. Also, in this particular case the creation of the park was tied to the land owner's tourism development plans.

The tension between environmental goals and economic realities as demonstrated by the Undara Experience case is likely to become commonplace in many rural, and especially remote, areas. Some form of public–private partnership might be required to ensure that developers who value principles of sustainable development can also manage profitable ventures. Without such arrangements there are very real risks of either economic failure or environmental degradation.

REFERENCES

Atkinson, A. (1991) *The Lava Tubes of the Undara Volcano: Far North Queensland*, Australia: published by the author.

Beeh, P. (1994) 'Tunnels to a wildlife underworld', *Geo Australasia* 16(4): 68–80.

Berle, P. (1990) 'Two faces of ecotourism', *Audobon* 92(2): 6.

Commonwealth Department of Tourism (1992) *Tourism Australia's Passport to Growth: A National Tourism Strategy*, Canberra: Commonwealth Department of Tourism.

—— (1994a) *National EcoTourism Strategy*, Canberra: Commonwealth Department of Tourism.

—— (1994b) *Rural Tourism Strategy*, Canberra: Commonwealth Department of Tourism.

Hall, C. M. (1995) *Introduction to Tourism in Australia: Impacts, Planning and Development*, 2nd edn, Melbourne: Longman Cheshire.

Hall, C. M. and McArthur, S. (eds)(1996) *Heritage Management in Australia and New Zealand: The Human Dimension*, Melbourne: Oxford University Press.

Hill, C. (1991) 'The legacy of Undara's rage', *Australian Geographic* 22 (June): 51–57.

Jealous, V. (no date) *The Undara Experience* (booklet).

Jenkins, J. (1996) 'Commonwealth government involvement in rural tourism and regional development', in C. M. Hall, J. Jenkins and G. Kearsley (eds) *Tourism Policy and Planning in Australia and New Zealand*, Melbourne: Irwin.

Joint Statement by Mr. Wayne Goss, Premier of Queensland, and Mr. Pat Comben, Minister for Environment and Heritage (1992) *Undara National Park to Add to Booming Eco-tourism* (9 August), Brisbane.

Queensland Department of Environment & Heritage (1993) *What's So Special About Undara?* (8 April), Cairns.

Romeril, M. (1989) 'Tourism: the environmental dimension', in C. Cooper and A. Lockwood (eds) *Progress in Tourism, Hospitality and Recreation Management*, vol. 1, London: Belhaven.

Savannah Guides (no date) *Protectors of North Australia's Gulf Savannah* (brochure).

Statement by Environment and Heritage Minister Pat Comben (1992) *Minister Promotes Ecotourism at Undara Lava Tubes* (11 April), Brisbane.

Valentine, P. (1992) 'Review: nature-based tourism', in B. Weiler and C. M. Hall (eds) *Special Interest Tourism*, London: Belhaven.

9 Rural tourism in New Zealand: rafting in the Rangitikei at River Valley Ventures

C. Ryan

INTRODUCTION

The main component of this chapter is an analysis of the problems and strategies of a rural adventure tourism operator located in the Rangitikei District on New Zealand's North Island. However, in order to understand the situation in which the operators, Brian and Nicola Megaw, found themselves, it is necessary to establish a context. The description thus moves from macro to micro considerations, starting with a brief description of tourism, first, in New Zealand, and then, second, in the Rangitikei. If any area offers the quintessential New Zealand that is sold through the brochures, then that location is the Rangitikei, a rural area on the North Island, New Zealand. Its advertising slogan 'The Undiscovered Secret' is well merited, as many thousands of tourists travel through it without stopping. Hence, for rural operators such as the Megaws, there is both the opportunity and the problem of being located in an area peripheral to the main centres of tourism in New Zealand. Having established this framework, the study finally concentrates on the product, marketing and operations of River Valley Ventures.

THE GREEN IMAGE OF A TOURIST DESTINATION: IMPLICATIONS FOR RURAL TOURISM

The overseas promotion of New Zealand by the New Zealand Tourism Board is one of a fresh, green, and unspoilt environment – a land of rural scenic splendour, fresh air and an exciting outdoors that can appeal to both the 'soft' and 'hard' adventurer. Add to this the appeal of a Maori culture unique to New Zealand, an opportunity to share a *haka* or watch a *poi* dance, and the ingredients are present for a unique tourist experience. Like many countries, New Zealand can boast of increased numbers of overseas tourists and a growing industry based upon increased visitor expenditure, but the question to be asked is how much of the tourists' experiences of New Zealand involve interaction with the 'rurality' implied by the green images – or is the countryside simply a backdrop, as is suggested by Oppermannn (1996) in his study of German farm tourism.

As Page and Getz note in chapter 1, to define 'rural tourism' requires considerations of place, economic structures, images, and the interactions of tourist and host with the image of 'rurality'. It is thus impossible to gauge from official statistics whether those holidaying in New Zealand interact with a reality of 'greenness'. Nonetheless, the available statistics do indicate that 'farm tourism' is not without importance. Data derived from the New Zealand Tourism Board (NZTB) indicates that in 1993, 3 per cent of all overseas visitor nights were spent in farm-stays, home-stays and historic homes (i.e. about 600,000 nights). Obviously many hotels and motels are located in rural locations, but the data base does not currently permit an analysis by type of location. Rural-based activities are of importance too. NZTB (1994) data reveal that:

- over 300,000 of New Zealand's 1.3 million overseas visitors in 1993 took a 'short bush walk' of less than half a day;
- 300,000 went on a scenic boat cruise;
- 45,000 went fresh-water fishing;
- 40,000 went tramping;
- 300,000 went to a farm show;
- over 550,000 visited a national, forest or maritime park.

Data on New Zealand's domestic tourists are currently less exhaustive, but current projects on domestic tourism being undertaken at Lincoln University, Canterbury, and Auckland University, New Zealand, reveal high levels of use of New Zealand's non-urban resources for leisure and tourist activities.

What has been shown by a number of researchers (e.g. Oppermann 1994; Pearce 1995; Ryan 1995) who have re-examined NZTB data is that distinctive spatial patterns exist for different groups of tourists. Currently much of the analysis has been based upon nationalities, as shown in Figures 9.1 and 9.2. Here, Oppermann (1994) indicated the flows of German visitors using escorted tours in New Zealand. Using the same data set, in a separate study Ryan (1995) reported that while an area like the Coromandel attracted only 8 per cent of overseas visitors, 48 per cent of German visitors went to the Coromandel, and Germans thus accounted for 28 per cent of all overseas visitors in that area. These spatial patterns and differing use by nationality of rural and urban districts of New Zealand can be explained in part by the differing tour characteristics of the nationalities. Up until 1996 more Germans than, for example, Taiwanese or Koreans go backpacking. The latter are more likely to go on escorted coach tours than Germans, Australians, Britons or Americans in New Zealand. Familiarity with English and with travel is also a factor. Additionally, research undertaken on behalf of the NZTB (1995) which involved focus groups of Asian tourists revealed that for some Asian

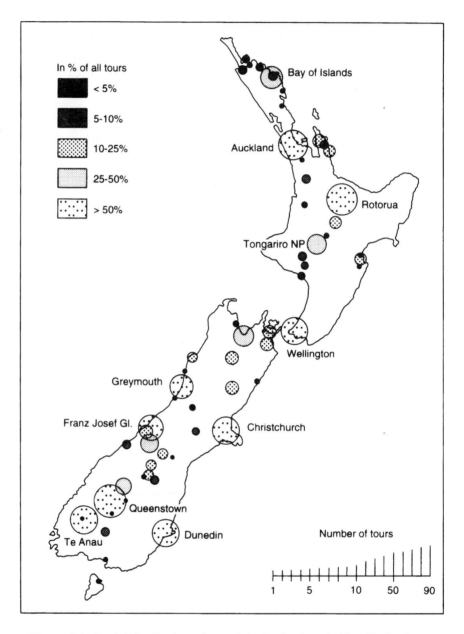

Figure 9.1 Spatial distribution of overnight destinations in New Zealand.

visitors their own highly intensive urban lifestyles with little contact with open spaces meant that the countryside is not only an attraction, but also a challenge. For example, Asians reported as their highlights 'hugging sheep, feeding lambs, watching sheep shearing and watching the dogs working' (NZTB 1995:18). Yet there was also a vague sense of uncertainty on the part of some respondents. For example, the report comments that:

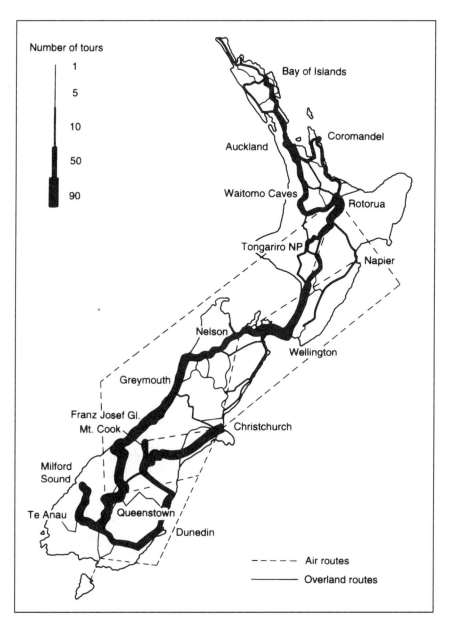

Figure 9.2 German escorted package tour flows in New Zealand.

interpreters/guides need to tell them what to expect before the [farm] stay, in order to reduce their anxiety. . . . Full communication of what an activity entails, as well as instruction or guidance usually provide a reassurance of safety, e.g., with a snow activity parents should be reassured that warm clothing will be provided so that the children will not get cold.

(NZTB 1995:19 and 40).

From these statements, it can be concluded that the differences identified between the nationalities as to their use of the rural tourism product may be explained by other interacting variables such as age, interest, levels of urbanization and past travel experiences, as well as simply by nationality and culture.

The potential importance of tourism to rural communities in New Zealand has been identified by Pomeroy (1996). She notes that from accounting for 80 per cent of exports in 1974, land-based products now provide New Zealand with 45 per cent of export income. While New Zealand exports have grown and diversified, the agricultural and forestry sectors have become relatively less important, and less financially secure for small farmers. The proportion of New Zealand's population living in rural areas dropped from 43 per cent in 1976 to 39.6 per cent in 1991 (Ministry of Agriculture and Forestry 1990). Additionally, from a sample of 619 farms, it would appear that 75 per cent of farms relied, in varying degrees, on off-farm income. The 'green image' of New Zealand, as promoted to tourists, is thus a resource of growing economic importance as part of rural diversification strategies aimed at generating revenue. Tourists jostle with deer, emu, llamas, ostriches and other exotica as a means of maintaining farm incomes. But rural tourism is not solely farm tourism. New Zealand offers many eco- and adventure tourism products within rural locations that are characterized by small communities, a lifestyle still based upon agriculture and forestry, and networks of local people. As Lane noted, rural tourism is multi-faceted, based upon special interest, adventure, heritage, and art-based activities (Lane 1994: 9). In spite of its geographical isolation, New Zealand is not so unique as not to share in the problems of a modern world, whether these problems are social, economic or political. Likewise, New Zealand suffers from threats to its green image. In 1993 the Department of Conservation (DOC), in its brief to the incoming Government, wrote of the challenge of increasing tourist numbers thus:

> overseas visitors may not find the predicted level of tourism acceptable from a social perspective because of crowding, particularly at huts and campsites. There is certainly a great deal of concern among traditional New Zealand users of the back-country over the level of contact with other users which will occur and the diminishment of the sense of isolation. . . . We must ensure that the clean, green image is matched by reality, or New Zealand's credibility with potential visitors will be destroyed.
>
> (Department of Conservation 1993: 21–2)

The challenge comes not only from the increased numbers of tourists. As an island, New Zealand developed a flora very susceptible to damage by imported predators, and the Ministry of Agriculture and Forestry (MAF) and DOC continually combat the ravages of insects and mammals such as opossum. DOC drops pellets of the chemical 1080 (sodium monofluoacetate) from helicopters or laces carrots with the chemical to rid areas of the ravages of the estimated 60 million opossums which devour the cabbage tree, rata and other trees of New Zealand. Agricultural practices also threaten the land. There is a high use of pesticides and herbicides as well as fertilizers, with consequent impacts upon water quality. Concern has also been expressed about agri-chemicals once perceived as safe (e.g. MAF 1990; Watts 1993). An increasing awareness of the problems that threaten the dollars that tourism brings to New Zealand is certainly present, as was clearly demonstrated in evidence provided to the Select Committee Review of the performance of the New Zealand Tourism Board in 1994. Mechanisms are being put into place to protect, sustain and, where possible, restore the environment. Most notable among these measures is the Resource Management Act (1991) (see Page and Thorn 1997), which in effect enables territorial authorities to require Environmental Impact Assessments for 'significant' developments. However, even these measures are criticized from both sides of the debate. For pressure groups such as the Royal Society of Forests and Birds, the measures are insufficient. On the other hand, for example, the New Zealand Tourism Board noted criticism of the way in which the Act is implemented for inhibiting capital investment in New Zealand's tourism industry. Thus the Board noted:

> from a tourism perspective, the frustrations faced by some developers and investors are occurring at a bad time. . . . The New Zealand Tourism Board (NZTB) has sensed a reluctance by Asian investors, in particular, to subject themselves to a planning process where the time-frame, costs, and outcomes are effectively outside their control.
>
> (NZTB 1994b: 6)

Hence, behind the scenic views that are used to promote New Zealand, considerable care, effort and often contentious debate characterizes policies that relate to the land and rural areas. New Zealand is no manicured land, but still possesses true wilderness, which is both an opportunity and a concern for tourism development.

At the time of writing, it might be said there is no policy for rural tourism in New Zealand. In part this arises from the 'user pays' policies of the National Party in government – a conservative party with a belief in the marketplace and hence one that does not address issues through national planning strategies in ways understood by parties with more interventionist policies. However, under the 1987 Conservation Act, DOC has as its responsibilities:

> [to] manage for conservation purposes all land, and all other natural and historic resources held under this Act [and]. . . to the extent that the use of any natural or historic resource for recreation or tourism is not inconsistent with its conservation, to foster the use of natural and historic resources for recreation, and to allow their use for tourism.
>
> (NZTB 1993: 1)

Thus DOC has direct responsibility for 30 per cent of the land area of New Zealand, and an influence over policies in other areas through the Resource Management Act (1991). As a result policies are being framed with implications for rural and outdoor areas – notably bush walks, as evidenced by the 1993 report on the Conservation Estate and International Tourism (NZTB 1993). Various bodies also exist to promote rural tourism, including New Zealand Farm and Home Host, Inc., an association of farms and other rural homes providing home-stay tourism.

WHITE WATER RAFTING IN NEW ZEALAND

Much of this debate may appear removed from the concerns of individual operators of white water and scenic rafting, especially of the smaller rural operators. But such appearances would be misleading, as will become evident in the case which is detailed below. White water rafting has featured strongly in the promotion of New Zealand, as representing the images of fun, excitement and the outdoors (see Figure 9.3). The number of overseas tourists who take a raft trip is estimated at over 80,000 a year (NZTB 1994a), which represents two-thirds of the total number carried by rafting companies. The major part of the market is based in the South Island, notably around the tourism honeypot of Queenstown, with major operators like Danes being based on the Shotover River, which is also home to New Zealand's leading jet boat company, the Shotover Jet. In 1994 the number of people carried by rafts was estimated by the Adventure Tourism Council at approximately 120,000, of whom about 45 per cent went rafting in the Shotover area. This means there is a significant skew in the statistics relating to the distribution of the the overseas market. On the Shotover there is a very high dependency on overseas visitors, whereas in areas such as the Rangitikei the business is more reliant upon the domestic market. However, there is a paucity of statistics on rafting operations in New Zealand. The International Visitor Survey (IVS) only incorporated a question about rafting in 1993, and no questioning was undertaken in 1994. The Adventure Tourism Council is currently unable to undertake much research because of a scarcity of resources, and in 1995 was more concerned with establishing industry safety procedures, although in 1995 it released a report based on market research into the motivations of its clientele.

Rafting is not a homogenous product, as is illustrated by the activities of River Valley Ventures, an operator based on the Rangitikei River some 27 km northeast of Taihape in the North Island New Zealand. Rapids on the river are graded in difficulty (see Table 9.1) from a gentle float to the very difficult, a grade 5, (and a further grade 6, beyond the reach of tourists) which in the words of the River Valley Ventures brochure is 'adrenalin pumping stuff' on a river described as being at times 'aggressive and challenging'. The grading of rivers is based on factors such as the flow of water, drop in gradient, nature of terrain and length of rapids. Further, fluctuations in water level due to rain can significantly change the nature of the rapids. Rides that are thrilling may become so dangerous that companies will have to reschedule or abort rides. Hence, responsible companies continually monitor water levels and have established their own measuring marks, which will be carefully checked during the day. Unfor-

Figure 9.3 White water rafting on the Rangitikei, New Zealand (courtesy of River Valley Ventures Limited).

Table 9.1 A grading of rapids for rafting operations

Grade	Description
1	Slow-moving lowland rivers. Rapids usually consist of riffles over shallows and the occasional boulder bank requiring some manoeuvring to pick a way through. Scarcely any white-water.
2	Waves breaking white but without obstacles, so does not require a great degree of boat-handling skills.
3	Requires precise boat handling. Generally technical boating with obstacles being either rocks, logs or stopper waves.
4	Big water, holes and hydraulics. The route through the rapid will be complex.
5	Big water where a swim could be hazardous. Difficult hydraulics that may hold a river craft. These rapids will generally have areas of extreme hazard which must be avoided, but with a logical route through the hazard.
6	Big water where a swim is potentially fatal. Most rapids will be extremely confused with no logical route through. Hazards will be frequent and extremely difficult to avoid.

Note: Problems exist with the grading system, which is always a topic of debate. Grades 4+ or 5− are being introduced. Also, as skill levels and equipment improve, a large number of rapids previously considered as unrunnable are now run more often. Some operators believe a more open system of grading akin to that used in rock climbing might be more appropriate. Additionally, water conditions can affect the difficulty of any given rapid.

tunately in the summer of 1994/95 problems occurred on the Shotover River, where, possibly, companies had not taken due cognizance of the problems of the proximity of rafts. The result was the death of two tourists in two separate incidents, and reports were filed of further accidents when two other tourists were washed down the river for over 100 m and, who, in consequence, suffered fractures. Concerns over safety have to be paramount. However, paradoxically the good safety record in itself poses a problem. Brian Megaw of River Valley Ventures comments that 'although we brief passengers as to the dangers involved in white water rafting, it is obvious that at least some do not perceive the dangers to be real'. Possibly some passengers view white water rafting as being something akin to a white knuckle ride at a theme park; that is, there is an adrenalin rush caused by a perception of danger, but that perception is not real because the ride is engineered to be safe. White water rafters are quick to point out that the rivers are not safely engineered environments and that the potential for accidents always exists no matter how careful they may be.

At the other extreme, the raft trip where passengers drift down a river, carried by the flow of the water over quiet stretches, offers another form of rewarding experience. Tourists are able to observe countryside and wildlife not otherwise seen, and to experience a sense of isolation and peace. Within these extremes of a continuum, other rafting products can also be offered (some of these are described below on pp. 175–83).

From a conceptual viewpoint the visitor experience can be analysed in terms of perceived risk and competence. In Figure 9.4, following Priest and Bunting (1993), the 'peak adventure' occurs when there is a balance between risk and competence. If the level of risk is above the individual's competence, then 'misadventure' can occur, and an even greater imbalance of risk and competence can lead to 'devastation and disaster'. At the other end of the scale, where the level of risk is low and within the competence of the participant, then a period of exploration and experimentation occurs where the 'paddler' learns about the responsiveness of the raft to paddling effort. Exposing the participants to more risk leads them to experience greater levels of 'adventure'.

Priest and Bunting's model was derived from white water canoeing, but in rafting there is another factor to be considered, and that is the skill of the guide. Most participants are inexperienced, and hence would be low on the competency scale. If the distance between the radii are interpreted as also meaning the increased probability of an event happening at any given skill level, then the incompetent rafter has only a small probability of sustaining a sense of 'peak adventure'. The ability to move significantly up the risk scale with only comparatively small movements to the right of the competency scale of the individual rafter thus depends upon the skill of the guide. Hence, in Figure 9.4, assuming no improvement in competency, movement to the peak adventure experience along the line *AB* is

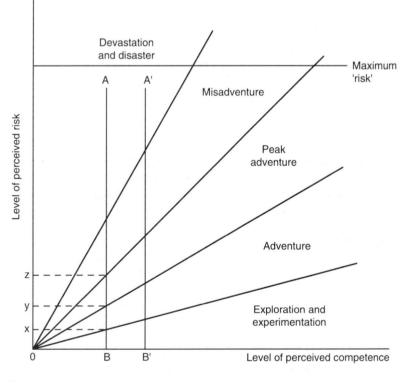

Figure 9.4 The rafting experience and the guides' role.

primarily in the hands of the guide. It is the guide's skill which permits the incompetent rafter to experience 'peak adventure' between risk levels Oy and Oz, where the distance zy represents the probability of peak experience at individual skill level OB. The guide is also able to select conditions that permit the inexperienced rafters to experiment safely at risk levels of Ox and less. The good guide, or rafting operation, might also be able to obtain some movement to the right of line AB to $A'B'$ within the time available, thereby again increasing the possibility of peak adventure and minimizing the range where risks exceed competence. Thus, any rafting operator must also take into account the training and retention of good guides.

THE RANGITIKEI: CHARACTERISTICS OF A RURAL TOURISM REGION

Rafting is thus a significant attraction within the portfolio of tourist assets that a rural area can offer. In New Zealand it is worth possibly NZ$8.7 million (Megaw, personal communication), although no real estimates exist. It is an attraction which can exist near to urban areas, in that a main determinant is the nature of the river. However, within New Zealand it is primarily seen as a rural-based activity, and it is in this context that the rest of this chapter discusses the way the product can be developed, and the advantages and disadvantages that accrue from being located in a rural area.

River Valley Ventures is based in the Rangitikei, which itself has many of the features of a rural area responding to the opportunities posed by tourism. It is located in the North Island of New Zealand, south of one the country's major tourist areas based upon Lake Taupo, a lake of over 600 sq. km. Running through the area is State Highway 1, the main road which runs through New Zealand in a north–south direction, and which links Auckland to Wellington.

Many independent travelling tourists using camper vans and hire cars, as well as coach-borne visitors, will use this route through the Rangitikei. New Zealand Transit (1994) figures show an average daily road usage rate of over 4,000 vehicles at Mangaweka, which is located within the heart of Rangitikei. During the summer months of December to February, this figure might be twice as high.

But while many tourists travel through the region, comparatively few stay. The Rangitikei possesses all the problems of a rural area sited between two major tourist honeypots. To the north lies Rotorua, with its bubbling mud pools and Maori culture, and Lake Taupo, with its large lake. Four hours' drive south from Taupo is Wellington, the country's capital and the location of the inter-island ferries that take tourists across the Cook Straits to the Southern Alps and other attractions of the South Island. The Rangitikei is part of the Manawatu-Whanganui Region, and in 1994 it was estimated that visitor spending in this region was NZ$180 million (Ryan 1994). Of this, approximately one-third was from overseas visitors (Ryan

1994). However, the region contains a national park, the Wanganui National Park, and, in Palmerston North, a major conference and sporting centre. It is difficult to estimate with any confidence the actual numbers of visitors, but since September 1994 a visitor monitoring survey has been established on a monthly basis. This not only covers accommodation providers, but also includes a telephone survey of residents to obtain information on the visiting friends and relatives (VFR) market. The results of this survey show that approximately 65,000 visitor bednights occurred in the Rangitikei in 1994/95. The average stay was 1.8 nights, and overseas visitors accounted for approximately 10 per cent of the total. However, there is a marked seasonality with overseas visitors, with the market share of such visitors being approximately 7 per cent in the off-season winter months and as high as 16 per cent in the summer peak.

Yet as an area the Rangitikei meets many of the expectations of overseas tourists to New Zealand. The International Visitors Survey (NZTB 1994a) indicates that the most popular activities undertaken by overseas tourists include visiting museums, going on short bush walks, jetboating, scenic flights and rafting. The Rangitikei provides opportunities for all of these activities. When surveyed, members of the Rangitikei Tourism Association identified the unique characteristics of the Rangitikei as being garden visits, spectacular scenery, white water rafting, fishing, peace and quiet, jet boating and bungy jumping, as shown in Table 9.2 (Getz and Ryan 1994). It will be noted that the Rangitikei's rural nature is foremost in such a listing. The area is known throughout New Zealand for its rhododendron and other gardens, and a number of large gardens are open to the public. It possesses spectacular scenery, of which few are aware when travelling east of State Highway 1. Indeed, in one location a deep gorge lies only 40 m from the highway, but probably few motorists are aware of it. It offers, in places like Woodleigh Farm, historic homes of great charm and character which are open to the public. Until the mid-1990s the area was not promoted, and it is comparatively unknown even to New Zealanders. The Rangitikei Tourism Association has therefore taken advantage of this relative obscurity to promote the area as 'The Undiscovered Secret'.

In addition to its rural and scenic charms, the area is unique within New Zealand for a strong military presence in the north and south of its district. In the north is the army base at Waiorou, complete with a major military museum, whereas in the south, at Ohakea, lies the New Zealand Air Force base, also with an aviation museum. To the west of the army exercise areas, near the Desert Road, lie the winter ski field areas of Turoa and Whakapapa, located in the Tongariro National Park. Although it is not in the Rangitikei, the park is a source of business for retail and accommodation units in the north of the district. The region also possesses fine golf courses, including one with a lift down a cliffside to reach holes that lie by the side of the river. The identifying theme of the district, however, is the Rangitikei River. It is this and its feeder streams that provide the context for fishing, jet boating and rafting, and it is also responsible in part for the spectacular scenery as the river has cut deep gorges through the limestone hills.

Table 9.2 Measurement of uniqueness: perceptions of the Rangitikei

Items	Compared to New Zealand			Compared to Rest of World		
	Mean	StD	Rank	Mean	StD	Rank
Garden visits	6.81	2.81	1	7.16	2.71	1
Spectacular scenery	6.63	3.06	2	6.84	2.91	6
White water rafting	6.61	2.69	3	6.53	2.70	9
Fishing	6.59	2.82	4	6.69	2.80	8
Peace and quiet	6.25	2.48	5	7.06	2.59	2
Jet boating	6.19	2.66	6	7.03	2.75	4
Bungy jumping	6.12	2.37	7	7.00	2.58	6
A wild river	6.11	3.00	8	6.07	3.11	11
Farm/home-stays	6.06	2.32	9	6.84	2.53	7
Rural lifestyle	5.97	2.64	10	7.06	2.42	2
Wilderness lodges	5.87	2.68	11	6.10	2.82	10
Tramping	5.72	2.49	12	6.06	2.61	12
Military presence	5.65	3.08	13	4.12	3.27	25
Volcanoes	5.41	3.66	14	4.86	3.47	20
Skiing	5.19	3.46	15	5.04	3.22	19
Museums/heritage	5.13	2.50	16	5.22	2.73	18
Small communities	5.13	2.60	17	5.33	2.67	17
Remote/wilderness	5.03	3.16	18	5.55	3.09	14
Festivals/events	4.97	2.79	19	4.66	2.94	21
Hunting	4.69	2.88	20	5.34	2.91	16
The railway	4.57	2.75	21	4.21	2.76	24
Interesting buildings	4.53	2.99	22	4.23	3.10	23
Native forests	4.45	2.64	23	5.39	2.90	15
Climate	4.04	3.32	24	4.24	3.19	22
Arts and crafts	3.47	2.51	25	3.67	2.40	26
Maori culture	2.97	2.46	26	5.75	3.59	13
Logging	2.04	1.79	27	2.32	2.44	27

Source: adapted from Getz and Ryan (1994).

Rafting in the Rangitikei

River Valley Ventures is not the only rafting company in the Rangitikei. At least two other operators exist, of which only one is of notable size. River Valley Lodge carried about 2,000 passengers on its rafts in 1994, compared to the approximately 800 carried by Rangitikei River Adventures. However, the latter company has no provision for accommodation and is a much more diverse business. John Eames, its owner, is currently developing a bigger bungy jump than that he currently operates, but faces many problems in developing an adventure product within a secondary tourist area with little accommodation near to his operation. The economic viability of Rangitikei River Adventure is underwritten by petrol and forecourt sales from a petrol station at Mangaweka which is heavily used because of its distinguishing feature of the 'cafe in a plane'. Most New Zealanders will know of Mangaweka, a small community of little more than 100 houses, because of the DC3 aircraft parked by the road. Previously a crop-spraying aircraft, it has for many years acted as a restaurant, serving teas, pies and soft drinks to New Zealanders and tourists alike as they travel down Highway 1.

The third operator based in the district is located at Flat Hills. Founded over a decade ago by Hilton Davis, this location will be known to many coach travellers, for it is a favoured stop for refreshments and use of toilets on State Highway 1 from Wellington to Auckland (see Figure 9.4). Flat Hills is a professionally run business that can serve a coachload of fifty passengers in 12 minutes – a feature much liked by coach drivers seeking to maintain schedules. Additionally, it stands in isolation, so passengers are not drawn to window-shopping down a street. Flat Hills offers some rafting and jet boating, but these are now very much secondary to its main business as a restaurant. However, in a new development that opened in 1995 in the paddock behind the restaurant, a 10-minute jet boat ride operates in a specially constructed small, shallow lake, which gives a thrill and a photo opportunity to coach passengers, while still allowing the coach driver to adhere to timetables. Both this and the other river-based activities are sub contracted through other businesses, notably River Valley Ventures and Rangitikei River Adventure. Other operators also use the Rangitikei River, but these appear to subcontract out or hire equipment from others.

RIVER VALLEY VENTURES: THE DEVELOPMENT OF THE RAFTING BUSINESS

River Valley Ventures was started by Nicola Megaw's parents, Brian and Robin Sage, in 1982. Brian and Robin were farmers and their home was located about 1.5 km from the Rangitikei River. However, the Sage's home was within a valley which allowed access to the river, and the final 1.5 km to the water lay across their land. They thus controlled access to the river, and access at this point by vehicular traffic is still within the control of the Megaws. The family constructed the road and, while they permit others to use it, a small toll is levied. Brian and Robin Sage entered the rafting business after initially providing meals, lunches and refreshments to other operators. In 1982, after purchasing two rafts, they formed their own rafting operation. Brian Megaw had met Nicola while he was a student at Auckland University, but by 1982 he was shearing sheep, bossing a sheep-shearing gang and had little relationship with the business. By then he and Nicola had purchased a house in Taihape and had started a family.

At first the rafting business went well. The location could not have been better for rafting, with some of the best white water rafting facilities in North Island accessible from their base – along a river which is equal in many parts to the more famous South Island locations. From the Mangaohane Bridge there is a 'gentle' introduction for a few kilometres, with a chance to gain confidence over 'Truck Rapids' and the 'Pop Up', after which come a series of rapids and falls, including 'Arch Rapid', 'Max's Drop', 'Dog Leg', 'Blind Canyon', 'Foo Fong Falls', 'Rock Slide' and others in quick succession. In 1987 the Sages decided to expand and provide accommodation. It was in that year that the River Valley Lodge was built, set within trees looking across to a waterfall tumbling down from the cliffs into the river (see Figure 9.5). It offered dormitory-style accommodation plus four double/twin rooms at opposite ends of a mezzanine. At ground level is a large recreational area and kitchen facilities, while outside are shower units and changing facilities. Electricity was provided by a diesel generator.

Unfortunately the budgets which formed the basis of the expansion bore little relationship to the reality of the situation. By 1989, although turnover had increased to NZ$350,000, losses had also accumulated. In 1990 annual operating losses were NZ$40,000, and the company was unable to service its borrowing. The family went through difficult times as creditors sought repayment of loans. Finally, Brian and Robin Sage, after having to sell their farm to repay the most pressing debts, sold the business to Brian and Nicola. Brian persuaded the creditors not to close the business, arguing that the assets were insufficient to meet the debts and that the best chance for repayment was to allow the business to operate under his management. The business had shown its potential to earn revenue, and tourism activity in New Zealand was continuing to grow. Many of the problems had arisen from a lack of proper cost controls and proper accounting and management practices.

As might be appreciated, the decision to take over the business was not one taken lightly. Indeed, Brian and Nicola had already examined the possibility of establishing a sea-kayaking business in the Bay of Islands, and had explored that area, identified locations and drawn up budgets. On the other hand, the threatened bankruptcy of Nicola's parents would have meant the loss of her parent's home and the loss of a business which had shown a potential to earn money. Brian and Nicola thus sold their own house and its 5 acres to raise money to meet the most pressing debts, and for a year juggled with debts, paid cash for everything, introduced proper accounting procedures, saved and scrimped, argued and survived.

Today, with a revenue less than that of 1990, the business has an operating profit, has repaid several outstanding loans, and is in a position to reconsider investment and upgrading of its assets. In 1994 a net profit after provision for tax in excess of NZ$30,000 was made on a turnover of NZ$230,000. This represented an increase in revenue of over 20 per cent on the previous year, but approximately one-third less revenue than in 1990. In short the business has retrenched, ensured debts were paid and permitted future expansion to be planned.

This experience in itself illustrates one problem of rural businesses moving into tourism. Many rural enterprises are based on farming and exist within a network of mutually supporting agricultural businesses. The networks are characterized by few buyer and supplier relationships. For example, sheep may be taken to one abattoir or sold to one meat stock company, and the suppliers of feedstuffs, herbicides and farm equipment are comparatively few in number and may well visit the farmer. There is little need to create advertising materials. In many communities business deals are done with a shake of the hand and paperwork is kept to a minimum. Contracts may be relatively few in number and of comparatively

Figure 9.5 River Valley Ventures lodge (courtesy of River Valley Ventures Limited).

high value. Tourism requires different types of business relationships and culture. The customers are many, and the transactions are often much smaller in value. They are more difficult to reach, and there is a need to advertise and promote the product. There may be intermediaries with whom an entrepreneur has to deal, and who certainly will want to negotiate individual details and prices. The clients will seek individual treatment and may complain. Tourism is a people-oriented business, and the solitude that is often associated with farming may not be the best preparation for such activity. Organizationally, and possibly temperamentally, there are important differences between tourism-based activities and farming. Both require their own sets of skills, but to do both poses different problems. On the other hand, those working on farms are used to working seven days a week, and all hours. But the 'cultural problems' may be exacerbated when tourism grows. What may originally have been perceived as a marginal activity may become the major business, and hence create different demands and a different lifestyle to that originally chosen.

River Valley Ventures – the tourism product

It has already been noted that rafting is not a homogenous product. River Valley Ventures Limited possesses a portfolio of products based upon the river and its accommodation. These include:

1 Outdoor Management Training: accounting for approximately 20 per cent of total business.
2 Day trips: these cover 'wild water' trips, which can be up to six hours' duration from 9.30 a.m. to 3.00 p.m. and 'scenic fun days', which take clients over quieter waters.
3 Multi-day trips, which are of different duration: the three-day River Magic Trip, the three-day Headwater Safari (the difference relates to geographical area and types of rapids covered) and the five-day Headwater Safari. Prices in 1995 ranged from NZ$290 for three days to NZ$695 for five days, which include all equipment, wet suits and other clothing, meals, vehicle and helicopter transport where required, and accommodation.
4 Complementary outdoor activities such as horse trekking, abseiling, kayaking and tramping. These activities are not primary products but are booked by clients staying at the Lodge, and hence are expected to increase as the numbers staying at the Lodge increase.

The one-day and multi-day trips appeal across market segments, and overseas independent tourists currently account for about 10 per cent of the business, tour groups for another 20 per cent, schools (primarily for the scenic fun day product) 30 per cent, with the remainder comprising social groups, clubs, family group bookings and the like.

Their marketing has been through a combination of word of mouth, advertising and serendipiditous contacts. As an example of the last, one of the tour operators with whom River Valley Ventures works is an Australian tour company bringing skiers to the ski fields of Mount Ruapehu, which are approximately two hours away, depending on which field is being used. A director from the company arrived at River Valley as a client and was so thrilled with the product that he now incorporates the rafting as part of his own tour package. However, operational problems exist in this case, in that the clients are usually keen skiers, and thus rafting is seen as an alternative when skiing is not practicable due to low clouds, mist on the mountains, or other similar adverse weather or conditions, such as the recent eruption of Mt Ruapehu. However, those same poor weather conditions can cause problems for rafting, and hence the profitability of the operation can be eroded if poor weather means higher transport costs in getting clients to safe rafting conditions.

Current advertising in magazines is being monitored through 'enquiry pads' and 'trip sheets'. Clients are asked how they found out about the company. Similarly, as part of the safety procedures before a trip, a client's name, address, age and contact phone number are recorded. Clients are again asked how they got to know of the company, and whether they wish their name and address to be recorded on a database so that they may receive circulars in the future. These surveys show that currently only about 8 per cent of clients come because of advertising, yet advertising takes up 80 per cent of the promotional spend. Hence, in 1996 the Megaws were considering abandoning their magazine advertising entirely, or at least cutting it down radically. Their brochure production will increase from 20,000 to 30,000, and more careful targeting of intermediaries will occur. Some of this is taking place through the Rangitikei Tourism Association, which since 1995 is engaging in new marketing initiatives such as being present at Tourism Rendezvous New Zealand (TRENZ). This is an annual tourism trade show where overseas tour companies and incoming operators meet, negotiate and trade with domestic companies. Targeted brochure 'mail-outs' will also occur, and familiarization visits with key intermediaries such as car rental staff, tourist information centre staff and others will also occur. The brochure will also help to locate the Lodge within the Rangitikei and make full use of the attractions of the area, and it is planned to finance the brochure in part by cooperative advertising paid for by other operators with complementary products. Thus, although brochure production will be increased the net cost will be approximately the same.

The current healthy financial position is also permitting a major redevelopment of current accommodation to allow River Valley Ventures to upgrade its market segments while retaining current business. The first stage has already begun, with the diesel generator being relegated to 'standby' duties as the Lodge is being connected to mainline electricity. Also, replanting of areas is being undertaken to screen off working and maintenance areas, and to enhance sightlines from the lodge. The careful planting of trees between the lodge, the new accommodation area and the river will also help direct attention to the very high waterfall on the cliffs opposite the lodge, soften the features of the cliff, and create areas of privacy for clients, while the overall panorama will still be seen from the verandas of the Lodge and new accommodation unit.

The major expense is in upgrading the Lodge and constructing new accommodation to ensure that, in Brian's words, 'River Valley is top of the league', that 'it is high in quality' and 'it will become the place to be'. The Megaws seek to capitalize upon their location, a beautiful river valley, and create a relaxing experience where people enjoy being in that environment. Currently the lodge is being used primarily by school and outdoor management groups. Many of the rafting clients come for the rafting, but not all stay for the accommodation. The business is now at a point where, as noted, it is beginning to attract tour groups. These include some new niche companies appealing to what have been termed 'ecotourists'. Such companies include New Zealand Nature Tours and the German operator Vieten Tours. Currently the present pattern of accommodation poses some problems. The dormitory-style accommodation is appropriate to outdoor management groups and schools, but smaller rooms that sleep two to four are still pertinent for such markets. However, the current number of four such rooms means that River Valley Ventures is unable fully to capitalize upon the accommodation requirements of other market segments. Building such accommodation, with some upgrading, will produce an effective accommodation mix, permitting River Valley Ventures to sustain higher occupancy rates and to offer an enhanced product to their tourists and tour company clients. Hence, instead of rafting and leaving, from 1996 there will be even more incentive for clients to remain, relive and continue a sense of experience by staying and eating at the Lodge.

It was possible that consent to develop the Lodge would have to be obtained under the Resource Management Act. In practice, as most of the development related to an upgrading of existing structures, and the area was being upgraded through new planting, no problems with the local authority materialized. Additionally, it should be noted that for the Megaws compliance with regulations designed to protect a natural environment are not perceived as an imposition, but rather a means of supporting what they, themselves, perceive as being essential for the place within which they live and work.

The upgrading of the Lodge will also allow for easier catering provision and overcome another problem that currently exists when dealing with management team-building groups. The present arrangement means that there are no 'break-out rooms'. The plans are to make the current two dormitories into two conference rooms, which can be better lit through the use of skylights, and the current small bedrooms will become break-out rooms for conference and team-building delegates. River Valley Ventures is already well established in a corporate market with the team-building exercises, and these contacts might allow the Megaws to enter into the small conference market. Current clients for team-building exercises include public-sector bodies such as the New Zealand Police and Department of Conservation, and private-sector companies, including Elders Pastoral and Sunbeam Industries. The upgrading of accommodation will also marginally expand, up to sixty, the numbers that can be hosted, thereby increasing revenue and profitability per employee but still retaining the atmosphere of comparatively small group operations.

One problem is how these different market sectors might be catered for by the same asset base. The traditional tourist pattern of seasonality is a factor in meeting this problem. The corporate market, whether for team-building or conferences, tends to become important outside the main tourism season. However, there is some temporal overlap with the school market. The school market is also more price-sensitive, but the Megaws will still be able to cater for sectors of that market through the provision of camping facilities. The schools market, in their experience, is a growth market, but unfortunately too much dependence upon it would mean the danger of going down-market, while also hindering attempts to maintain a high standard of equipment. This is because of a higher usage rate to achieve any given level of revenue, while schools also tend to be 'hard' on equipment.

The changing role of guides

Part of the upgrading is a change in promotional emphasis as well as a form of product change. A new 'eco-tour' rafting trip is to be introduced, but essentially the same route and equipment will be used as for the current scenic fun trip. What changes is the role of the guide. Instead of 'splash fights' there will be a commentary on history, flora and fauna. Across from the Lodge the land belongs to Maori *iwi* (tribe), and thus possesses an interest and history that would appeal to many 'ecotourists'. Rangitikei Maori have, until very recently, had neither much interest nor much involvement in tourism. However, in 1995 some Maori in the district mooted the idea that conservation-based tourism might represent potential for the *iwi* and *hapu* (family groupings). Currently the *iwi* will permit visitors to the Lodge to cross the river and tramp through their lands subject to certain conditions; Brian Megaw is able to arrange this and a small payment is requested by the *iwi*. At present a quite serviceable footpath wends its way up the cliffside, and an upgrading of this route has begun.

However, the development not only of 'eco-tours' but also of possibly higher numbers of overseas tourists, particularly European, means a changing role for the guides. Traditionally guides have been attracted to the job by the thrill of white water and the enjoyment of isolation. Increasingly they are expected to be knowledgeable not only about flora and fauna, but also possibly about a foreign culture; that is, as *pakeha* (European) they must have some knowledge of Maori tradition and custom. From a Maori perspective, any such knowledge *pakeha* possess is, by necessity, incomplete and possibly inaccurate. This means that the training of guides becomes even more complex. Conventionally training is, and must continue to be, concerned with the safety of the client. The industry has recognized the need to respond to a changing market – from one in the late 1960s, when enthusiasts with 'gung-ho' attitudes rafted, to one today involving tourists of all ages and levels of fitness in much larger inflatable rafts. Safety has taken the form of improvements and changes in equipment. While less manoeuvrable, larger rafts are more stable (and economically more viable in that they hold more visitors), and self-bailing rafts have been developed. Nonetheless, rafting remains a potentially hazardous activity, and safety lies essentially in selecting conditions within the capabilities of staff and equipment.

Thus, safety procedures are being established as a response to market needs and recent changes in occupational health and safety legislation. Employers are responsible for the safety of their employees and visitors to the workplace. Two events in 1994 led to a reappraisal of the legislation by the tourism industry. First, following helicopter crashes and rafting incidents in the summer of 1994/95, which together caused the death of at least nine tourists, the concept of Tourism Occupational Health and Safety (TOSH) was developed by the New Zealand Tourism Industry Association and the New Zealand Civil Aviation Authority. Second, court decisions implied that a 'workplace' could be defined as any place where an employee worked. The New Zealand Tourism Industry became aware that this meant that, for example, a jet boat or raft could be considered to be 'a workplace'. Hence the client was a visitor to the 'workplace' and therefore covered by the legislation. Indeed, there is an emerging view that failure to demonstrate the establishment and implementation of proper safety procedures is prime facie evidence of negligence, which may lead to a company being sued. The potential importance of this in New Zealand cannot be underestimated, as New Zealand has no concept of suing for negligence as it is understood in many countries like the USA and the UK. This is because of the existence of a state-funded system (Accident Compensation Corporation (ACC); see Page and Meyer 1996) which is supposed to give automatic rights to compensation in the case of accident without a need to prove negligence and thereby sustain the costs of uncertain court action. This 'blanket' system of protection for all was granted in return for the surrender of the right to sue. Today, however, increasing financial stringency has meant that the protection afforded has become increasingly criticized as being inadequate even while the costs of administering the scheme have climbed – with the result of increasing demands for abolition of the scheme in its present form. From the viewpoint of small rural operators in adventure tourism, any legal action arising from the death of a client might end their business. On the other hand, a move away from ACC would mean high insurance costs, which would again potentially put small operators out of business. In March 1995, in a claim against one of the Shotover River companies, damages of NZ$10,000 were awarded to help meet expenses arising from an accident – a modest award, but one with legal significance.

River Valley Ventures had already established safety procedures, which are documented and which have to be followed by all guides. These include the checking of all equipment before and after trips, the need for either a minimum of two guides in a raft or one raft plus a safety kayaker for grade 4 and above rapids, a minimum age limit of 13 for customers (other than for a grade 1 course), weather and water-level checks prior to commencement of a trip, a checklist of equipment, certain guide–client ratios on given sections of water, and the carriage of a first-aid kit, which must be checked prior to the trip to ensure all its contents are present. Guides must hold current first-aid qualifications. Equipment is used only if it conforms to certain New Zealand standards.

Prior to the trip, guides have a checklist of instructions to be followed in a briefing session with clients, and for each set of rapids embarkation points have been identified where passengers can alight if they wish and join the raft once it has passed the rapids. Clients are taken only on rapids classified as 1 to 5, no higher. Guides must thus be fully versed in these procedures, and possess the technical skills required to guide a raft through the waters.

River Valley Ventures employs eight guides, only one of whom is on a full-time contract during eight months. Rafting guides are similar to ski instructors in that some travel following the season. Thus rafting guides from River Valley Ventures would work there, in Australia at sites such as the Tully River, and then in areas such as the Zambezi or northern hemisphere countries such as the USA or Canada. Brian Megaw regards this as an advantage, as it means not only that guides are retaining their technical skills but also that New Zealand companies are able to learn from the guides experiences of what other international operators are doing. However, of the eight guides, six are local people who have other occupations but are also experienced rafters. They have the advantage of being able to identify with the Rangitikei and its culture and history, and some have already expressed interest in further studying the area so as to be able to cater for the interests of 'ecotourists'. Nicola Megaw is also training to become a guide, and in March 1995 took her first group on a trip.

DISCUSSION

Lane (1992) noted that a third phase in tourism is taking place – the rise of cultural tourism. In this phase rural tourism offers more jobs, a pluri-activity of work patterns, a more diversified employment structure for rural areas and a means of sustaining services, farming and forestry. Rural tourism produces pressure to enhance conservation measures, while it provides a stimulus for arts and crafts and helps sustain small communities. Against this, the negative elements are what Lane calls 'death by numbers', the issues of incoming entrepreneurs and who controls the growth of tourism. There are associated problems of housing costs, the management of change and, of course, potential environmental problems.

These are not new problems. In one sense Lane is incorrect when he points to a new concern with rural areas as tourist resorts. As Travis (1993) points out, 'Nimbyism' (Not in My Back Yard) was exercised by new-comers to Devon in the nineteenth century just as it is elsewhere today. And in the 1880s concerns were also expressed about environmental impacts and sewage disposal. However, to note the replication of concerns does not make those concerns any the less real. At its current stage in the destination life-cycle the Rangitikei has few, if any, problems with tourism, and the case study of River Valley Ventures confirms the positive contribution to tourism that Lane noted. The guides are pluriactive in having more than one job, and the income from rafting helps to sustain their families as part of a rural community. The Megaws were able to develop new marketing and management skills which are now being used in their home community and which enable them to play a role in the development of new initiatives being undertaken by the Rangitikei Tourism Association. Lane (1992) and Ryan (1991) have noted how tourism creates new opportunities for female workers, and Nicola plays a major role in the management of the business. However, as with the operator of all small businesses, Brian and Nicola are not only managers, but also cooks, bed-makers and rafting guides, as well as being parents. However, both are now beginning to look forward to the stage when it might become possible to employ a manager, which will give them time for themselves – indeed in 1995 they were able to leave for a family holiday of a couple of days for the first time since taking over the business.

Rural tourism in the Rangitikei is still about family-based operations, and the costs in terms of encroachment upon family time cannot be underestimated. In the case of home-stay businesses, it means that the tourist is indeed entering MacCannell's (1976) 'back-room', but while the individual tourist does it but once, the host deals with the intrusion many times during the season. The Megaws are able to deal with this by not living on the premises of the business, and it might be significant that another successful entrepreneur in the area concluded that an answer to his problems was not to sell the business, but simply to move his home away from the business.

CONCLUSIONS

The policies being adopted by River Valley Ventures represent an increasing professionalism to sustain and develop a product in the face of increasing demands and competition. Rural tourism in New Zealand appeals to overseas and domestic markets because it represents an escape to a more natural surrounding – an environment where it is possible to have both adventure and peace. In one respect, existing operators face problems because the barriers to entry into rural tourism are comparatively low, and thus growing demand does not necessarily translate into growing profits, but rather increased supply. Yet, as markets mature, client demands change. Many of those rafting today seek assurance about safety and wish to prolong their stay in a comfortable, albeit scenic, setting so as to enhance the total experience of being 'away'. For today's tourists 'rafting product' is not simply one of river experience divorced from the other components of the trip, but one where anticipation, action and recollection become one continuous process of bonding with others who share the trip. This requires that entrepreneurs deliver a product which can sustain this totality of experience, and this is what River Valley Ventures is increasingly providing. What is being formulated is a complete experience of good, comfortable accommodation linked to its physical setting by careful planting of trees and shrubs that creates both views and privacy. The trip is a highlight led up to, and subsequently shared in retrospect over drinks and good food.

Yet the quality of the product needs a market to sustain it, and the Megaws link into the wider rural community not simply as a provider of jobs, but as part of joint marketing initiatives shared with other operators in the community. A synergy is sought whereby the operators within the Rangitikei mutually support each other in the development of packages which enable the visitor to experience what they have termed 'The Undiscovered Secret'. The Rangitikei Tourism Association is primarily an association of small, rurally based independent operators. Not all are solely in tourism – many are farmers. However, they appreciate that if they wish to provide an enhanced product it is in their interests to link together. The Megaws are part of this process, and today they and their colleagues are gaining a good reputation for being a dynamic, rurally based organization, able to offer products based upon small, friendly and individualized attention. It is the linking together of people for whom the Rangitikei is not simply a place of work, but also their home – a place with which they strongly identify – that provides the tourist with experiences not to be found in more commercialized urban areas. It is also this sense of identification that guards against an overexploitation of the river and the surrounding countryside. The case study also illustrates many of the issues identified by Page and Getz in Chapter 1. Citing Long and Nuckolls (1994: 19), they note that key factors in organizing success for rural tourism planning are the leadership of individuals, education, the adoption of strategies that fit a local situation, and access to technical information. The case study illustrates how important these are at an operational level. The Megaws are university-educated, they use computer technologies, they are entrepreneurial, but they have roots in their local community and are aware of the attitudes of that community. They have planned their steps, while retaining flexibility that permits responses to opportunities that are consistent with longer-term aims. The business is small; its ability to grow is limited by the need to preserve an environment, and hence growth can be achieved by product duplication in other geographical areas or through complementary products. Thus, from many perspectives they typify the current state of many successful small operators in New Zealand's rural tourism sector.

ACKNOWLEDGEMENTS

The author wishes to acknowledge the help given by Brian and Nicola Megaw, River Valley Ventures, Taihape, David and Sue Sweet, Rangitikei Tourism Association, John Eames, Rangitikei River Adventure, Mangaweka, and Christine Beech, Manawatu-Wanganui Regional Council. Without their help, especially that of Brian and Nicola Megaw, this case study would not have been possible. However, any interpretation of the material and the views expressed are solely the responsibility of the author, unless they are specifically attributed to other parties. It should be noted that the situation described relates to the period up to May 1996.

REFERENCES

Department of Conservation and Te Papa Atawhai (1993) *Greenprint Overview – The State of Conservation in New Zealand*, Wellington: Department of Conservation.

Getz, D. and Ryan, C. A. (1994) *Preliminary Report into Rangitikei Tourism*, Report for the Rangitikei Tourism Association, Palmerston North, Massey University.

Lane, B. (1992) 'A philosophy for rural tourism', *Tourism on the Farm*, Tipperary, Ireland: University College Dublin Environmental Institute.

—— (1994) 'What is rural tourism?', *Journal of Sustainable Tourism* 2(1): 7–21.

Long, P. T. and Nuckolls, J. (1994) 'Organising resources for rural tourism development: the importance of leadership, planning and technical assistance', *Tourism Recreation Research* 19(2): 19–34.

MacCannell, D. (1976) *The Tourist: A New Theory of the Leisure Class*, New York: Shocken Books.

Ministry of Agriculture and Forestry (1990) *Effects on Earthworms of Herbicides, Fungicides and Insecticides Including Round-Up*, Levin, near Palmerston North: Levin Horticultural Research Station.

New Zealand Tourism Board and Te Papa Atawhai (1993) *New Zealand, Conservation Estate and International Visitors*, Wellington: New Zealand Tourism Board and Department of Conservation.

New Zealand Tourism Board (1994a) *New Zealand – International Visitors Survey*, Wellington, New Zealand Tourism Board.

—— (1994b) *Tourism Investment and the Resource Management Act 1991*, Wellington: New Zealand Tourism Board.

—— (1995) *Product Development Opportunities for Asian Markets*, Wellington: New Zealand Tourism Board.

New Zealand Transit (1994) *Traffic Counts on State Highway 1*, Wellington: New Zealand Transit.

Oppermann, M. (1994) 'Comparative analysis of escorted tour packages in New Zealand and North America', *Proceedings, Tourism Down Under: A Tourism Research Conference*, Palmerston North, Department of Management Systems, Massey University, December.

—— (1996) 'Rural tourism in Southern Germany', *Annals of Tourism Research*, 23(1): 86–102

Page, S. J. and Meyer, D. (1996) 'Tourist accidents: an exploratory analysis', *Annals of Tourism Research* 23(3): 666–90.

Page, S. J. and Thorn, K. (1997) 'Towards sustainable tourism planning in New Zealand: public sector planning responses, *Journal of Sustainable Tourism* 5(1): 1–19.

Pearce, D. (1995) *Tourism Today – A Geographical Analysis*, 2nd edn, Harlow: Longman.

Pomeroy, A. (1996) 'Farm adjustment strategies in the rural context', in R. Le Heron, and E. Pawson, *Changing Places: New Zealand in the Nineties*, Auckland: Longman.

Priest, S. and Bunting, C. (1993) 'Changes in perceived risk and competence during whitewater canoeing', *Journal of Applied Recreation Research* 18(4): 265–80.

Rojek, C. (1993) *Ways of Escape – Modern Transformations in Leisure and Travel*, Basingstoke: Macmillan.

Ryan, C. (1991) *Recreational Tourism: A Social Science Perspective*, London: Routledge.

—— (1994) 'Tourism in the Manawatu-Wanganui Region', unpublished paper presented to the Economic Sub-Committee, Palmerston North City Council.

—— (1995) 'The German visitor and farm stays', address at the Annual General Meeting of the New Zealand Farm and Home-Host, Inc., Dunedin.

Travis, J. (1993) *The Rise of the Devon Seaside Resorts*, Exeter: University of Exeter Press.

Watts, M. (1993) 'Roundup and other socially acceptable poisons', in K. J. Smith (ed.) *Super Foods*, Auckland: Auckland Institute of Technology Press.

Conclusions and implications for rural business development

Conclusions and implications for rural business development

D. Getz and S. J. Page

INTRODUCTION

In the preceding chapters the various authors examined the context of rural tourism and the operation of tourism businesses using a case study method. In this concluding chapter the editors have drawn upon the case studies and introductory literature review to address several objectives:

- to summarize the nature of rural tourism with particular reference to the perspective of rural tourism businesses;
- to identify the key issues and opportunities facing tourism enterprises in a rural environment;
- to recommend strategies and actions for governments and destination marketing/development agencies to better foster, plan and market sustainable rural tourism.

The international case study approach taken in this book allows a unique examination of the field of rural tourism and, in particular, constitutes the first examination of rural tourism from the perspective of individual business owners and managers. Also, the international scope of the authors, all of whom possess direct experience in researching rural tourism, permits an unparalleled synthesis of views on rural tourism issues. The results, as summarized in this chapter, should prove valuable to a global audience. Rural tourism is clearly very important throughout most of the world, and is likely to become more important as countries and destinations compete for niche markets. Furthermore, mass-tourism developments continue to occur in once-rural areas, both threatening their rurality and presenting new opportunities for spin-off benefits in the remaining communities. Business opportunities, both small and large, will therefore continue to expand for rural residents and those preferring to set up businesses in rural areas. Without the sharing of experiences, many mistakes will be repeated and successful strategies missed. Without synthesis, the field cannot be advanced. Many of the issues discussed in Chapter 1 are beyond the scope of the case studies and our focus on entrepreneurs and business operations, so we do not attempt to address every theoretical concern here. The following summary and conclusions stress the contributions of the case studies.

WHAT IS RURAL TOURISM?

A theoretical perspective on rural tourism was taken in the introductory chapter, whereas at this point some very practical conclusions can be drawn from the cases. To a large degree, the question of what is rural is irrelevant to rural tourism business operators. They face a set of environmental and market forces which are different from those in cities and large resorts, and while there are certain global commonalties in rural tourism business there are also many place-specific issues. Furthermore, the theoretical question of who is a rural tourist is not an issue for the operators – their concern is with attracting the optimal mix of market segments, and that might cover any and all segments. And defining rurality is not really of importance to the visitors either. They are seeking specific opportunities or environmental attributes which, regardless of the position of the setting on an urban–wilderness spectrum (see Figure 10.1), might equally satisfy their needs and preferences. Defining rural is therefore more of a

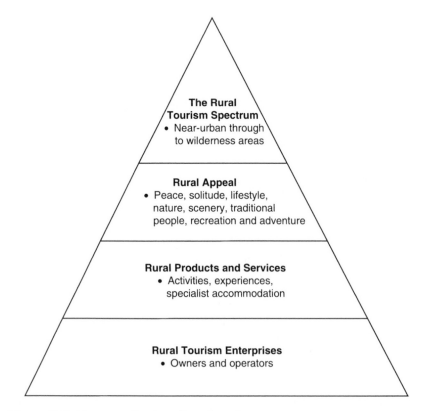

Figure 10.1 Conceptualization of rural tourism.

concern for policy-makers who want to do something about so-called rural problems. Nevertheless, an understanding of the issues discussed in Chapter 1 is important to planners, policy-makers and business operators, who all need a better understanding of forces and trends to reach their goals.

Each of the chapters revealed something different about actual tourism business operations in rural areas, and although the cases are not representative of all possible rural tourism ventures, they do cover a very wide range. Perhaps the most obvious, and to some observers the most rural of rural tourism enterprises, is that of farm-based holidays or farm visits. In Germany, Opperman examined this phenomenon and noted that it was the overnight stay in rural areas that differentiated tourism from excursions, and that rural tourism by definition occurred in non-urban settings where human activity (e.g. farming) was present. His research revealed differences between farm-based holidays, where the rural activity itself was part or most of the attraction, and the simpler provision of self-catering or bed and breakfast accommodation on farms and in small towns. For many rural tourists the farm accommodation is a base for touring, so that the presence of other attractions, notably mountains, water and recreational opportunities, helps explain patterns of supply and demand.

Other rural-based accommodation was featured in the cases, including a campground, both for touring and as the destination (the USA), remote lodges (Australia and New Zealand) for ecotourism, 'outback experiences' and recreation, and temporary teepee accommodation for those seeking a native experience (Alberta, Canada). These are primarily small in scale and not the main attraction, which clearly differentiates them from resorts. However, the Undara Lava Lodge case in Queensland revealed the difficulty of developing and operating a larger and profitable rural accommodation business without providing resort-like features. Clearly the form of accommodation can be part of the rural tourism experience, which is quite distinct from urban and large resort types, but the nature of the rural setting is more important.

Beyond accommodation, other services form an integral part of rural tourism. In China (Chapter 7), once official policy permitted private enterprise, numerous accommodation and services sprung up in rural areas and small towns to meet rising demand from domestic and foreign visitors. Long and Edgell (Chapter 3) noted how the touring corridor concept in the USA gave rise to the need for many touring-oriented services, including accommodation, food, fuel, shopping and recreation. However, unlike accommodation services, other forms of services for rural travellers are unlikely to be an attraction in themselves unless they are unique and authentic, as in the case of local foods and beverages.

Recreational activities constitute a major rural attraction. In New Zealand the basis of River Valley Ventures is white water rafting and other outdoor pursuits. As shown by Ryan, this business provides an expanding list of activities that can be considered adventurous and eco-friendly. Its isolated setting edges it into the category of wilderness lodge, although the operators came from a farming background and farming is an obvious part of the Rangitikei environment. At Undara Lava Lodge, Getz and Sofield (Chapter 8) found the owners to be devoted to true ecotourism experiences but planning more and more 'outback' opportunities, including wildland expeditions and horse-based activities. Many forms of rural recreation are unique to the great outdoors and can be experienced in areas occupied by humans or in wilderness. Guiding is an essential part of many rural recreational experiences, either where the activity itself requires it (e.g. rafting) or as part of a management and conservation plan (e.g. controlling access and providing interpretation at Undara Lava Lodge).

Cultural attractions were highlighted in several of the cases. The appeal of gaining contact with indigenous peoples and traditional cultures is strong, as revealed in both China and Canada. Getz and Jamieson (Chapter 5) showed that demand for native tourism 'products' is increasing, but there are problems (see 'The supply–demand balance', p. 199) with the development of supply. At its heart, 'native tourism' involves direct contact with the culture of indigenous peoples, including arts and crafts, visits to communities and historic sites, and special events held for the public. Direct involvement and contact with native peoples heightens the experience, and might even be necessary – as in the case of the community tours and adventure camps operated by Hal Eagle Tail in Alberta (Chapter 5). It can also be concluded that the natural resources owned or controlled by native people are an inherent part of the appeal, giving rise to adventure and ecotourism opportunities. The land base of native peoples around the globe is primarily rural and often wilderness in nature, constituting an increasingly scarce and valuable attraction. Sightseeing in general is a major element in rural tourism, involving both natural and cultural resources. More specific is the 'pilgrimage' to sacred places in China, as demonstrated by Sofield and Li (Chapter 7). This traditional form of domestic tourism is very well established and is now being overlaid by international tourism to the same sites as well as to ethnic enclaves.

Some evidence was also presented in the cases on the question of who the rural tourist is. Little evidence was found to support the contention that rural tourists are especially affluent or seek high quality. Indeed, it appears that rural experiences attract everyone, as is reflected in the large domestic and international business of rural tourism in China, and the evidence in North America that native tourism has very broad appeal. Specific products might appeal because of their lower relative cost (i.e. farmstays and B&B in Germany), their ecological uniqueness (Undara Lava Lodge), thrills (white water rafting) or convenience (camping). Because the range of rural environments and experiential opportunities is very broad, so too will be the market appeal. The need for market segmentation and yield management is as important to rural tourism operators as it is in all other tourism settings (see Yield management, p. 204). There does not appear to be any well-defined 'rural tourist' segment.

The case studies allow a reassessment of Lane's (1994) criteria for defining rural tourism:

1 We need to extend the scope of rural tourism beyond the farmscape to more remote and even wilderness areas, thereby creating a spectrum similar to the well-known recreation opportunity spectrum.

2 The emphasis on being 'functionally rural' – that is, built upon small-scale enterprise, open space, contact with nature, heritage and traditional societies and practices – remains central, but we need to allow for isolated instances of resorts and services which do not reflect these characteristics but are functionally part of the rural tourism environment.

3 We need to modify slightly the criterion that operations should usually be small in scale, by adding the caveat that enterprises must be sufficiently large to be economically viable.

4 It is often the case, and perhaps it is the ideal, that businesses are traditional in character, grow organically and are connected with local families, but this will not always be practical;

5 The cases examined in this book corroborate the point that enterprises should be diverse, reflecting the complex rural environment.

Rural tourism therefore consists of much more than travel and related businesses in rural areas. The cases demonstrate the importance of the rural setting and atmosphere, which is tangibly and emotionally separate from urban or resort tourism. While there is overlap, it is the combination of environment, unique experiences and traveller expectations that makes rural tourism a separate and identifiable phenomenon. It is not merely the absence of urban and resort-like elements, such as large-scale development and mass tourism, but rather the positive qualities of the rural product that define rural tourism.

To conclude, the following conceptualization is presented. Figure 10.1 suggests a 'nesting' of rural tourism subjects, from the broad nature of defining the rural environment, through a more specific analysis of rural appeal from the consumer's perspective and an inventory of rural tourism products, to more focused concern on rural tourism enterprises and, finally, the entrepreneurs/operators themselves.

KEY ISSUES FACING RURAL TOURISM ENTERPRISES

Collectively, the cases provide a clear overview of the important business issues and opportunities facing the rural tourism enterprise or entrepreneur. This is the area in which little research has been completed, and so these findings are particularly useful. In terms of problems and challenges, the case of native tourism in general seems to be the most extreme. Many native communities and individuals are getting into tourism for reasons of community and economic development, as well as for personal profit, but the development of this sector can be especially difficult. Many native communities lack the experience and training necessary to develop businesses, particularly where the community has traditionally relied on collective activity and decision-making. Native communities face a number of other unique challenges, including a strong desire to balance development with cultural and resource preservation, and the difficulty of fostering tourism development without losing control to outside investors or agencies.

Getz and Jamieson (Chapter 5) documented the entrepreneurial efforts of Hal Eagle Tail in his attempt to provide a number of deliverable products to tourists and the tourism industry. Entrepreneurship of this kind is not common in many native communities, and it might have to be stimulated and supported. This operator faced particular challenges in the marketing of his products, finding it necessary to form an alliance with an outside tour operator. By acting as a private company, on the other hand, much more could be done – and more quickly – than if community decision-making processes had to be followed. Real opportunities exist for involving more community members and family groups in tourism among the Tsuu T'ina, and for greatly expanding the range of services and products. Among the Treaty Seven nations of Southern Alberta, considerable scope exists for developing major attractions in the form of cultural centres and other attractions, although it remains to be seen if a situation of over-supply might be created.

Financing rural tourism enterprises

For native tourism, obtaining loans and investment is often difficult, owing to a lack of community and personal capital, to an inability to secure conventional loans against real property, or to the absence of government grants and subsidies. In Alberta native communities have turned to corporate sponsorship to help realize their development plans. Many entrepreneurs must rely on family resources and income to finance rural tourism businesses, thereby exposing themselves to potential financial ruin. On the other hand, family enterprises can have strengths that conventionally financed businesses do not, including total commitment to the venture and a sharing of risks among family members and generations. In the Undara case (Chapter 8), the family pastoral business had to support the tourism operations, but a separation of the two was felt to be desirable.

Higher costs

Remoteness and normal rural conditions such as the distance between settlements and businesses can impose many additional costs on rural businesses, including the need for independent utilities and services, provision of staff accommodation, access improvements and general communications. For example, Undara Lava Lodge (Chapter 8) requires costly water-supply expansion and its access road needs upgrading.

Profitability

Many rural tourism businesses fail to achieve acceptable profitability. This makes it difficult to attract loans and investors, and causes entrepreneurs to invest a great deal of their own land and time. The Undara case in Australia (Chapter 8) revealed that expansion of the attractions and services offered was necessary to attract longer stays and generate more revenue. Various researchers have noted that many people develop or buy tourism and hospitality businesses for lifestyle reasons. Their lack of experience or training might very well limit the potential for profit, although some might be willing to reduce their incomes in order to live and work where they prefer. In some native communities casinos are viewed as holding more promise of profits than other, more culturally authentic, products. Although cultural attractions used to be dominant in Alberta (Chapter 5), a number of casino proposals have been put forward, and elsewhere in North America native-run gaming has become big business. The lesson is that rural tourism must generate monetary benefits for the host communities and for entrepreneurs or other forms of development will become more appealing.

Labour and training

The training problem in rural tourism stems from a combination of remoteness (making communication difficult), inexperience of operators and staff, and the wide range of largely small, family-run businesses. Specific effort is required to solve these problems, as documented in the Australian policy study (Chapter 8). Lack of proper cost controls and proper accounting and management practices was shown to be a serious problem in the New Zealand case (Chapter 9), along with overextended borrowing. These are primary training needs, especially for operators getting into tourism from other activities. Training for guides is important, including recreation guides and those providing interpretive services. Increasingly, as shown in the Australian and New Zealand cases (Chapters 8 and 9), guides will figure prominently in providing and enhancing the rural tourism experience. Ecotourism will depend on qualified guides, many of whom will be the service and attraction owners. Seasonality can be more pronounced in rural tourism, resulting in special problems with the recruitment and retention of staff. This problem can be exacerbated by remoteness, poor housing supply, low wages and low profitability. At Undara Lava Lodge (Chapter 8) staffing became more difficult as needs increased, and this resulted in increased turnover and the need to recruit further afield. The case of the KOA campground in Colorado (Chapter 3) illustrated the value of a franchise in gaining training and other support services.

Organization of the sector

Tourist organizations are a vital element in the development of a market profile for an area, promoting its qualities, attractions and products. Yet such organizations are often dominated by cities and resorts, leaving rural tourism operators without an adequate voice or support mechanisms. In particular, native tourism in Canada (Chapter 4) and elsewhere has lagged behind other sectors in terms of organization and coordination. Rural tourism operators can band together, as they have in the Rangitikei District of New Zealand (Chapter 9), to overcome many obstacles facing individual operators.

Marketing

There is no simple, easily identifiable rural tourism market segment. Operators must engage in increasingly sophisticated research, segmentation and communications to understand and reach their appropriate segments. The Megaws in New Zealand (Chapter 9) learned that a form of yield management was needed to increase revenues, raising questions about which segments to promote and how to balance the mix of segments imposed by seasonal demands, established versus new markets, and segments differentiated by price. At Undara Lava Lodge (Chapter 8) a mix of visitor types was also noticed, but the main issue became one of attracting visitors for longer stays and thereby generating essential revenue. This case raised the question of whether there were sufficient numbers or high-enough spenders in the ecotourism market to justify major ecotourism developments.

Conservation and green practices

A global issue in rural tourism is the need to balance resource conservation with development, especially because it is clear that rural tourism depends on a special ambiance and access to natural environments. Native people are acutely aware of the need for both cultural and landscape conservation. Ecotourism products, such as Undara Lava Lodge, must maintain very high development standards and 'green' management practices in order to attract true ecotourists and preserve their special natural attraction. But these cost more and do not necessarily get a satisfactory return on investment. In the case of River Valley Ventures in New Zealand (Chapter 9), the operators proved to be advocates for nature conservation and high standards, and this is likely to be an increasing role for rural tourism operators. Unfortunately, in many countries it seems likely that environmental standards and development regulations are inadequate to fully protect rural areas and communities from the potential negative impacts of unregulated or mass tourism. Specific risks include disruption of community life, especially in native and traditional communities, despoliation of natural resources and scenery, and loss of solitude and peacefulness. The Undara Lava Lodge case (Chapter 8) clearly illustrated the high cost of environmental sustainability. It remains an open question whether ecotourism can actually be profitable in this context, as remoteness, high costs and low average visitor spending threaten the viability of the enterprise. Defining the carrying capacity of a resource, such as Undara Lava Tubes (Chapter 8), or of a rural community, is extremely difficult. This is both a conservation issue and one that can affect the bottom line of tourism businesses.

Family enterprise

Many rural tourism families decide to add a tourism enterprise to their existing activities. This might be done to supplement farm income, or perhaps for lifestyle reasons such as meeting new people. Family cohesion and traditional gender roles can easily be affected, and privacy can suffer. The KOA campground owners (Chapter 3) were specifically looking for a retirement opportunity – a going concern where they could live on site. However, the need for competent and trustworthy employees becomes an issue when families want to get away from the business. As discussed above (see 'Financing rural tourism enterprises', p. 196), family financing of rural tourism enterprises is common; this can lead to potentially serious risks but it also broadens the base of commitment.

Regulations

The KOA campground owners in the USA (Chapter 3) found that paperwork, conflicting requirements and standards which required costly improvements were all potential problems for the small business operator. In the Undara case (Chapter 8) the owners had to work very closely with the state and its national park service, and this sometimes resulted in strain.

The supply–demand balance

Owing to ease of entry, supply in rural tourism can easily increase to exceed demand. This is not a unique problem, as it can apply to businesses of all kinds, but in rural areas it might be exacerbated by the low costs associated with offering, for example, farm-based accommodation, tours or access to resources.

Lack of data and research

Oppermann (Chapter 6) noted that a lack of research and data on farm tourism in Germany restricted analysis of this important sector. It appears to be a global problem, in that rural tourism has not been separated for data collection or statistical analysis. This is of concern to individual business operators as well. They will find it difficult to monitor supply and demand trends, to gauge the competition or to seek out opportunities.

Lack of policy and support strategies

Ryan noted the absence of a rural tourism policy in New Zealand (Chapter 9). Other countries like Canada have not developed anything specific to this sector, although in the past a number of programmes were directed at rural tourism planning and development. Australia (Chapter 8) seems to be more active than most countries in pursuing ecotourism and rural tourism strategies, while in the USA a number of very recent initiatives, described in Chapter 3, are generating results. Sofield and Li (Chapter 7) noted that in China tourism growth was not accompanied by adequate investment in infrastructure and organization. Governments in developing nations will have to plan for, and often directly provide, essential services in order to avoid serious problems, or they will have to facilitate private initiatives through tourism development strategies.

Accessibility

In itself, remoteness can be a major attraction. However, it not only imposes additional costs upon rural tourism, but also affects the flow of travellers, the organizational capacity of operators, and the means of access to services and attractions. Achieving the right balance between accessibility and isolation is a major planning challenge in rural tourism.

Natural hazards

The vagaries of weather, the seasons and other natural phenomena can have a more serious impact on rural tourism businesses, many of which are linked directly to the resource base (e.g. river rafting, hunting, fishing and skiing). Water supply is a critical concern in Australia, while in other countries forest fires might be a major threat.

Opportunities for rural tourism

The cases suggest that a number of opportunities exist for rural tourism, both in terms of business potential and destination development. The training and employment of guides, both recreational guides and interpretors, appears to be of growing significance. Guides might also tend to become investors and operators, or vice versa. Given increasing emphasis on rural tourism as a distinct experience, guides and interpreters are required to provide access to restricted or remote areas, interpret nature, ensure safety and comfort, and outfit the visitors. Traditional hunting and fishing outfitters might find it advantageous to expand their qualifications and offer new services based on adventure and ecotourism. Many alternative forms of rural accommodation exist, and demand for these is likely to expand. There is considerable opportunity to add accommodation to existing farm operations, construct small eco- and adventure tourism lodges, convert heritage buildings or develop small resorts. The aim is to provide sustainable development with rural/wilderness appeal or access to rural lifestyles. A danger is unregulated proliferation and inadequate design and environmental standards.

Mobility has been increasing globally, so it can be expected that touring will continue to grow. As a consequence, a major opportunity exists – especially in newly developing destinations like China – for entrepreneurial provision of services for travellers. Cultural, ethnic and native tourism are certainly gaining in popularity. The major limitation to date appears to be a lack of supply, particularly of deliverable 'products' that can be sold reliably to tour operators. With some degree of assistance or investment, many native communities can provide services and access to attractions, while native entrepreneurs can be encouraged through the provision of training and various support mechanisms. The recent experience of China (Chapter 7) suggests substantial potential for development of 'informal' rural tourism enterprise. In some countries this occurs outside the law, while in others it is condoned. Although many individuals can participate informally, the absence of regulations and controls could easily result in harm to tourists and the industry (e.g. health problems). It seems preferable to harness private enterprise and encourage more formal and stable business operations, perhaps at the community level through cooperatives.

Strategies for destinations

Government agencies should enter into partnerships with industry groups and communities to address the special needs of rural tourism businesses. The following strategies and actions have been suggested largely by the case studies.

Facilitating private enterprise

The China case (Chapter 7) shows how growth in services, accommodation and attraction development can be realized through official sanctioning of private enterprise. This requires accompanying decentralization of decision-making in some countries, while in others it will require more proactive support services or incentives.

Financial assistance

Schemes of financial assistance specific to rural tourism are likely to be required in many destinations if the documented financing and profitability obstacles are to be overcome. Options include the kind of development bank operating in China, or government grant and loan schemes. Indirect assistance, such as for joint marketing initiatives and training/advice, could also be very effective in improving financial performance.

Management training

The cases revealed a strong need for management training, as many rural tourism operators lack previous experience and formal business education. Programmes will have to be customized to the special needs of rural business operators, for example through distance education, use of the Internet and specially designed material including case studies such as those contained in this book. Management training could be combined with standards and certification of operators/guides, and quality ratings for enterprises. Many rural tourism operators are in the business part time, and many are women. These circumstances dictate a training scheme with flexibility and receptiveness to many varied learning needs.

Marketing assistance

Many rural tourism operators need assistance with marketing (Chapter 2). In native communities the development of deliverable product and assistance with joint marketing efforts appear to be critical. In terms of destination marketing, organizations could link native entrepreneurs and communities with inbound tour companies. Native tourism organizations should be formed and their close working with broader-based organizations facilitated. Packaging rural tourism should be a priority, on the basis either of similar products (e.g. adventure, ecotourism, cultural, native or farm themes) or of the area (e.g. experience the undiscovered country), as in the case of the Rangitikei and its promotion as 'The Undiscovered Secret' (Chapter 9). Individual operators might also need advice on how to package their own products and services.

Standards

Standards can be developed for classifying rural tourism operations (based on type and quality), operators (based on training) and sustainability factors (based on environmental and social impact audits). Standards should recognize the innate special qualities of rural tourism and the need to preserve the environmental appeal of rural areas. Consumers should be better informed about distinct rural opportunities and the special developmental and management standards needed to deliver high-quality sustainable product. Standards should be accompanied by certification procedures, and awards can be instituted for superior compliance.

Demonstration projects

Taking a lead from the Australian rural tourism strategy (Chapter 8), demonstration projects might be beneficial in destinations launching rural tourism initiatives. Successful enterprises can also be documented and held up for emulation.

Infrastructure

Rural areas often require heavy government investment in basic infrastructure, including roads, airports, water supply, sewage treatment, electricity and communications. Where possible, industry can be required to contribute – especially when developing in more remote areas. New facilities and services should be planned for joint resident–visitor use.

Direct provision of services and attractions

Many public facilities and resources serve the tourist industry, but governments are not always attuned to market forces or amenable to increased usage. Industry has a role in advising government on the value and management of public lands and facilities for visitors. Public agencies should have tourism goals and programmes specifically incorporated in their mandates and planning processes.

Organization

Small rural tourism operators in particular are likely to require assistance in getting organized for planning, marketing, training and other initiatives. Leadership will often be a key factor, so government agencies, industry associations or broader-based destination organizations might have to become actively involved in the early stages. Otherwise, the training of rural tourism operators should generate leaders as well as better operators.

Community-based planning

Rural communities should respond well to community-based planning for tourism, particularly where there is strong cultural homogeneity or an already-identified need for economic development. The scenic corridor programme in the USA (Chapter 3) provides such a model, and notably encourages industry–community dialogue on goals and means. Logically, a variety of partnerships should evolve from the planning exercise – witness the Peak to Peak case (Chapter 3). In terms of community-based planning for rural areas, the necessary factors are education in advance of commencing the process, achievement of balanced community representation, leadership, access to information and expertise, and formulation of locally appropriate visions and strategies.

Sustainability and green practices

Industry–government partnership might be needed to launch green operations such as recycling and to promote sustainable development principles. Codes of conduct for tourism operators and visitors are very important in rural and remote areas.

Focal points

Because of the accessibility and isolation challenges of many rural areas, development of one or more focal points (attractions and services) could be a primary strategy. Where an existing resort or service town performs this function, attention can be directed more quickly to use of the centre as a base camp for hinterland exploration and tours, and to development of the touring/access corridors and minor nodes. In the case of Colorado, the concept of a scenic corridor became the focal point for tourism planning and development.

Marketing innovation

As is demonstrated by the United States USTTIN a website can be a major marketing strength for rural areas (see Chapter 3). Individual attractions and services otherwise unable to develop an Internet presence can be linked through a destination home page, or a home page defined by a theme (such as adventure or native tourism). Database marketing is often beyond the reach of small operators, so a joint destination database of past and potential customers can be a valuable marketing tool. In New Zealand the Megaws were developing their own database to facilitate communications and more sophisticated yield management.

Yield management

Because rural tourism markets are highly segmented, operators and destinations must increasingly manage these segments for maximum revenue yield. Different segments at different times of the year, each with their own interests and needs, are common in rural tourism. The operator wants to be able to cater to the mix which generates the best returns. While this tends to shift the operation up-market and raise consumer prices, it might be essential for long-term viability because of higher costs.

Image

Rural destinations must work harder to develop a positive, clear image. Cities and resorts, in comparison, can rely on major attractions, sport teams, cultural and convention centres, major events (Getz 1997) and corporations to foster an image (Page 1995). But rural areas might lack a major focus of attention. In New Zealand the Rangitikei Tourism Association developed a good slogan and launched a unified image campaign to overcome the absence of consumer awareness and identity.

Farm-based tourism

As this sector is very widespread and closely associated with rural tourism, focused strategies are warranted. As the two cases in Canada (Chapter 4) and Germany (Chapter 6) reveal, farm-based tourism has a number of dimensions, including forms of accommodation and actual farm attractions. Farm households will have unique needs for financing, training and marketing, and their motivations for developing a tourist clientele might not be strictly economic. Concern about the impact of tourism on the farm operation and family should be addressed, as well as the likelihood of low profitability. Given the challenges, encouragement of and assistance to a farm tourism association could be very rewarding for destinations. It is quite possible that only collective action within this sector can effectively address all the concerns.

On the value of being different

As a final point, the discussion and cases in this book highlight the importance for rural areas and businesses of being different. There is indeed a special quality to rural tourism, both from the supplier's perspective and in the perceptions and desires of consumers. Individual enterprises and rural destinations must strive to enhance their authentic character and to differentiate themselves, in particular, from resort and urban competitors.

The major factors which give rural tourism its special appeal can be used by destinations and businesses in their planning and marketing strategies; these include:

- remoteness/isolation;
- peace and quiet;
- solitude;
- authentic culture (ethnic, traditional, native);
- heritage sites and buildings;
- alternative lifestyles, including food and beverages;
- undisturbed nature;
- hospitable residents;
- safety;
- exclusivity (not mass tourism);
- excitement;
- aesthetically pleasing landscape.

These are the resources of rural tourism which must be nurtured and preserved.

REFERENCES

Getz, D. (1997) *Event Tourism*, New York: Cognizant Publishing.

Lane, B. (1994) 'What is rural tourism?', *Journal of Sustainable Tourism* 2: 7– 21.

Page, S. J. (1995) *Urban Tourism*, London: Routledge.

Place index

Subject index

Map section

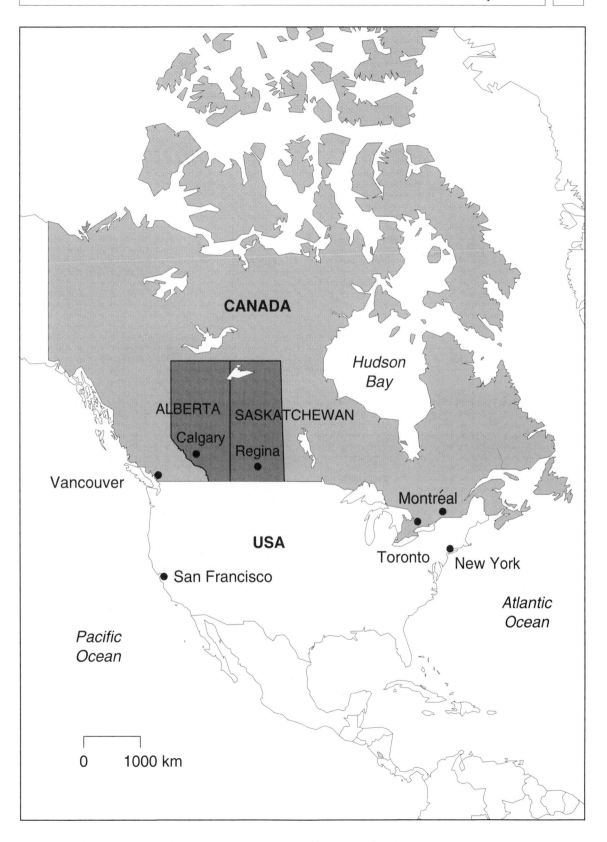

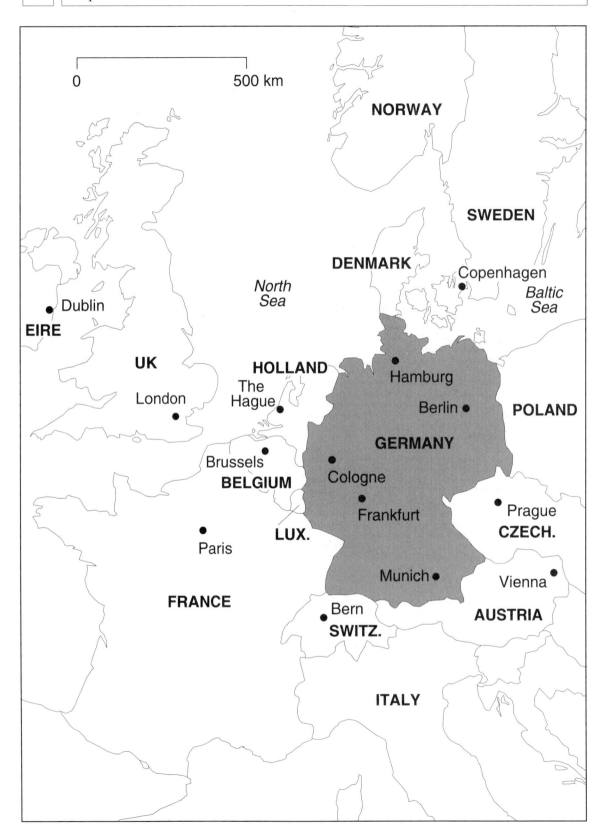

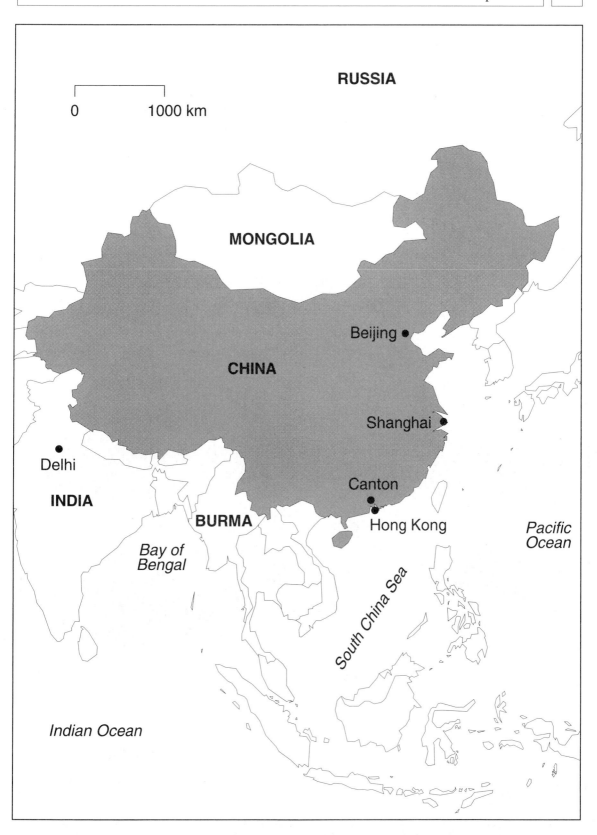

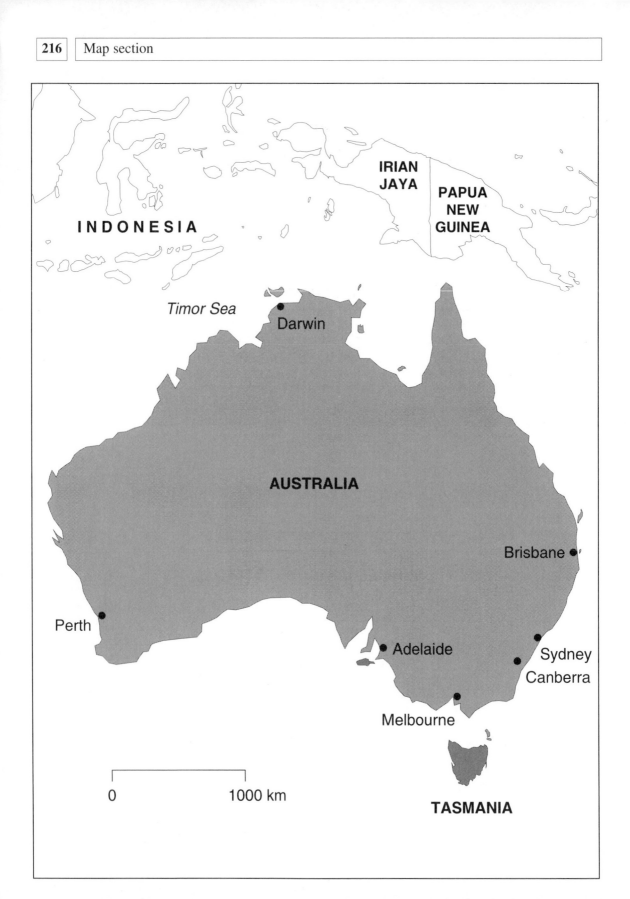

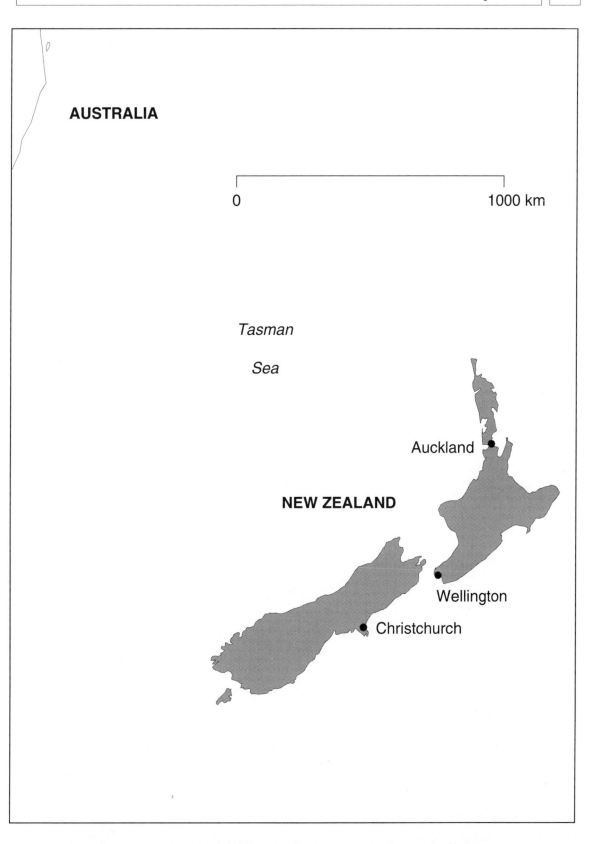

AUSTRALIA

0   1000 km

Tasman

Sea

Auckland

NEW ZEALAND

Wellington

Christchurch